Rousseau and Representation

ROUSSEAU
AND
REPRESENTATION

A Study of the Development of
His Concept of Political Institutions

RICHARD FRALIN

COLUMBIA UNIVERSITY PRESS
New York   1978

The Andrew W. Mellon Foundation, through a
special grant, has assisted the Press in
publishing this volume.

Library of Congress Cataloging in Publication Data

Fralin, Richard, 1939–
Rousseau and representation.

Bibliography: p.
Includes index.
1. Rousseau, Jean Jacques, 1712–1778—Political
science.   2. Representative government and representation.   I. Title.
JC179.R9F7   320.5'1   78–15903
ISBN 0–231–04474–7

Columbia University Press
New York   Guildford, Surrey

To the memory of my father,
for my mother,
and for Marylou

ACKNOWLEDGMENTS

THIS STUDY BEGAN as an essay for a seminar in eighteenth-century political thought taught by Professor Julian H. Franklin, who aided and encouraged me throughout the long process of transforming this initial essay into the present work. Professor Herbert A. Deane, who cosponsored my dissertation, read the entire work chapter by chapter through several revisions and offered valuable advice along the way. To both I am deeply grateful. I would also like to thank my dissertation readers, Professors Isser Woloch, Louis Henkin, and Tom Horne, for their criticism and helpful suggestions.

CONTENTS

Rousseau and Representation

INTRODUCTION

ROUSSEAU'S basic political concepts, above all, his concept of the indivisibility and inalienability of popular sovereignty, have earned him a reputation as one of the most radically democratic of all the great political philosophers. Unlike other theorists, who talk abstractly of popular sovereignty but who for all practical purposes relegate the people to the role of voting for representatives who make all important political decisions, Rousseau is thought to have carried the concept of popular sovereignty to its logical conclusion by insisting that the people participate directly in the exercise of sovereignty. His intense opposition to representative government in the *Contrat social,* his best known and most influential political work, is widely regarded as one of the most distinctive features of his political thought.[1] It is acknowledged that he occasionally voiced less hostile opinions of representation, but these are explained as straightforward concessions to circumstances rather than as indications of a fundamental change of view. His acceptance of a mandate system of representation in the *Considérations sur le gouvernement de Polgne,* for example, is seen as a deliberate compromise necessitated by Poland's enormous size, not as approval of the principle of representation *per se.*[2] Other commentators point to several curious passages in *Économie politique* that indicate that he once ac-

1

cepted representative assemblies as a legitimate alternative to popular assemblies, but his acceptance of representation in this early political work is dismissed either as an aberration from his main view or as an indication that his political thought had not yet matured.[3]

Even two recent studies by prominent Rousseau scholars that appear to take exception to this dominant interpretation of Rousseau's view of representation prove, on closer inspection, not to be genuine exceptions. Thus Robert Derathé contends that Rousseau abandoned the rigid opposition to representation expressed in the *Contrat social* and, in his constitutional proposals for Poland, eventually came to accept it not only as a matter of political expediency but also as a matter of principle.[4] Roger Masters goes even further, arguing that, despite appearances to the contrary, Rousseau did not reject representation even in the *Contrat social.* According to Masters the system of government Rousseau called "elective aristocracy" is "merely another name for parliamentary or representative government."[5] The dissenting opinions of Derathé and Masters are, however, based on definitions of representative government that differ in key respects from most modern definitions.

The definition of representation, as Hanna Fenichel Pitkin makes clear in her book-length study of the term,[6] is not a simple matter, and this definitional problem is compounded by differences between eighteenth- and twentieth-century conceptions of representation. Among other significant differences, present-day conceptions usually stress the freedom of representatives to make decisions without referring to the instructions or even the wishes of their constituents, whereas in much of eighteenth-century Europe some form of mandate system was prevalent, and even in Britain, the major exception to this rule, the modern system of representative government existed only in embryo.[7] Although Rousseau never clearly defined representation, he did provide sufficient information from which a definition faithful to his own understanding of the term can be constructed. In his view a representative government was one in which the citizenry, instead of approving or disapproving proposed laws directly in a popular assembly of all citizens, elected officials who were authorized to approve or disapprove proposals in behalf of their constituents.

2

Neither Derathé nor Masters defines representative government, but Derathé notes Rousseau's insistence on a strict mandate
system, which would accord with eighteenth-century usage but
would not meet the criterion of decision-making independence
stressed by most twentieth-century writers. Masters views what he
calls representative assemblies as essentially institutions that prepare laws for popular enactment, which is clearly not the way most
twentieth-century representative institutions normally function. In
short, Derathé and Masters differ with the dominant interpretation
of Rousseau's view of representation for terminological rather than
substantive reasons.

Closely associated with the view of Rousseau as a staunch opponent of representative government is the view of him as an advocate of direct or participatory democracy.[8] He rejected representative government, it is argued, because he believed that the value
of personal participation in the political process outweighed any
possible inconveniences of popular assemblies. Here too certain
oddities are noted, for example, his belief in the necessity of a superior individual to act as lawgiver at the institution of a legitimate
state and his corollary belief that government should play a leading
role in the legislative process, but these too are dismissed as aberra-
tions from his usual position that political participation has not
only a positive instrumental value but possibly an intrinsic value as
well.

My contention is that both these interpretations of Rousseau's
political thought are misleading, that he was in reality far more ambivalent about both representation and direct citizen participation
in the political process than is generally thought, and that this ambivalence in turn stemmed from his profoundly ambivalent view of
the political capacities of ordinary citizens. This ambivalence is particularly evident if one focuses on his institutional thought rather
than on the basic political concepts—the social contract, the general
will, sovereignty, and the like—which are, quite properly, the focus
of most studies of his political thought. This focus on abstract principles, however indispensable, can easily lead to serious misconceptions, for Rousseau repeatedly made sweeping claims in his statement of basic political principles that he elsewhere sharply

qualified or modified. In the *Contrat social*, for example, Rousseau presented the institutional ideal of Books III and IV as the logical fulfillment of the basic political concepts set forth in Books I and II. If his institutional ideal were no more than this, if in fact one could deduce it from a careful study of his basic political principles, a focus on Rousseau's institutional thought might provide a more concrete idea of what he intended to say but otherwise could be expected to provide few significant new insights into his basic political concepts. In reality, however, the institutional principles of Books III and IV frequently clash with, or at the very least sharply qualify, the sweeping general principles of Books I and II. However one explains these contrasts between his institutional principles and his basic political concepts, whether one calls them inconsistencies or contradictions or tensions or simply indications of ambivalence, they offer an important key to understanding not only his institutional thought but also his political thought as a whole.

That Rousseau himself attached great importance to political institutions is beyond doubt. When, in 1743–1744, he first conceived the idea of writing a major work on politics, he called it *Institutions politiques* because he was convinced that political institutions determine the nature of a people. The key to reform of the corrupt society in which most moderns live was thus institutional reform, and Rousseau accordingly set himself the task of devising political institutions that would elevate men above their present sorry state.[9] Only people like the peasants of Neuchâtel or the Haut-Valais, isolated people whose simple way of life was not yet greatly affected by modern civilization, could dispense with political institutions. Such fortunate people achieved spontaneously in their daily lives what most people could achieve, if at all, only with the aid of carefully designed political institutions.

Rousseau's view of political institutions was largely neglected until a little over a decade ago, when a spate of articles on his critiques of eighteenth-century institutions appeared in conjunction with the bicentennial commemoration of the publication of the *Contrat social*. A number of the papers presented at the "journées d'études" at Dijon in 1962 dealt with various aspects of his institutional thought,[10] and several other articles on the subject were published in the journal *Le Contrat social* in the same year.[11] These and subsequent publications[12] have helped to clarify the institutional aspects of his thought, but much remains to be done.[13] If it is less common to see Rousseau referred to simply as an advocate of direct democracy, which is at best misleading, it is still far from clear how he expected his institutional ideal of "elective aristocracy" to function, or how this proposal set forth in the *Contrat social* differs from his proposals in other writings.

One of the most striking features of Rousseau's concept of political institutions is the tension between his insistence on personal participation in the political process, particularly in the legislative process which he considered the heart of every legitimate political system, on the one hand, and on the other, his adamant opposition to various forms of popular political initiative, notably the right to propose laws or nominate candidates for public office. He opposed assemblies of representatives because they deny the average citizen the opportunity to participate directly in the political process, but at the same time he denied the average citizen the political initiative without which participation in the popular assemblies was largely devoid of meaning. He opposed legislative representation only to insist all the more forcefully on executive representation, that is, the delegation of responsibility for execution of the laws. True, he drew a sharp distinction between legislative and executive representation, arguing that the executive was simply the instrument of the people's will, but elsewhere he argued that the executive must have a will of its own, that it must be relatively independent vis-à-vis the people to provide the strong leadership that all governments should provide. Not the least of the executive's broad discretionary powers would be a preponderant role in legislation, which tends to render meaningless his distinction between legislative and executive representation.

Just as Rousseau was ambivalent about representation, he was also ambivalent about the value of direct citizen participation in the political process, which is, so to speak, the other side of the coin. Representation is of course a form of indirect participation and in that sense is a type of political participation, but in Rousseau's view, at least in the *Contrat social*, representation was opposed to

5

participation because he considered the indirect participation of a representative system to be virtually identical with nonparticipation. If he had managed to complete the *Institutions politiques*—and he apparently did complete an important fragment on confederation, which unfortunately was destroyed—it is probable that he would have combined direct participation at the local or city-state level with representation at the national or international level. This is in effect what he proposed for Poland, with direct participation in the dietines and representation in the diet.

Apart from the *Contrat social,* then, Rousseau tended to see direct and indirect participation as complementary rather than opposed, although he usually stressed the virtues of direct participation and only grudgingly acknowledged the virtues of representation. Despite his celebration of the virtues of direct participation, however, Rousseau was far more ambivalent about this form of political participation than is often thought. He may have ridiculed the English for thinking themselves free because they had the opportunity to vote for members of Parliament only on very infrequent occasions, but the citizen in his ideal popular assembly would have little more to do than the English voter whose freedom he considered illusory. Direct participation was at once crucial and inconsequential. Government was in principle subordinate, but in practice it monopolized all important political initiatives. It is a curious mixture, and the explanation, it seems to me, lies in Rousseau's ambivalence toward the ordinary citizen.

Rousseau's trust in the political capacities of ordinary citizens was genuine, but it was balanced by a deep distrust of those same citizens that is easy to overlook if one concentrates solely on his basic political concepts. The tension between these contrasting views runs throughout his political writings as he alternates between praising the fundamental good sense of the common man and warning against the danger of mob violence by the unsophisticated masses. Whereas Rousseau's faith in the political capacities of ordinary citizens has often been stressed, a number of recent studies have protrayed Rousseau as a social and political conservative who recoiled at the prospect of entrusting the common man with real political power.[14] This swing of the pendulum has

6

brought to light important qualities of Rousseau's political and social thought that were too often neglected by those who saw in
Rousseau a radical democrat or even a revolutionary, but it is just as
misleading to portray Rousseau as a thoroughgoing conservative as
it is to portray him as a radical democrat. With regard to the political capacities of ordinary citizens, he was both conservative and
radical, and he was both simultaneously, so that to classify him as
essentially one or the other is to distort his thought.

The ambivalence or tension in Rousseau's social and political
thought has received increasing attention in recent years.[15] Bernard
Groethuysen's *Jean-Jacques Rousseau*,[16] published posthumously in
1949, was a major contribution and stimulus to this approach to the
study of Rousseau. Groethuysen focused on the tension between
conflictng values in Rousseau's thought, values associated with the
alternative and mutually exclusive ideals of "l'homme naturel" and
"l'homme social."[17] Groethuysen argued that, although Rousseau
recognized that these ideals and their corresponding values could
not be reconciled and even insisted on the necessity to choose between them, Rousseau himself was equally committed to both,
hence the tension tension throughout his work. Rousseau's preoccupation with himself in his extensive autobiographical writings
has made him a prime candidate for psychological investigation,
and a number of studies using this psychological approach have
brought to light various tensions and conflicts in his personality
and thought. Perhaps the best known of these is Jean Starobinski's
Jean-Jacques Rousseau: la transparence et l'obstacle,[18] which focuses
on Rousseau's lifelong struggle to overcome the discrepancy between appearance and reality.[19]

One of the more interesting attempts to employ the psychological approach in the study of Rousseau's political thought, which
is not the primary focus of Starobinski's important study, is an
essay by Fred Weinstein and Gerald M. Platt, "Rousseau: the Ambivalent Democrat," which focuses on the tension in Rousseau's
thought between freedom and control, autonomy and authority.
They argue that Rousseau wanted man to be free and autonomous,
but at the same time he was convinced that man lacked the moral
courage to be free. Man was capable of self-government only if con-

science dominated all aspects of his existence, but conscience was not strong enough to dominate the passions, and so Rousseau resorted to various mechanisms—the lawgiver, censorship, civic religion—to compensate for this weakness. Rousseau's strong commitment to both freedom and control was in turn an accurate reflection of the value conflict in Enlightenment society, which was also committed to both of these goals.[20] A study of Rousseau's concept of political institutions leads to similar conclusions. Rousseau sincerely wanted the people to be sovereign, and he believed it essential that the people participate personally in the exercise of sovereignty, but he also sincerely feared the consequences of untrammeled popular sovereignty. Despite his distaste for "intermediaries"—by which he meant variously political parties, representatives, or the executive, among other things—he considered intermediaries essential to prevent the people from abusing their sovereignty.

The value conflict between freedom and control was especially acute for those eighteenth-century political thinkers who, like Rousseau, were deeply influenced by the classical republican tradition. If the heyday of classical republicanism was the seventeenth century, the tradition persisted throughout the eighteenth century as well, especially among dissidents in England and the American colonies.[21] There is little indication that Rousseau was greatly influenced by these English writers. Neither Harrington nor Milton nor any of the Levellers are mentioned in his political writings, although he does refer several times to Algernon Sidney, whose *Discourses Concerning Government* he used in writing the *Discours sur l'inégalité*.[22] Far more important for Rousseau than these English writers was Machiavelli, who had also been a major source of inspiration for the English classical republicans, and, beyond Machiavelli, the writings of the Greek and Roman republicans.

Like other classical republicans, Rousseau generally preferred to restrict citizenship to those whom he considered to be economically autonomous, but Rousseau's concept of citizenship was more ambivalent than that of most classical republicans, primarily because he developed a more radical concept of popular sovereignty that tended to undermine the traditional distinction between citizens and noncitizens. On the one hand, Rousseau accepted Geneva's denial of citizenship to a large bloc of its self-sufficient residents, the *natifs* and *habitants,* at least up until Geneva's condemnation of the *Contrat social* and his own renunciation of Genevan citizenship. He was apparently not altogether happy with Geneva's criteria for citizenship, however, for some years later, in his constitutional proposals for Poland, he urged that the entire adult male population be enfranchised, arguing that even the lowly Polish serfs were potentially just as capable of citizenship as their masters were.

That Rousseau was more deeply influenced by the classical republican tradition than most of his fellow Encyclopedists were was largely due to his birth as a citizen of the Republic of Geneva. The nature and extent of Geneva's influence on Rousseau's social and political thought remain a matter of controversy. In the late nineteenth and early twentieth centuries Geneva's influence was frequently and heavily stressed by admirers and detractors alike. Whereas critics of this view were not entirely lacking, it was not until the publication in 1934 of John Stephenson Spink's *Jean-Jacques Rousseau et Genève* [23] that the importance of Geneva's influence on Rousseau's political thought was seriously questioned. Spink acknowledged that the Genevan bourgeoisie exerted an important influence on the development of Rousseau's political thought, but he contended that the Genevan constitution could not have played a significant role prior to the condemnation of the *Contrat social* simply because Rousseau knew very little about it prior to that time.[24] Perhaps even more important than Spink's thesis was the use made of it by Robert Derathé in his *Jean-Jacques Rousseau et la science politique de son temps,* which was first published in 1950 and which remains one of the classic studies of Rousseau's political thought. Derathé accepts Spink's contention that Geneva was not a major source of Rousseau's political thought and documents in great detail Spink's suggestion that Rousseau was deeply indebted to the natural law theorists for his political ideas.

Although Spink and Derathé have made a profound contribution to our understanding of Rousseau's political thought, they have unfortunately seriously understated the importance of Geneva's influence in the process of demonstrating the important role of the natural law theorists in the formation of Rousseau's views. Granted that the natural law school exerted a great influence on Rousseau, the nature of this influence was to a large extent shaped by Rousseau's Genevan background. This is also true of other major influences on Rousseau's social and political thought. The particular way in which Rousseau reacted to the classical republican tradition was surely affected by his intense identification with Geneva, which was, after all, a living if somewhat perverted embodiment of this tradition. The same can be said of the ferment of ideas that the Genevan Rousseau encountered as an Encyclopedist living in or near Paris, the center of the Enlightenment and in many ways the antithesis of Geneva, during many of his most productive years as a writer. Many of Rousseau's most distinctive political ideas were also distinctly Genevan in origin, especially his concept of political institutions, which he first set forth in the *Dédicace,* elaborated in much greater detail in Books III and IV of the *Contrat social,* and modified in his subsequent writings on Geneva, Corsica, and Poland. In all these writings the Genevan influence is manifest. Even in his constitutional proposals for Corsica and Poland, nations whose very size rendered the Genevan city-state model less relevant, the Genevan influence is still significant. Nor is this surprising, for it was Genevan institutions on which he had based his idea of elective aristocracy, the guiding principle of his broader concept of political institutions, and this principle applied in Corsica and Poland as well as in Geneva.

Whatever the sources of Rousseau's concept of political institutions, whether Geneva or the natural law theorists or some other influence was predominant, it is important to recognize that his view of political institutions was among the last aspects of his political thought to mature. His attitude toward representative institutions, perhaps the most distinctive feature of his broader concept of political institutions, was not always one of hostility. In the early 1750s he had very little to say about political institutions, probably because his thinking on the subject was still very tentative, but what little he did have to say strongly suggests that at that time he not only approved of representative government but also shared the general Lockean conception of government that was so highly esteemed by his then close friends among the Encyclopedists. Several passages from *Économie politique* are little more than paraphrases of Locke's argument in the *Second Treatise* that a government may levy taxes only with the consent of the people or their representatives.

Not until the *Contrat social,* published some seven years after *Économie politique,* did Rousseau present his well-known case against representation. He now opposed representation on the grounds that will cannot be represented, a contention that is either irrelevant or at best highly questionable as an argument against representation. In any event his real objection to representation was not theoretical but practical; he was convinced, rightly or wrongly, that popular assemblies are more effective than representative assemblies in preventing or retarding executive usurpation of popular sovereignty, which in the *Contrat social* he identified as the chief threat to the body politic.

Because his objections to representative government were essentially pragmatic, the way was left open for a change of heart if he should ever come to perceive representative assemblies as more effective than popular assemblies in achieving the basic goals of the *Contrat,* and there is abundant evidence that this is precisely what happened. In the *Lettres écrites de la montagne,* which he wrote in the wake of Geneva's condemnation of the *Contrat,* he argued that the British Parliament, the eighteenth-century example *par excellence* of a representative assembly, was more effective than the Genevan Conseil Général, the primary assembly on which he had modeled the institutions of the *Contrat,* in restraining the executive. Later, in his constitutional proposals for Poland, he reluctantly approved a mandate system of representation. These changes indicate that his vehement opposition to representation in the *Contrat social* was an extreme position, not the characteristic feature of his political principles that it is usually thought to be. These same changes also suggest that Rousseau's thinking about representation evolved from an initial passive acceptance in *Économie politique* to overt hostility in the *Contrat social* to qualified opposition in the *Lettres écrites de la montagne* to qualified approval in the *Considérations sur le gouvernement de Pologne.*

11

To demonstrate this evolution in Rousseau's political thought more clearly, and also to emphasize the historical context in which his institutional thought developed, I discuss his writings in chronological order. In Part I, I argue that, up until the *Dédicace*, and possibly even later, Rousseau's institutional ideal was not significantly different from that of his fellow Encyclopedists. Not that he went out of his way to extol the virtues of representative institutions in these early writings, for certainly he did not, but for want of a well-thought-out alternative ideal of his own he passively accepted the prevailing view of his closest friends, who were overwhelmingly sympathetic toward representative government. In the *Dédicace* he presented for the first time the Genevan model of political institutions that he would use some years later in the *Contrat social*, much embellished and refined, to be sure, but still recognizably the same basic model, the main difference between the two being that in the earlier work he did not elevate the Genevan primary assembly into a universal ideal that excluded representative assemblies.

Part II is an analysis of the *Contrat social*, beginning with the general principles in Books I and II that underlie Rousseau's concept of political institutions, then proceeding to a more detailed analysis of his institutional views in Books III and IV. The final chapter in Part II evaluates the various influences that contributed to the distinctive concept of political institutions set forth in the *Contrat*. My purpose is not so much to trace the historical lineage of his institutional views, however interesting that might be in its own right, but rather to clarify his concept of political instiutions by showing which influences were most important.

In the final section, Part III, I examine the three writings in which Rousseau applied the institutional princples of the *Contrat*, either in the analysis of an existing constitution, as in the case of the *Lettres écrites de la montagne,* or by recommending new constitutions, as in the cases of his proposals for Corsica and Poland.

The Early Writings

ONE

Child of the Enlightenment: Économie Politique

POLITICAL PARTICIPATION in mid-eighteenth-century Europe was typically limited to an aristocracy whose size varied from thorities, he declared, with his usual flair for the dramatic, that if he segment of the population. In Eastern Europe the right to participate in the political process was virtually a monopoly of the nobility, and the nobility in turn was dominated by a few families of wealthy landowners. In the great monarchies of Western Europe political rights were enjoyed by a somewhat larger spectrum of the population, but there too the majority of the population was excluded from the political process. France was still in principle a divine right monarchy, and in practice political participation was the prerogative of a privileged minority of members of the various orders or estates.[1] In England the franchise in the counties extended to all those who owned a freehold worth at least forty shillings per year, a standard that was first established in 1430 when forty shillings was a far greater restriction on the franchise than it was in the eighteenth century, and in some boroughs the standards for the franchise were still less restrictive. Despite the broader franchise in England, however, there was a definite trend toward parliamentary oligarchy in the eighteenth century, and most Englishmen still remained outside even the formal political process.[2] Even in the few small European republics, citizenship was confined to an aristocracy that in most cases was hereditary and in all cases constituted only a minority of the population.[3] In terms of Rousseau's distinction between citizens and subjects—citizens were those who participated in making laws, while subjects simply obeyed laws enacted for them by higher authorities—eighteenth-century Europe had far more subjects than citizens.[4]

Representative institutions were either nonexistent or moribund in most of Continental Europe. The French Estates General had not met since 1614, and the few provincial assemblies that continued to function exercised only limited powers within their jurisdictions and in any event were little more than the political instruments of the higher nobility.[5] The preeminent eighteenth-century example of a modern representative assembly—that is, one whose members are elected by the citizenry and authorized to make decisions binding on their constituents—was the British Parliament, or more precisely the House of Commons, the great exception to the general decline of representative institutions throughout Europe in recent centuries. Even in Britain modern representative government existed only in embryo. The king still exercised wide-ranging powers and had substantial influence in Parliament, and the electoral process was rife with corruption. Large landowners purchased seats in Parliament with such regularity that a system of borough brokers developed to regulate this profitable business. Disputed elections were rare, most elections being decided by country gentlemen in private bargaining. Tenants, a class which included most freeholders, were commonly bribed or blackmailed into voting according to the wishes of their masters.[6]

The leading conception of representation in the middle of the eighteenth century was not the modern but the corporate conception, which viewed representatives as simply the agents of one or another corporate body or estate—the clergy, nobility, bourgeoisie, or some other legally defined category of the population. Whether a

16

representative was elected or not was of no consequence in this conception of representation; in practice many representatives held their positions through inheritance or appointment. Representatives of each estate were bound by a system of imperative mandates to express the views of their respective estates rather than their personal views and had to account for their conduct at the conclusion of an assembly. Since each estate met separately and each representative could speak only for his own constituency, each estate possessed a veto power over the other estates.[7] This was the conception of representation of the then defunct French Estates General, and also of the Swedish Riksdag and the Estates General of the United Provinces, both vital institutions during the eighteenth century, and, apart from the British Parliament, perhaps the best known contemporary examples of representative assemblies.[8]

The corporate conception of representation was closely associated with the trend toward aristocracy that characterized much of Europe prior to the French Revolution. Corporate bodies were dominated by aristocracies that found this conception of representation convenient because it confirmed the superior status of the existing estates or corporations. The corporate conception was more useful to those who opposed social change than to those who favored it because it gave each corporation the right to veto any change it perceived to be unfavorable, and, since it did not insist on election, it did not threaten the existing hierarchy of each estate with the specter of internal upheaval. For the French aristocracy, at least for the French nobility, the lack of a regularly assembled national representative body—the Estates General, like most representative assemblies in this period, could assemble only if summoned by the king—posed a special problem, for without it the nobility was hampered in its efforts to maintain its position vis-à-vis the royal court and its agents, on the one hand, and the increasingly demanding bourgeoisie on the other. A solution was found in the parlements, the regional courts of France, all of which were thoroughly under the sway of the robe nobility. The Parlement of Paris, largest and most influential of the parlements, declared that in the absence of the Estates General it represented the entire nation, and it used its power to defend the interests of the nobility against

17

the claims and demands of both the monarchy and the bourgeoisie. This parlementary theory of representation was basically a variation of the corporate conception, but at the same time it introduced an important new element by claiming to represent not just another corporate body but all the corporate bodies together.[9]

This, in brief, was the institutional setting and the climate of opinion regarding political participation and representation in mid-eighteenth-century Europe. If one were an Encyclopedist living in Paris, as Rousseau was at this time, and if in addition one were critical of the existing social and political system and concerned to reform it, as Rousseau was also, there were several basic choices available. One could support the *thèse nobiliaire,* which held that corporate bodies were the indispensable intermediaries between the people and the king and that these intermediaries were responsible for protecting the liberties of the people by ensuring that the king adhered to the fundamental laws of the nation. By far the most prominent spokesman for this view was Montesquieu, who set forth a moderate version of the *thèse nobilaire* in his Esprit des lois.[10]

A second possibility was the *thèse royale,* which called for an alliance between the bourgeoisie and a strong, centralized monarchy capable of subduing the aristocratically dominated corporate bodies that blocked the path to needed social reform. In its extreme form this view held that the king alone represented the French nation and that, in fact, as Louis XV would later proclaim, the king alone was the sovereign power, the source of public order, and the guardian of his subjects, whose interests were naturally the same as his own.[11] The *thèse royale* did not necessarily imply enlightened despotism, but it certainly lent itself to this view. Bourgeois advocates of the *thèse royale,* among them Voltaire and the Physiocrats, were less concerned about the possibility of enlightened despotism, however, than they were about the corporate aristocracy's stranglehold on social reform.

A third possibility was an intermediate thesis that would retain the corporate structure of society but reform it to eliminate the nobility's dominance and make it more responsive and responsible to the people as a whole. One of the key demands of the moderates was for revival and reform of the Estates General to ensure the representation of all significant social groups. Diderot and d'Holbach were among the leading proponents of the moderate view, and in the early 1750s Rousseau's own position was probably closest to that of the moderates, although he later broke with them, especially on the issue of representation, and developed a political theory that differed in fundamental respects from all three of the principal contenders at mid-century.

Montesquieu exerted a greater impact on the development of Rousseau's political thought than any other French political theorist. Several chapters of the *Contrat social* are little more than summaries of portions of the *Esprit des lois*,[12] and the relativism of Rousseau's later works on Geneva, Corsica, and Poland may indicate, as Vaughan has argued, that Montesquieu's influence on Rousseau increased with the passage of time. If so, however, it is important to add that this relativism does not accord well with the abstract quality of Rousseau's principles, especially in the *Contrat social*. As Derathé observes, Rousseau never succeeded in harmonizing or reconciling these two tendencies which coexisted in his political writings, one toward severe abstraction and the other toward an extreme relativism.[13] On other issues, for example, the account in the *Contrat social* of the social and economic conditions requisite for a democracy, Rousseau's debt to Montesquieu is less ambiguous.[14] Yet, despite his admiration for and debt to Montesquieu, Rousseau vehemently criticized the *thèse nobiliaire* that was so dear to Montesquieu. The only intermediate body that Rousseau tolerated in the *Contrat social* was the executive power, and even this he considered a continuing threat to popular sovereignty. Rousseau's well-known antipathy toward "partial societies" within the state in all probability reflected his hostility toward the corporate bodies that Montesquieu praised as the bastion of the people's liberties. For Rousseau as for Helvétius, a friend of Montesquieu but also Montesquieu's severe critic on the matter of the *thèse nobiliaire,* the essential thing was to ensure the predominance of *l'esprit civique* over *l'esprit de corps.*[15]

On the specific issue of representation, which Rousseau naturally associated to some extent with the *thèse nobiliaire,* Rousseau differed profoundly with Montesquieu, refuting virtually line by line Montesquieu's observations on representation in Book XI, Chapter 6 of *Esprit des lois*. Thus Montesquieu held that it is impossible for the whole body of the people to exercise legislative power in large states, and subject to many inconveniences even in small states. The people should therefore choose representatives to do for them what they cannot properly do themselves. Rousseau agreed that large states are not suitable for primary assemblies and even acknowledged minor inconveniences of primary assemblies in small states, but in the *Contrat social* he emphatically disagreed that these inconveniences justified representatives. Second, Montesquieu held that the people as a whole are unfit to discuss public affairs and participate directly in the process of legislation and should therefore choose the most capable of their betters to act as legislators.[16] Rousseau also had doubts about the capacity of ordinary citizens to initiate legislation and also strongly opposed giving them a role in the execution of the laws, but he did have sufficient faith in the legislative capacity of the people to insist that they personally approve or disapprove laws proposed to them by the executive.[17] Third, Montesquieu opposed tying representatives to the instructions of their constituents because he believed this would entail serious practical problems for the legislative process.[18] Rousseau acknowledged the impracticalities but still insisted on the *mandat impératif* when he reluctantly accepted the need for a system or representation in Poland.[19] Fourth, Montesquieu favored restricting the franchise to those with sufficient means to demonstrate their independence[20]; Rousseau vacillated on the question of property requirements, but when forced to take a stand on this matter in his proposals for Poland, he questioned the need for specifying a fixed amount of property as a qualification for citizenship and asked plaintively whether a poor man was any less a citizen simply because he was poor.[21] Finally, and perhaps most significantly, Montesquieu argued that the votes of those distinguished by birth, honors, or wealth should count for more than the votes of the common people, that the nobility should have a voice in legislation proportionate to its other advantages in the state[22]; Rousseau vehemently opposed a privileged status for the nobility or any other group of citizens.[23]

Among the supporters of the *thèse royale,* none advocated it with more fervor than Voltaire. If Voltaire had one political concern that took precedence over all others, it was probably that men of letters be free from government censorship and oppression.[24] If this and other civil liberties could be guaranteed by an absolute monarchy, it was of little importance to him whether these guarantees were backed up by institutional mechanisms.[25] Voltaire may not have been a defender of enlightened despotism, as some have claimed, but he unhesitatingly sided with the Bourbon monarchs when confronted with the same unhappy choices as Diderot, d'Holbach, and other reformers who were at least as uneasy with absolute monarchy as they were with the nobility. A sympathetic critic of Voltaire's politics characterizes his position as "constitutional absolutism" but acknowledges that Voltaire's failure to provide for institutions to determine whether or not a king abides by the laws leaves him open to a serious objection: "his royalism seems to leave him almost defenseless against despotism, enlightened or unenlightened."[26]

In practice, if not in theory, Voltaire's constitutional absolutism differed little from the *despotisme légal* of the Physiocrats.[27] For Rousseau, "legal despotism" was a self-contradictory phrase[28]—a regime is either legal or despotic, but not both—and Diderot and d'Holbach voiced similar criticism of the phrase as well as the Physiocrats' support of absolutism. Not all Physiocrats were opposed to the representative institutions of the *ancien régime,* but those who did favor some form of representation tended to regard the power of representatives as purely consultative in the tradition of the French monarchy.[29]

Rousseau's views on political participation and representation thus differed sharply from those of staunch advocates of the *thèse nobiliaire* and the *thèse royale,* from those of Montesquieu as well as from those of Voltaire and the Physiocrats. At mid-century and on through the early 1750s Rousseau's views were much closer to the mainstream of Enlightenment thought.

The heart of the Enlightenment during this period was the *Encyclopédie.* Apart from Rousseau, whose relationship to the *Encyclopédie* terminated after his article on *Économie politique,* none of the major Encyclopedists was primarily a political thinker. Diderot, d'Holbach, Jaucourt, and Saint-Lambert, who together contributed the bulk of the political articles to the *Encyclopédie*, all borrowed heavily from Montesquieu and from the writers of the natural-law school, especially Grotius, Pufendorf, Locke, and Burlamaqui.[30] The authorship of the last ten volumes of the *Encyclopédie*, which were published together in 1765, is often difficult to determine. D'Holbach's contribution to these volumes numbered more than 1100 articles, including many on political and religious questions. Jaucourt's contribution to the entire seventeen volumes numbered more than 17,000 articles totaling some 4.7 million words, but, as these staggering figures suggest, he was essentially a compiler of other people's views. His moderate views on political issues were generally also those of his fellow contributors. Regardless of the specific authorship of each article, the imprint of Diderot, the editor and moving force of the *Encyclopédie*, is evident throughout the work.[31] Like his fellow contributors, Diderot was a monarchist, but his and their emphasis, in contrast to that of Voltaire and the Physiocrats, was always on limited monarchy. His support of the French monarchy did not prevent him from supporting the constitutional contentions of the *parlements*, especially the Parlement of Paris, which, despite their shortcomings and privileged status, were virtually the only institutions capable of legally restraining the absolute powers of the crown. He also favored the provincial assemblies as another intermediate representative institution that could temper the ambitions of the monarchy.[32] Diderot's practical proposals were generally quite moderate. He believed that a constitution like England's was the best guarantee that a king would act in the interest of his subjects, even though he was no less aware than Rousseau of the corruption of Parliament.

The most important single article in the *Encyclopédie* that dealt with representation was one entitled "Représentants," an article that was long attributed to Diderot but is now believed to have been written by d'Holbach.[33] Whoever of the two was in fact the author, it probably reflects the views of both. It has been described as "the most positive attempt in the whole of the *Encyclopédie* to set forth in detail an alternative to the absolute monarchy under which

Frenchmen of that age lived."[34] The article begins with a definition of representatives:

> Les *représentants* d'une nation sont des citoyens choisis, qui dans un gouvernement tempéré sont chargés par la société de parler en son nom, de stipuler ses intérêts, d'empêcher qu'on ne l'opprime, de concourir à l'administration.[35]

Representative institutions take various forms—diets, estates general, parliaments, senates—in different countries. In an absolute monarchy the king is the sole representative of the people, while in a *monarchie tempérée* such as England the king has full executive power but shares legislative power with the people's representatives, namely, Parliament.[36]

Following these preliminary remarks, d'Holbach traced the history of representative institutions in Europe. The kingdoms founded by the barbaric Germanic tribes that conquered Gaul, Spain, England, and other nations following the collapse of the Roman Empire were originally military governments without representative institutions. These conquerors, the ancestors of the present nobility, initially claimed for themselves alone the right to represent the people but later allowed the clergy to choose its own representatives in an effort to reinforce their domination of the lower classes.

> Voilà pourquoi dans toutes les monarchies modernes nous voyons partout les nobles, les grands, c'est-à-dire des guerriers, posséder les terres des anciens habitants et se mettre en possession du droit exclusif de représenter les nations; celles-ci, avilies, écrasées, opprimées, n'eurent point la liberté de joindre leurs voix à celles de leurs superbes vainqueurs. Telle est sans doute la source de cette prétention de la noblesse, qui s'arrogea longtemps le droit de parler exclusivement à tous les autres au nom des nations. Elle continua toujours à regarder ses concitoyens comme des esclaves vaincus, même un grand nombre de siècles après une conquête à laquelle les successeurs de cette noblesse conquérante n'avaient point eu de part.[37]

The situation during feudal times was thus one in which those who contributed least to society, namely, the nobility and clergy, had all the rights, while those who contributed most, that is, the farmers,

23

bourgeois, and manufacturers, had no rights and no representation. Kings had relatively little power, and the great majority of the people were oppressed by a useless aristocracy. As time passed, kings united with their people against the nobility and increasingly sought the advice of representatives of their productive subjects.[38]

This brief historical sketch is of particular interest because it helps to fill in a significant gap in Rousseau's remarks on the origins of representation. Rousseau several times referred to the feudal origins of representation and condemned the feudal system as the worst of all forms of government,[39] but he nowhere explained in any detail what it was about feudalism that rendered it so objectionable. D'Holbach's account, which stressed the role of conquest and heredity in the early development of representative institutions and the exclusion of the productive majority in favor of a privileged and useless minority, may well reflect Rousseau's own view and in any case is fully consistent with what is known of Rousseau's view.

Following this historical introduction, d'Holbach presented what was in effect an argument for the revival and reform of the Estates General in France. He acknowledged the right of the nobility and clergy to elect representatives but urged that this right be extended to include separate representation for magistrates, merchants, and farmers, at least those who met specified property requirements. He warned against the danger of having one class of citizens represent its own particular interests as the common interest of the nation, as was true of the feudal system, and urged adoption of a system in which no one class would predominate but which would rather permit all to coexist in a state of equilibrium.[40] As for the function of representatives, he insisted that they were simply the agents of their constituents:

> Quels que soient les usages ou les abus que le temps a pu introduire dans les gouvernements libres et temprérés, un *représentant* ne peut s'arroger le droit de faire parler à ses constituants un langage opposé à leurs intérêts. Les droits des constituants sont les droits de la nation, ils sont imprescriptibles et inaliénables. Pour peu qu'on consulte la raison, elle prouvera que les constituants peuvent en tout temps démentir, désavouer et révoquer les *représentants* qui les trahissent, qui

abusent de leurs pleins pouvoirs contre eux-mêmes, ou qui renoncent pour eux à des droits inhérents à leur essence. En un mot, les *représentants* d'un peuple libre ne peuvent point lui imposer un joug qui détruirait sa félicité; nul homme n'acquiert le droit d'en représenter un autre malgré lui.[41]

Although d'Holbach did not specifically call for the *mandat impératif*, and may even have preferred, as Montesquieu did, that representatives have somewhat more freedom to express their own views than was allowed by the *mandat impératif*, his emphasis throughout was that the primary function of representatives is to express the views of their constituents, not to arrogate to themselves the right to decide what is best for their constituents. Rousseau went a step further by insisting that Poland's national representatives be bound by imperative mandates, but he and d'Holbach were in fundamental agreement on the need to prevent representatives from substituting their own views for those of their constituents.[42]

D'Holbach's reference to "les gouvernements libres et tempérés" in the first sentence of the preceding quote was a reference to England, specifically to Parliament, whose members were considered free to vote their own opinions. And yet it was precisely these representatives with their vaunted freedom who often betrayed their constituents to their oppressors. With a vehemence worthy of Rousseau, d'Holbach railed against the corruption, the traffic in votes and offices, and other evils of some representative bodies, clearly referring to England. He concluded with a warning that, whenever the members of a representative body enjoyed the uninterrupted right to represent the nation, they would soon become masters of that nation. Periodic elections were therefore essential to prevent representatives from exceeding or abusing their powers.[43]

The parallels between d'Holbach's view of representatives and Rousseau's own view are striking. Both traced the origins of representation to feudalism; both condemned the nobility's domination of representative institutions, feudal and modern; both urged that the right of representation be extended to include additional classes of citizens; both sharply criticized the best known contemporary example of representative government, England; and both insisted that representatives express their constituents' wishes, not their own. These parallels indicate that Rousseau differed with the mainstream of Encyclopedist thinking on political institutions less than is generally thought. Despite all these similarities, however, the spirit that pervades Rousseau's constitutional proposals is not that which inspired d'Holbach's proposal to revive and reform the French Estates General. D'Holbach embraced the principle of representation without reservation and saw restoration of the long defunct Estates General as the key to reestablishing a healthy body politic in France. Rousseau accepted representative government with great reluctance, arguing in effect that it would work only if accompanied by the kind of public-spiritedness and citizen participation traditionally associated with the city-state.

Even during the early 1750s, when Rousseau was still on good terms with most of his fellow Encyclopedists, he attached more importance to the city-state ideal than his coworkers did, but his admiration for the city-state did not, at that time, lead him to reject the institutional ideal of the Encyclopedists—limited monarchy tempered by representative assemblies—in favor of the primary assemblies of the city-state. According to his *Confessions,* he conceived the idea for the *Institutions politiques* as early as 1743 or 1744 while working in Venice as secretary to the French ambassador, but at mid-century he had made little progress on this great project, which he saw as the major work of his life, the one that would put the seal on his reputation. He never completely finished the *Institutions politiques,* although parts of it were eventually published in his *Discours sur l'économie politique,* his *Lettre à d'Alembert,* and, above all, the *Contrat social.* The idea for this *magnum opus* originated in his intuition that "everything is radically dependent on politics" and that consequently "no people would ever be anything but what the nature of their government made them." The problem was to determine what kind of government would create the most virtuous and enlightened people. It would necessarily be the government that adhered most strictly to the rule of law, but then the question arose, "What is law?" It would take many years to work out the implications of these insights. He kept at it because it was a labor of love, a service to humanity, but in the early 1750s he was still very much unclear about the nature of the ideal government and its institutions, and accordingly he tended to follow the lead of his then close friends among the Encyclopedists.[44]

In the *Préface à Narcisse,* completed in late 1752 or early 1753, Rousseau reflected on how difficult it had been for him to overcome the prejudices of his century and recognized that his own political thought was still very much in the process of development.[45] Whether one sees the celebrated illumination of Vincennes which occurred in 1749 as a kind of divine inspiration or as merely another, perhaps decisive, moment in the evolution of his thought,[46] the *Discours sur les sciences et les arts* did not exhaust this vision, which would not be fully revealed until *Émile* and the *Contrat social.*[47] The prolonged controversy over the first *Discours* forced him to reflect on the ideas he had there stated so boldly, often hyperbolically, and to develop little by little what he was to call his *grand système.*[48] In one of his responses to critics of the first *Discours* he recognized that it would be necessary to consider many basic political questions in order to properly defend and explain the positions he had taken in this initial publication. The necessary research could not be undertaken in his present circumstances, however, but had to await a more favorable working environment like Geneva.[49]

While the first *Discours* did not reveal his mature political thought, it did contain important indications of the direction in which his thought was evolving. His lament that there were few citizens left in the world, and that even these few usually died indigent and despised in an abandoned countryside,[50] reflected the special significance he would attach to the title "citizen" throughout his life. So rare were citizens in the cosmopolitan monarchies of the eighteenth century that he adopted the title as a mark of distinction.[51] His identification with Geneva was apparently less nearly complete than it would become later, however, for he referred to the French as "our nation," although this may have been nothing more than the exaggeration of a foreigner competing in a prize essay contest sponsored by a French academy of learning.[52] And even in the first *Discours* he did not completely forget about his homeland, which he praised on two occasions, once as "that rustic nation"[53] and again as "a group of poor mountaineers."[54]

Rousseau wrote the *Discours sur les sciences et les arts* as an obscure figure seeking recognition from the very world of arts and sciences that he called into question through the astute use of paradox and sophism. When he wrote the *Discours sur l'inégalité* he was an accomplished author who no longer needed to prove himself and who instead sought to give a philosophical and scientific foundation for his critique of society.[55] His political thought was still not fully formed, but he now had a solid foundation on which to build. What remained to be done was to determine the nature of a legitimate society and its institutional arrangements, a far more difficult task than the criticism of existing social and political institutions. The tentative quality of his political thought at this time can be seen in his discussion, toward the end of the second *Discours,* of the terms of the fundamental laws or constitution for a legitimate society:

> Without entering at present into the researches yet to be undertaken concerning the nature of the fundamental compact of all government, I limit myself, in following common opinion, to consider here the establishment of the body politic as a true contract between the people and the chiefs it chooses for itself: a contract by which the two parties obligate themselves to observe laws that are stipulated in it and that form the bonds of their union.[56]

Rousseau's reference here to a contract between a people and its government suggests that he had not yet completely rejected the legitimacy of a pact of submission, a concept that he would explicitly refute in the *Contrat social.*[57] It is possible, of course, that even here he presupposed a social contract prior to this contract between the people and its magistrates and that he meant to dissociate himself from the traditional notion of a pact of submission when he limited himself to "following common opinion." The continuation of the passage quoted above lends some support to this interpretation:

> The people having, on the subject of social relations, united all their wills into a single one, all the articles on which this will is explicit become so many fundamental laws obligating all members of the State without exception, and one of these laws regulates the choice and power of magistrates charged with

watching over the execution of the others. This power extends to everything that can maintain the constitution, without going so far as to change it.[58]

As Masters points out, the contract by which the people "united all their wills into a single one" logically precedes and is superior to the laws regulating "the choice and power of magistrates," who are denied the power to change the constitution. According to Masters, then, "Rousseau had already thought through, at least in a rough way, his understanding of the principles of political right."[59] Perhaps so, provided that emphasis is placed on the qualifying phrase "in a rough way." For even if Masters is correct in arguing that Rousseau here distinguished between a prior social contract and a subsequent contract between the people and its government, the fact remains that he used the traditional concepts and terminology. It thus seems best to take seriously Rousseau's claim that there were "researches yet to be undertaken concerning the nature of the fundamental compact of all government."

Even the *Discours sur l'économie politique*, which was not published until November 1755 in Volume V of the *Encyclopédie*, reflects a strong continuing Encyclopedist influence on Rousseau's view of political institutions. The precise dates of composition of *Économie politique* are unknown. René Hubert, who has probably devoted more attention to this matter than anyone else, contends that Rousseau wrote it in the early months of 1754, that is, prior to the completion of either the *Dédicace* or the *Discours sur l'inégalité*, although he concedes that the original draft may have been toned down at a later date by either Rousseau or Diderot, the latter in his capacity as editor of the *Encyclopédie*.[60] Most commentators prefer a later date for completion of *Économie politique* but acknowledge that substantial portions of it may have been written as early as Hubert contends.[61]

Without pretending to solve this mystery, I shall discuss *Économie politique* prior to the *Dédicace*, which Rousseau completed on June 12, 1754, just before his return to Geneva, because it seems to me that the *Dédicace* marks an important watershed in the development of Rousseau's view of political institutions. Even if *Économie politique* was not completed until a later date, it does not reflect several important changes that came about as a result of Rousseau's re-newed interest in Geneva. These changes are not fully evident in the *Dédicace* either, but it was in the *Dédicace* that Rousseau first presented his conception of the Genevan model that was to play a crucial role in all his later writings on political institutions, and it was also in the *Dédicace* that he first clearly expressed his preference for primary over representative assemblies, a preference that was to become perhaps the most distinctive feature of his mature view of political institutions.

While his discussion of political institutions in *Économie politique* agrees on many points with his discussion in the *Dédicace*, he took a very different view of primary assemblies in *Économie politique*, disparaging their value and accepting representative assemblies as a legitimate alternative. This may have been due in part to the fact that *Économie politique*, as an article in the great French *Encyclopédie*, was addressed to a much larger and more varied audience, one that would not be so appreciative of the value of primary assemblies as would the Genevans for whom he wrote the *Dédicace*. This cannot be the whole of the explanation, however, for *Économie politique*, like the *Contrat social*, is an abstract treatise setting forth the basic principles of political institutions, principles that are supposedly of universal validity, and Rousseau's position on the issue of primary versus representative assemblies differs sharply in the two works. I shall argue that this difference was largely due to the increasing importance Rousseau attached to Genevan political institutions and that he in fact modeled the political institutions of the *Contrat social* on Genevan institutions, or, more precisely, on Genevan institutions as they were perceived by the bourgeoisie, but first it is important to note the Encyclopedist influence on his view of political institutions during the early 1750s.

Much of what Rousseau had to say about political institutions in both the *Dédicace* and *Économie politique* simply reflected prevailing opinion among the Encyclopedists. One of Rousseau's primary goals in the opening section of *Économie politique* was to demonstrate the importance of establishing an identity of interests between governors and governed, which he believed could best be achieved by subjecting everyone alike to the rule of law, "the most sublime of all human institutions." He tried to convince the princes of Europe that a government which bound itself by the law was far stronger than any tyrannical government. "It is certain that all peoples become in the long run what the government makes them," and if a government makes them love the laws it will assure itself of the most absolute authority.[62] Saint-Lambert expressed the same view in his article on the "Législateur," in which he observed that, whenever the spirit of community reigns in a country, the people perceive the law as their friend rather than as their master.[63] Similarly, the social welfare and tax measures proposed in the latter part of *Économie politique* were for the most part borrowed from the Encyclopedists. Despite Rousseau's reputation as a radical egalitarian, the Encyclopedists were hardly less concerned than he to prevent or reduce extreme economic inequality and advocated many of the same measures to achieve this goal. Both Rousseau and Jaucourt, author of the article "Impôts," the most important in the *Encyclopédie* dealing with taxes, favored tax exemptions for the poor, a progressive income tax, luxury taxes, and other taxes that would reduce economic differences as well as increase state revenues.[64]

Rousseau's emphasis in *Économie politique,* like that of other political articles in the *Encyclopédie,* was on the need for government to respect the rights and persons of the governed. He declared it the duty of the state to ensure the security of even the least of its members and concluded a long excursus on this theme with this admonition to governments: "Show respect, therefore, to your fellow-citizens, and you will render yourselves worthy of respect; show respect to liberty, and your power will increase daily. Never exceed your rights, and they will become unlimited."[65] At the same time, however, Rousseau argued for a very active role for government and allotted it extremely broad discretionary powers.[66]

If the first duty of government was to govern in accordance with the laws and to bind itself by those laws, there were an infinity of administrative details that must be left to the wisdom of the government. Governments have two basic rules to guide them in applying the laws: (1) decide individual cases in keeping with the spirit of the laws and (2) consult the general will when all else fails. But, he went on, this does not mean that the whole nation must be assembled every time some unforeseen event makes it necessary to consult the general will, partly because there is no guarantee that the decisions of such an assembly would express the general will, and partly because it would obviously be impracticable to hold such assemblies in large states. In any case, it is hardly ever necessary to resort to this extreme remedy in a state whose government is well intentioned, since such a government can easily recognize the decision most favorable to the public interest and therefore to the general will.[67] The cavalier manner in which Rousseau dispenses with primary assemblies in this passage is in sharp contrast to the position he would take in the *Contrat social*, where he insisted on primary assemblies even at the risk of the ridicule of those moderns who consider them impracticable.[68]

While his position in the passage above is odd in view of his later and better known position in the *Contrat social*, his approval, in three other passages of *Économie politique*, of the use of representatives as a legitimate alternative to primary assemblies is even more surprising. In the first of these, he contended that "Before any use is made of this fund [i.e., the funds derived from the public domain] it should be assigned or accepted by an assembly of the people, or of the estates of the country, which should determine its future use."[69] The term *estates* presumably refers to representative institutions like the Estates General of France or its provincial or other national counterparts. Since the act of approving the use of public funds may or may not be seen as a legislative act, which would be an act of sovereignty in Rousseau's understanding of the term, Rousseau's acceptance of representatives in this situation does not necessarily conflict with the principle that he would proclaim in the *Contrat social* to the effect that sovereignty can never be represented. Still, it is somewhat surprising that he should juxtapose a primary assembly and a representative assembly as equally valid alternatives, as though he were simply trying to cover the range of existing political institutions that might be used in similar situations.

The other two passages in which he accepted the use of representatives are less ambiguous, although even here it is not possible to say unequivocally that he accepted representation in *Économie politique* in precisely the same sense in which he rejected it in the *Contrat social*. In both passages the issue was whether or not popular approval was required for the institution of new taxes. In the first of these two passages, Rousseau rightly observed that popular approval was traditionally required and added that this approval could be given either directly by the people or indirectly by their representatives.

> That taxes cannot be legitimately established except by the consent of the people or its representatives, is a truth generally admitted by all philosophers and jurists of any repute on questions of public right, not even excepting Bodin.[70]

This requirement was one of the principal sources of power of the representative institutions that flourished in the fourteenth through the sixteenth centuries in most of Western Europe. Although most of these representative assemblies had since succumbed to increasingly centralized monarchies that were able to dispense with them, others, notably the British Parliament, had not only survived but also had displaced the monarch as the effective sovereign and had achieved this largely through the skillful use of their power of the purse. Within a decade after *Économie politique* was published, the slogan "no taxation without representation" was to become one of the principal battle cries of the American revolutionaries, and not many years later the French monarchy would founder and eventually collapse when confronted by a militant Estates General summoned to relieve the monarchy's financial problems. Popular consent to taxation had also been at the center of Geneva's political controversies in the eighteenth century; indeed it was one of the few powers that the Genevan primary assembly had managed to retain despite the determined efforts of the ruling patriciate to dispense with it or get around it. All this makes it highly unlikely that Rousseau viewed popular consent to taxation as simply an administrative procedure and correspondingly increases the likelihood that he was speaking in this case of the legitimate exercise of sovereignty by representatives.

This likelihood is increased still further when one considers the context in which he accepted representation, for this acceptance was in effect the conclusion of an argument in the preceding paragraph that was obviously borrowed from John Locke's *Second Treatise*, a work that was widely known and respected by the Encyclopedists. Locke had declared that "The great end of Mens entring into Society" was "the enjoyment of their Properties in Peace and Safety." [71] Similarly, Rousseau held that "the foundation of the social compact is property; and its first condition, that everyone should be maintained in the peaceful possession of what belongs to him." [72] Several paragraphs later, Locke added that "The *Supream Power cannot take* from any Man any part of his *Property* without his own consent." [73] This would appear to rule out taxation altogether and compel governments to rely on voluntary contributions, but Locke avoided this awkward conclusion by redefining "consent":

> 'Tis true, Governments cannot be supported without great Charge, and 'tis fit every one who enjoys his share of the Protection, should pay out of his Estate his proportion for the maintenance of it. But still it must be with his own Consent, *i.e.* the Consent of the Majority, giving it either by themselves, or their Representatives chosen by them. [74]

Again, Rousseau followed Locke's argument:

> It is true that, by the same treaty [i.e., the social compact], every one binds himself, at least tacitly, to be assessed toward the public wants: but as this undertaking cannot prejudice the fundamental law, and presupposes that the need is clearly recognized by all who contribute to it, it is plain that such assessment, in order to be lawful, must be voluntary; it must depend, not indeed on a particular will, as if it were necessary to have the consent of each individual, and that he should give no more than just what he pleased, but on a general will, decided by vote of a majority, and on the basis of a proportional rating which leaves nothing arbitrary in the imposition of the tax. [75]

Rousseau's assertion "That taxes cannot be legitimately established except by the consent of the people or its representatives" came immediately after this quote. The parallels between these passages from Locke and Rousseau are too striking to be coincidental. If any additional confirmation were necessary, Rousseau provided it with a note in the margin of the manuscript, "Voyez Locke," which was not included in the published version[76]; in the preliminary version of this section of *Économie politique* Rousseau specifically mentioned Locke along with Grotius and Pufendorf as philosophers who had acknowledged the principle of no taxation without popular consent.[77]

All of these factors—the widely recognized principle of no taxation without popular consent and its close association with the development and power of representative institutions; the fact that it had figured prominently in Genevan politics within Rousseau's lifetime; and the indisputable influence of Locke, whose *Second Treatise* was an integral part of the Encyclopedists' political bible—suggest that in 1754–1755 Rousseau accepted the principle of representation. There is no indication that he had given much thought to the question, that he had carefully weighed the pros and cons and decided in favor of representation. On the contrary, all the evidence suggests that his acceptance was passive, that he simply followed the majority opinion of the Encyclopedists with whom he was still closely associated at that time, and this opinion was overwhelmingly favorable to representative government. Passive or not, there is no reason to doubt that this acceptance was genuine, especially since it appeared in a theoretical treatise rather than a *livre de circonstance*.

Rousseau's third reference in *Économie politique* to the use of representatives qualified the position he took in the second reference just discussed. After first reasserting the need for "the express consent of the people or its representatives" before instituting new taxes, he modified this requirement by claiming that it applied only to the necessities of life, not to "articles the use of which we can deny ourselves," namely, luxuries.[78] Since no one is obligated to indulge in luxuries, taxes on luxury items[79] can be considered voluntary, and hence individual consent takes the place of majority consent.[80] With the exception of taxes on luxury items, however, Rousseau in this passage reaffirmed his basic position that new taxes must be approved by the people or its representatives, so that once again primary and representative assemblies are treated as equally legitimate alternatives. Although none of his three references to representatives in *Économie politique* clearly states that representatives may exercise sovereignty, that is, approve legislation in behalf of their constituents, all three references, and especially the latter two, seem to justify this inference. If representatives can legitimately act on a matter affecting the very foundation of the social compact—for that is what he claimed was involved in the principle of no taxation without popular consent—then it becomes a moot question whether or not this constitutes an act of sovereignty.

TWO

Reborn Genevan: The Dédicace

WHEREAS *Économie politique* reflects the continuing influence of the Encyclopedists on Rousseau's view of political institutions, the principal inspiration of the *Dédicace* to the *Discours sur l'inégalité*, which was written at approximately the same time, was clearly Geneva. Undoubtedly Rousseau had formed a somewhat idealized conception of his native city during his long absence, and he may have deliberately exaggerated its virtues to ingratiate himself with his erstwhile fellow citizens, who were preparing to welcome the prodigal back to the fold. However that may be, he remembered or had learned enough about the reality of Geneva to use its institutions as a model, and the Genevan model of the *Dédicace* was his first systematic presentation of the model of a political society based on a primary assembly, which would become the hallmark of his view of political institutions. The *Dédicace* thus provides vital insights into his thinking about political institutions, but only in the context of Genevan institutions and the political struggles that had been fought over these institutions, particularly in the first half of the eighteenth century. This necessitates a rather lengthy digression into Genevan political and institutional history, since this history is crucial for understanding not only the *Dédicace* but also his later political writings, especially the *Contrat social* and the *Lettres écrites de la montagne,* in which the Genevan model figures prominently.

Geneva in the eighteenth century was divided into five political orders: (1) *citoyens,* who held their status by virtue of having been born in Geneva of *citoyen* fathers and who alone had the right to serve as magistrates; (2) *bourgeois,* who could vote as members of the primary assembly, the Conseil Général, but could not hold any major political office; (3) *habitants,* foreigners who had bought the right to live in Geneva and engage in certain economic activities but who had no political rights; (4) *natifs,* the sons of *habitants,* born in Geneva and having the same rights as their parents; and (5) *sujets,* or rural people living outside the city but subject to its government. *Citoyens* and *bourgeois* together constituted the Conseil Général, which numbered no more than 1,500 out of a total population of perhaps 25,000.[1]

Superimposed on this fivefold political division was a more significant division into three major social classes: (1) the patriciate or aristocracy, a self-perpetuating oligarchy composed of a small number of *citoyen* families, mostly descended from French and Italian refugees of the sixteenth century, who lived in the upper city (*haute ville*), wore distinctive clothing forbidden to other classes, and dominated politically through control of the two principal executive organs of the city, the Petit Conseil and the Grand Conseil (or Conseil des Deux Cents) (during the eighteenth century the patriciate came increasingly under the cultural, intellectual, and political influence of France); (2) the bourgeoisie, as those *citoyens* and *bourgeois* who were not members of the patriciate were collectively known, their participation in the political life of Geneva being limited for the most part to membership in the Conseil Général; (3) *natifs, habitants,* and *sujets,* often collectively known as *natifs,* who were mainly workers who possessed no political rights and only limited social and economic rights.[2]

The political system by which Geneva was governed in the eighteenth century had taken shape two centuries earlier in the wake of the Reformation. In 1526 a pro-Swiss faction successfully defied the Genevan bishop and entered into a pact of *combourgeoisie* with Bern and Fribourg. This political revolution was followed in the 1530s by a religious revolution that culminated in May 1536 with a unanimous vote of the Conseil Général to reject papal authority. In the course of this crucial decade in Genevan history the citizenry had claimed for itself virtually all the political prerogatives formerly exercised by their rulers under the episcopate.[3] The first years of this newly created Republic of Geneva were marked by almost continual political upheaval. Not until the Conseil Général approved the Edicts of 1543, whose principal author was Calvin, did Geneva have a system of stable political institutions, although these proved to be remarkably stable, lasting until the end of the eighteenth century with virtually no major changes.[4]

The Conseil Général had once functioned as the real legislative power of Geneva in the fourteenth and fifteenth centuries, and even as late as 1539 it had rejected a proposal that would have deprived it of the legislative initiative. During this long interval, however, it had relinquished one after another of its former prerogatives, and in 1543 it finally acquiesced to the proposition it had rejected only four years earlier by approving the provision of Calvin's aristocratically inspired edicts, which mandated that no proposal could be considered by the Conseil des Deux Cents until it had been approved by the Petit Conseil, and could not be considered by the Conseil Général until it had been approved by both the Petit and Grand Conseils. Approval of this provision effectively ended the legislative sovereignty of the Conseil Général by depriving it of the power to initiate legislation.

The Edicts of 1543 also confirmed the long-standing practice by which the Petit and Grand Conseils nominated the candidates for the four syndics, who were then elected by the Conseil Général. At the time that the bishop Adhémar Fabri codified Geneva's liberties in 1387, the syndics were the only officially recognized municipal authorities other than the Conseil Général, which nominated and elected the syndics annually and held them accountable for their conduct in office. In the early fifteenth century, however, the Petit Conseil, which previously had functioned as a purely consultative body, gradually emerged as the cog wheel of administration, and from that time onward the syndics could achieve little without its assent. In 1457 the Conseil Général created the Conseil des Cinquante as a means of mobilizing support to face an external threat. This council was enlarged to sixty members in 1502 and remained in existence until the end of the republic, although it never played a decisive political role. It did, however, establish a precedent for another expanded council, the Conseil des Deux Cents or Grand Conseil, which was created in 1526.

In 1530 the Conseil des Deux Cents claimed the right to choose members of the Petit Conseil, who had previously been chosen by the syndics, and the Petit Conseil simultaneously claimed the right to choose members of the Grand Conseil and thus created a tandem of ostensibly advisory bodies which nevertheless already exercised important political functions. Both councils were recognized by Calvin's edicts of 1543, and since they also controlled the initiation of legislation and the nomination of syndics and other important magistrates, they became, in practice if not in theory, a self-perpetuating oligarchy that could dominate Genevan political life so long as those excluded from the oligarchy could not mount a united challenge to their authority. During the first decade of the Calvinist republic there was widespread opposition to this arrangement, especially since Calvin and his fellow French refugees progressively replaced native Genevans on these councils. By 1555 this opposition was crushed, and the newly formed patriciate then entrenched in power was able to maintain its domination until the end of the eighteenth century.[5]

Conflict between the ruling patriciate and the remainder of the *citoyens* and *bourgeois* had occurred sporadically ever since the patriciate consolidated its hold on the government in the sixteenth century, but early in the eighteenth century this conflict erupted with a new intensity as the result of pressures exerted by the influx of thousands of French Protestants seeking refuge in Geneva following the revocation of the Edict of Nantes in 1685. Many of these newcomers were men of substance and spirit who were less willing than earlier generations to accept the oligarchic rule of the patriciate, even if this rule were usually benevolent. In 1704 protests by the bourgeoisie led to the repeal of recently imposed taxes on wine. Encouraged by this easy success, the bourgeosie soon radicalized its demands, which culminated in a petition circulated by one François Delachenaz calling for secret elections in the Conseil Général to ensure more freedom of expression, election of members of the Grand Conseil by the council itself instead of by the Petit Conseil, limitations on the number of family members who could belong to these councils, and publication of all edicts. When Delachenaz tried to present these demands at a meeting of the Conseil Général in January 1707, he was silenced on the technicality that no proposal could be presented to the Conseil Général until it had been examined by the Petit Conseil.

The fight initiated by Delachenaz's petition was now joined by more capable persons, led by the patrician Pierre Fatio, who roused public opinion and eventually succeeded in having three of the four demands of the original petition accepted at a meeting of the Conseil Général in May 1707. Fatio also proposed reforms that went far beyond those of Delachenaz. He called for annual meetings of the Conseil Général and insisted that the Conseil Général be able to debate and vote on any proposal that was supported by at least three members of the Petit Conseil (composed of twenty-five members) or ten members of the Grand Conseil or fifty members of the Conseil Général.

Implementation of these proposals would have radically altered Genevan politics. Instead, a compromise was agreed on whereby the Conseil Général was to meet as a deliberative body every five years instead of the annual deliberating sessions proposed by Fatio—the Conseil Général already met annually, but only to elect syndics from a list of candidates submitted by the Petit and Grand Conseils—and the Petit Conseil retained full control of the legislative initiative. The patriciate was thoroughly alarmed by these challenges to its monopolization of political power, for it was clear to patriciate and bourgeoisie alike that Fatio's reforms were designed to make the Conseil Général sovereign in fact as well as in theory—for even the patriciate spokesman, the Second Syndic Jean-Robert Chouet, conceded that the Conseil Général was sovereign in some abstract sense. With the support of troops from Bern and Zurich,

41

the patriciate arrested and executed Fatio and other leaders of the bourgeoisie and exiled or cowed the remaining dissidents.[6]

The issues that led to this confrontation between the patriciate and the bourgeoisie in 1707 led to similar confrontations throughout the eighteenth century. The crux of this conflict was the role of the Conseil Général, which remained an ineffective check on the Petit and Grand Conseils despite the reforms of 1707. Its ineffectiveness was made painfully apparent in 1712, the year of Rousseau's birth, when the Conseil Général, meeting in the first of the quinquennial meetings agreed to five years earlier, allowed itself to be persuaded by the patriciate to dispense with this requirement and thus voluntarily relinquished one of the important concessions secured by Fatio.[7]

From 1712 until Rousseau's departure from Geneva in 1728 there were no confrontations between the patriciate and the bourgeoisie comparable in intensity to that of 1707, although the imposition of new taxes in 1714 led to several years of protests of one kind or another. At least two anonymous letters were circulated in the city condemning the Petit Conseil as despotic, and in late 1718 the ancient tradition of *représentations* was revived; that is, grievances were formally submitted by groups of citizens to the syndics and attorney general. The leaders of these well-organized but unsuccessful protests were nearly all from the Saint-Gervais quarter of the city, *la basse ville*, and included Jean-Jacques' grandfather David Rousseau as well as other relatives and close friends of the family. Jean-Jacques had moved to Saint-Gervais in 1717 when his father was no longer able to maintain residence in the *haute ville* where Rousseau was born. There can be no doubt that the experience of growing up in this quarter left a lasting impression on Rousseau. Everything about the life of Saint-Gervais, from the games children played to the books they read to the ideas they were exposed to at public meetings and in the more intimate *cercles*—small political discussion groups in which the memory of Pierre Fatio was kept alive—conspired to imbue Rousseau with the political outlook of the bourgeoisie.[8]

The next major confrontation between the patriciate and the bourgeoisie began in 1734 with a *représentation* by the bourgeoisie demanding that new taxes have the consent of the Conseil Général. The Petit Conseil replied with a report written principally by Jean-Jacques Burlamaqui, who argued that the Genevan constitution was based, not on the sovereignty of the Conseil Général, as the bourgeoisie contended and as even many patricians had once conceded, but on "a mutually binding agreement between those who govern and those who are governed."[9] Sovereignty was thus shared by the Conseil Général, the Petit Conseil, and the Conseil des Deux Cents. In his celebrated work *Principes du droit politique* Burlamaqui made the same point in different terms, arguing there that Geneva was neither a pure democracy nor a pure aristocracy but a mixture of the two, an "aristo-démocratie."[10]

Burlamaqui's thesis was countered by an anonymous pamphlet, *Réflexions communiquées à un nouveau citoyen de cette ville*, published in 1734 and reflecting the views of the more radical among the bourgeoisie, which asserted the inalienability of popular sovereignty. The author contended that a free people can change the laws as it pleases, even without the consent of the magistrates. True, the constitution requires that matters presented to the Conseil Général be discussed first by the Petit and Grand Conseils, but if the people insist, these matters must be submitted to the Conseil Général whether the other two councils approve or not. In other words, the Conseil Général had not forfeited its legislative initiative by agreeing to this celebrated provision of the Genevan constitution. Not surprisingly, the Petit Conseil condemned the pamphlet as seditious.[11] The dispute intensified in July 1734 as a result of the *tamponnement* affair in which government troops secretly spiked the cannon in the Saint-Gervais quarter in an attempt to prevent their use by the bourgeoisie in the event the dispute led to violence. Discovery of this by the bourgeoisie led to repeated demands for punishment of the Tamponneurs, as those responsible were called, and severely embittered relations between the patriciate and the bourgeoisie. The threat of an armed uprising by the bourgeoisie in December 1734 compelled the patriciate to yield to the demand to punish the Tamponneurs, but fundamental differences remained unresolved.

As long as the bourgeoisie was united in its objectives, the continued supremacy of the patriciate was threatened. The disunity that appeared in the ranks of the bourgeoisie in 1735 as a result of the Micheli affair was therefore a temporary reprieve for the patriciate. Jacques-Barthélemy Micheli du Crest, like Pierre Fatio before him, was a patrician who had broken with his peers, originally over the system of fortification begun in 1714, which as an engineer he criticized on technical grounds, and later as a dissident who became a radical critic of the oligarchy's monopolization of political power.[12] Micheli contended that the Conseil Général alone was the supreme legislative power, that it could annul any acts of the Petit or Grand Conseil it considered to be in violation of the laws, and that the four syndics alone constituted the executive power since only they were elected by the Conseil Général.[13] In December 1731 Micheli was condemned in absentia to life imprisonment and confiscation of his property, and two of his Genevan supporters were exiled.[14]

After the successful protests by the bourgeoisie in December 1734, Micheli sought support for a review of the 1731 proceedings against him in the belief that the time was propitious for a more favorable verdict. It soon became apparent that only a minority of the bourgeoisie supported Micheli, that most thought it better to leave well enough alone. The result was a split between "Michelistes" and "Temporiseurs," and the patriciate lost no time in taking advantage of this division. In addition, the patriciate encouraged the efforts of a former officer of the Swiss guards of France, the Comte de Montréal, to recruit a small army among the *natifs* and *habitants* for use against the bourgeoisie. This blatant attempt to play the game of divide and conquer once again united the bourgeoisie, and in August 1737, following the arrest and condemnation of four citizens who dared to molest the Count in the streets, the bourgeoisie mobilized the citizen militia and seized control of the city. Only the intervention of the French representative in Geneva, La Closure, prevented the bourgeoisie from imposing reforms that would have substantially altered the Genevan form of government in favor of the bourgeoisie and would have extended important economic rights to the *natifs*. While La Closure openly sided with the patriciate, the man appointed as official French mediator, the Comte de Lautrec, quickly won the trust of both sides and successfully negotiated an agreement, the *Règlement de l'illustre Médiation pour la pacification de la République de Genève*, which was approved by the Conseil Général on May 8, 1738, by 1316 votes to 39.[15]

On the face of it, the *Règlement* appeared to grant extensive powers to the Conseil Général, or rather to confirm many of its traditional powers, including the power to accept or reject laws and taxes, to elect syndics and other magistrates, and to vote on all declarations of war and peace. On the other hand, the power to propose new laws remained solely in the hands of the Petit and Grand Conseils. True, the bourgeoisie was guaranteed the *droit de représentation,* in other words, the right to formally present grievances, which was potentially a form of legislative initiative; but even this right was severely limited in scope by Article VI, which stated that nothing could be considered by the Conseil des Deux Cents until it had been approved by the Petit Conseil, and nothing could be considered by the Conseil Général until it had been approved by the Conseil des Deux Cents. This too was the reaffirmation of longstanding practice; it could and would be used by the patriciate at a later date to negate the apparent gains of the bourgeoisie. In 1738, however, this was not evident to most of the bourgeoisie, which enthusiastically hailed the *Règlement* as the basis of civil peace and prosperity.[16]

Among the strongest supporters of the *Règlement* was Jacques-François De Luc, one of the leaders of the moderate majority of the bourgeoisie. De Luc took it upon himself to refute Micheli's biting critique of the *Règlement*—Micheli had argued that it rendered the Conseil Général effete and made the Petit Conseil a veritable tyrant—in a work published in 1747, *Réfutation des erreurs de M. Micheli Du Crest sur le Réglement de l'Illustre Médiation.* De Luc attributed Micheli's unhappiness with the *Règlement* to his unsuccessful attempt to gain amnesty. Significantly, De Luc explicitly praised the wisdom of the mediators for confining the legislative initiative to the Petit Conseil.[17]

Rousseau shared his friend De Luc's admiration for the *Règlement.* In *Le verger de Madame de Warens,* written in 1739, Rousseau lamented the frenzy and rage that had overtaken his former coun-

45

trymen and praised the beneficial effects of the French intervention of 1737–1738.[18] Even after the condemnation of *Émile* and the *Contrat social* made it clear to many moderates among the bourgeoisie that the *Règlement* had failed to deal with the crux of the political problem that periodically shook the city, the problem of the location of sovereignty in the Genevan constitution, Rousseau's view of the *Règlement* remained closer to De Luc's view of the 1730s and 1740s than to that of Micheli.[19]

Rousseau had left Geneva to make his way in the world six years prior to the conflicts of 1734–1738, but he visited the city at least twice during this period, once in June 1734 and again in the summer of 1737. On both occasions he remained aloof from the political struggle that engulfed Geneva at that time and was to engulf his own life in the 1760s. If his *Confessions* and his correspondence of the time are an accurate guide, he was quite oblivious to the controversy provoked by the *représentations* in 1734 and was at most a reluctant witness to the street fighting of August 1737. The main purpose of his visit in 1737 was to claim the inheritance left by his mother.[20] While it is understandable that, as a renegade and ex-citizen, he should have curried favor with those who might help him in this regard, it is still somewhat odd that he should refer to the French representative La Closure, staunch supporter of the patriciate, as one of the good friends he made during this stay.[21] His only comment in the *Confessions* on the armed uprising in which the bourgeoisie seized control of the city was to recall his unhappiness at seeing two friends, father and son, take up arms on opposite sides, and his subsequent vow never to take part in a civil war for any reason, not even in the defense of liberty.[22]

Rousseau returned to Geneva in June 1754 as the prodigal who had made a name for himself in the wider world. His reception was little short of triumphal. As he described it in the *Confessions:*

> On my arrival in that city [Geneva] I gave myself up to the republican enthusiasm that had led me there, and that enthusiasm was increased by the welcome I received. Fêted and made much of by all classes, I surrendered entirely to patriotic zeal. . . .[23]

Members of the consistory and of the Petit and Grand Conseils, ministers and magistrates, syndics and ordinary citizens, *haute ville* and *basse ville* alike extended their hospitality. He was readmitted to communion and reinstated as a Genevan *citoyen* with a minimum of the formalities usual in such cases. His closest Genevan friend at the time was De Luc, the bourgeois critic of Micheli du Crest, but he also listed several ministers, professors, and other members of the bourgeoisie as the principal acquaintances he made during his four-month stay. He was so moved by all this that he made plans to settle his affairs in Paris and return to Geneva to live the rest of his life, and for several years he even paid the taxes that only citizens enrolled in the guards were entitled to pay. Yet when he departed from Geneva in October 1754 he was never to set foot in the city again.[24]

With him Rousseau had brought the *Dédicace,* completed just prior to his return, and during his stay he confided it to a few close friends. He had originally intended to follow customary procedure and seek the permission of the Petit Conseil to dedicate the *Discours sur l'inégalité* to Geneva, and in fact this was one of his purposes in making the trip, but within a short time after his arrival he realized that to request formal approval of the *Dédicace* would almost certainly bring a refusal. Rather than abandon his project, he decided to act as his own censor, publish the *Dédicace* without formal approval, and accept the consequences, trusting in the integrity of the councillors to recognize that the work was inspired by the purest patriotism. This, at least, is the explanation he gave in a letter to the Genevan pastor, Jean Perdriau, written in November 1754 soon after his return to Paris. In the same letter he claimed that he had decided to dedicate the *Discours* to Geneva because he had been struck by the conformity between his own political principles and the reality of the Republic of Geneva. Perdriau had evidently objected in an earlier letter that publication of the *Dédicace* might revive the internecine political struggles that had plagued the city earlier in the century. Rousseau now replied that this might well have been the case had he taken sides in the internal politics of Geneva, but since he had taken great care to be impartial, praising

47

magistrates and ordinary citizens alike, there was no reason for anyone to take offense. To dedicate such a work to the Republic rather than to the Petit Conseil might be unusual, but under the circumstances it was quite fitting. By not asking approval in advance of the contents of the *Dédicace*, he was leaving everyone free to denounce any or all of it as he saw fit.[25]

Rousseau's explanation for writing the *Dédicace*, that it was to honor a republic that happened to conform to his own political principles, is less than fully convincing. As R. A. Leigh points out in his notes to Rousseau's letter to Perdriau, Rousseau was almost certainly aware that Geneva was less than the earthly paradise portrayed in the *Dédicace*. Even before his journey to Geneva he was probably reasonably well informed about Genevan political life through the contacts he maintained with a number of politically knowledgeable Genevans, including the exiled dissident Lenieps.[26] If he was ignorant about Genevan politics, it was not for lack of information but rather lack of understanding, and this shortcoming he shared with the majority of the Genevan bourgeoisie. It could hardly have come as a surprise to Rousseau when the former first syndic of Geneva, Jean Du Pan, wrote him that in the *Dédicace* he had portrayed Geneva as it ought to be rather than as it was in reality.[27]

Why, then, did he paint Geneva in such glowing colors? Was it simply the flattery of a renegade eager to return to the good graces of his fellow Genevans?[28] If so, his praise of the magistrates, who held it in their power to welcome him back or exclude him, is understandable but not his equally warm praise for the members of the Conseil Général, to whom, after all, the work was dedicated.[29] When the *Dédicace* was finally published, in June 1755, Rousseau sent a copy to the First Syndic Jean-Louis Chouet and asked him to present it to the Petit Conseil. Confronted with this *fait accompli*, Chouet, speaking for the Petit Conseil, thanked Rousseau for the *Dédicace* and praised the elegance and feeling with which he had celebrated the virtues of the fatherland.[30] Rousseau in turn thanked Chouet and the Petit Conseil for agreeing to the *Dédicace* and exclaimed that all the considerations shown to him in this affair were "the happiest events of his life."[31] Rousseau later claimed that

Chouet's letter had been "polite but cold,"[32] and many commentators have agreed, usually adding that the Petit Conseil had little reason to be happy about the *Dédicace*, which was in fact a skillfully written statement of the bouregoisie's view of the Genevan political system.[33] But Rousseau was also unhappy about the response of the bourgeoisie, only two of whom, De Luc and a pastor named Jallabert, bothered to compliment him.[34] Rousseau's view of the whole affair had obviously changed when he wrote the *Confessions*. In reality he could hardly have hoped for a more favorable response from the Petit Conseil under the circumstances, and the fact that the councillors not only formally approved the *Dédicace* but praised it as well is fairly convincing evidence that they did not see it as simply a tract of the bourgeoisie.[35]

A more plausible explanation for Rousseau's writing the *Dédicace* is that he was deliberately idealizing Geneva as the antithesis of all he disliked about Paris. To praise the republican virtues of Geneva, virtues that Paris could never hope to imitate, was a way of criticizing the high society toward which he already had mixed feelings and with which he was soon to break. Yet this explanation is not altogether satisfactory either, partly because he was not yet as thoroughly disenchanted with Paris as he would later become[36]— and, after all, he did return to live in Paris but never returned to Geneva—and partly because it does not explain which Geneva Rousseau was idealizing, for there were in effect several, none of which corresponded to the ideal sketched in the *Dédicace*.

There was, first of all, the Geneva of the patriciate, the élite who actually governed, relatively efficiently and honestly for the most part, but who were not in any meaningful sense responsible to those they governed. Rousseau admired the way they ran the government and apparently believed it quite proper that the reins of government be confined to such an élite, but he also believed they should ultimately have to account to those they governed. While Rousseau had friends among the patriciate, his closest ties were undoubtedly with a second Geneva, the Geneva of the bourgeoisie, with whom his family background and upbringing in the Saint-Gervais quarter as well as his closest friendships inclined him to identify. This identification was, however, qualified in at

least two important respects. In the first place, he did not fully identify with the bourgeoisie or any other group. At the time he wrote
the *Dédicace* he still saw Geneva as a *unity*, and it was with this
unity, which no doubt existed only in his imagination, that he truly
identified.[37] A second important qualification is that to the extent
Rousseau did identify with the bourgeoisie, it was primarily with
the moderate majority personified by De Luc that he identified, not
with radicals like the exile Lenieps. As for the third Geneva, the
Geneva of those noncitizens collectively known as *natifs*, Rousseau
had little to say, but the *Dédicace* as well as his later political writings make it clear that he did not object to their inferior political
status.

In the *Dédicace*, then, Rousseau sought to remain above the factional struggles that lay just beneath the seemingly calm surface of
Genevan politics. The Genevan political institutions as he envisaged them, his ideal institutions, presupposed harmony in order
to function. If any fundamental conflict should arise between these
institutions, the system was bound to break down because it was
not designed to deal with severe conflict. Neither Rousseau nor the
moderate bourgeoisie had to face up to this unpleasant fact in 1754,
and even the *Contrat social* could plausibly ignore it. Ironically, it
was precisely the controversy engendered by the condemnation of
the *Contrat social*, which was based to a large extent on this false
conception of Geneva, that compelled Rousseau and his friends
among the bourgeoisie to see the Genevan political system in a
clearer light. In 1754 Rousseau could still see Geneva's political institutions as a model for others to imitate; in 1762 this model disin-
tegrated and he was forced to reconsider his views on political institutions.

Rousseau's desire to see Geneva as a unity, to remain above the
factional struggle, becomes clearer when the Genevan model of the
Dédicace is analyzed in the light of the preceding discussion of the
city's institutional and political history. For convenience I list the
characteristics of the Genevan political system as perceived by
Rousseau in the order in which he discusses them in the *Dédicace:*

(1) the combination of natural equality and socially instituted
inequality in "the manner most approximate to natural law and

most favorable to society, to the maintenance of public order and the happiness of individuals";

(2) a territory and population of limited size;

(3) a low degree of economic specialization, hence a high degree of functional autonomy;

(4) intimate social relations among citizens;

(5) identity of interests between the sovereign and the people, who are in fact one and the same; Rousseau describes this as "a democratic government, wisely tempered";

(6) everyone without exception subject to the law, with freedom defined as this special kind of subjection;

(7) the antiquity of Geneva's political system;

(8) noninvolvement in international power politics, either as a major military power or as the pawn of other powers;

(9) the right of legislation common to all citizens, meaning that all citizens have the right to sanction laws proposed to them by their magistrates, though Rousseau opposes plebiscites of the sort held at ancient Rome because magistrates were there excluded from deliberation on proposed legislation; he also opposes the right of popular legislative initiative such as existed at Athens and favors instead the Genevan system, which restricts the legislative initiative to magistrates;

(10) no popular participation in the administration and execution of the laws;

(11) popular election of magistrates;

(12) no extremes of wealth or poverty among the citizens;

(13) deep respect of the people for their magistrates.[38]

Elaborating on this last point, Rousseau went on at some length to urge the citizenry to trust and esteem their wise magistrates and to sustain that perpetual unity between the people and their leaders that was the very foundation of Geneva's political system:

> If there remains among you the least germ of bitterness or distrust, hasten to destroy it as a deadly leaven which sooner or later would result in your misfortunes and the ruin of the State. I implore you to look deep into your hearts and consult the secret voice of your conscience. Does anyone among you know a more upright, more enlightened, more respectable body than that of your magistracy? Do not all its members give you the example of moderation, of simplicity of morals, of respect for the laws, and of the most sincere reconciliation? Then give such wise chiefs, without reserve, that salutary confidence which reason owes to virtue; bear in mind that they are of your

choice, that they justify it, and that the honors due to those whom you have established in dignity necessarily reflect upon yourselves.[39]

In a thinly disguised attack on those bourgeoisie who were dissatisfied with the *Règlement* of 1738, Rousseau warned the citizenry to beware the venomous discourses of those dissidents who sought to arouse the people against their leaders. He then turned to the magistrates, that is, the members of the Petit and Grand Conseils, whom he congratulated on their gentleness and condescension as ministers of the laws, although he reminded them that they held their preeminent position only because their fellow citizens recognized their superior merit.[40]

Most of the characteristics he mentioned occasioned little or no controversy,[41] but on at least two key issues he took a stand that was either highly favorable to the status quo or avoided addressing the real issue that had kindled opposition in the past and would do so again in the near future. Thus when he rejected the popular legislative initiative in characteristic 9, he was rejecting a demand that not only the reputedly cantankerous Micheli du Crest but also the legendary Pierre Fatio had recognized as essential if the heralded legislative sovereignty of the Conseil Général was to have any meaning. Rousseau was well aware that this was a controversial issue. His good friend Lenieps was living in exile in Paris in part for having supported Micheli in this demand, and it is reasonable to assume that his upbringing in Saint-Gervais had made him cognizant of Fatio's unsuccessful attempt to secure the legislative initiative in 1707. And yet he went out of his way to condemn those who wanted to revive this demand. In doing so, of course, he was simply accepting the passive role that the great majority of the bourgeoisie had accepted when they approved the *Règlement* in 1738. Rousseau shared both their illusions about the *Règlement* and their overwhelming desire for civil peace that had fostered this illusion. The effect was to leave the oligarchy firmly entrenched in power, since the laws could not be changed unless the oligarchy itself proposed the changes. The bourgeoisie did not see this, because it believed that the *droit de représentation* guaranteed by the *Règlement* provided a mechanism by which the bourgeoisie could initiate changes. Not until the 1760s did the bourgeoisie realize that the effectiveness of the *droit de représentation* also rested on the good will of the oligarchy.[42]

The issue Rousseau avoided relates to characteristic 11, popular election of magistrates. As Rousseau knew, the Conseil Général elected magistrates, but only from a list of candidates proposed by the magistrates themselves. This system made a mockery of the electoral process. Fatio, Micheli, and other dissidents had tried to change this to permit some form of popular initiative in the choice of candidates, or at the very least to make the Petit and Grand Conseils more independent of each other so as to break up their tightly held monopoly of power. Perhaps because the magistrates were of generally high caliber and enjoyed the respect of most citizens, the undemocratic manner in which they were chosen was less of an issue than the legislative initiative, and Rousseau could therefore safely ignore it. That he could do so, however, did not mean, unhappily for him, that the interests of the sovereign and the people were one and the same, as he contended in characteristic 5. The paragraph on which this characteristic is based is worth quoting in full because it summarizes much of what he wished to say in the *Dédicace.*

> I would have wished to be born in a country where the sovereign and the people could have only one and the same interest, so that all movements of the machine always tended only to the common happiness. Since that would not be possible unless the people and the sovereign were the same person, it follows that I would have wished to be born under a democratic government, wisely tempered.[43]

This might appear to be an unqualified assertion of popular sovereignty, made in the belief that this was the only way to achieve the perpetual unity that Rousseau desired so intensely. Translated into Genevan political insitutions, it would be a plea for the supremacy of the Conseil Général. But the key phrase in the paragraph is the final one, "wisely tempered." Rousseau wanted a democratic sovereign, but only if it was tempered by institutions that prevented the sovereign from getting out of hand. The tempering institutions in the Genevan system were the Petit and Grand

Conseils, whose members played a dual role in the city's political life as members of both the ostensibly sovereign legislative body and ostensibly subordinate executive.

If reality had corresponded to theory, this dual role would have presented no problems for Rousseau's portrayal of the city's institutions. But of course the allegedly subordinate councils were superior in fact; not only was there not an identity of interests among citizens, but the city was in effect divided into two separate bodies, each contending for power. Burlamaqui had provided the more accurate theoretical description of the Genevan system when he contended that sovereignty was divided among the Conseil Général, the Petit Conseil, and the Grand Conseil. He had erred only in saying that a balance of power existed among the three, when in reality that balance was heavily weighted in favor of the latter two councils. Rousseau may have been correct when he argued in the *Contrat social* that sovereignty is logically indivisible,[44] but as a description of the Genevan system Burlamaqui's model was closer to the truth. Genevan democracy was so thoroughly tempered that it had ceased to be democratic in any meaningful sense. In the *Contrat social* Rousseau would introduce several important revisions of the Genevan model of the *Dédicace,* among them a demand for periodic meetings of the primary assembly, a demand that he evidently considered too radical or provocative—or perhaps simply unnecessary—at the time he wrote the *Dédicace.* Even so, the model of the *Contrat social* was still recognizably the same basic model as that of the *Dédicace.*

THREE

The Years of Withdrawal

IN THE SPRING of 1756 Rousseau withdrew from Paris to live in the Hermitage at Montmorency. His departure was symbolic of his severance of personal ties with his former friends among the Encyclopedists, a break that would be virtually complete within a year. His break with the Encyclopedists also marked the beginning of a new stage in Rousseau's intellectual development during which he was to work out some of his most distinctive political concepts. At the Hermitage he immediately set to work editing and preparing for publication the twenty-three volumes of disorderly manuscripts and notes of the Abbé de Saint-Pierre that had been given to him in the fall of 1754. Rousseau was an avowed admirer of the Abbé, indeed one of the few contemporaries who took him seriously. Although Rousseau was critical of much that Saint-Pierre had written, the fact that his prolonged confrontation with the Abbé's writings occurred during an important period in the development of his own political thought probably heightened the impact of the Abbé's political views, especially his views on confederation.[1]

The only one of the Abbé's writings dealing primarily with national political institutions that Rousseau extracted and criticized was the *Polysynodie*,[2] in which Saint-Pierre proposed the creation of a number of councils as the key element in a reform designed to introduce a republican style of administration into monarchical rule. The idea was to divide administrative responsibility and authority among some eight functional councils, plus a ninth coordinating council, all of whose members were to be elected, promoted on the basis of merit, and rotated from one council to another. The result, according to Saint-Pierre, would be a new system of administration in which the particular interests of each council would somehow neutralize the particular interests of the other councils and thereby compel agreement on the public or common interest.[3]

Precisely how the public interest was to emerge out of this process was not made entirely clear, and Rousseau took the Abbé to task for not coming to grips with this problem. Rousseau agreed that a council was more likely to decide in favor of the public interest than was a single minister or even the king himself, since individuals tend to confuse their private interests with the public interest. It was for this reason that he considered republics more stable than monarchies, for republics always involve collective decisions. On the other hand, he saw Saint-Pierre's plurality of councils leading to nothing but administrative chaos and indecision. The common interest is not always obvious, Rousseau declared, and because of this each council would tend to define the common interest in terms that gave priority to its own function, whether finance, commerce, war, justice, or whatnot. Only a council concerned with the interrelation of these various functions could be expected to discern the common interest. Saint-Pierre's ninth, coordinating council might have served this purpose, but not as he conceived it, with constant rotation of membership and of the presidency of the combined councils.[4]

Rousseau's criticism takes for granted the need for a strong, decisive executive capable of acting with one will, whether the will of one person, as in a monarchy, or of a council, as in a republic. As Hendel remarks, Rousseau's insistence in the *Jugement sur la Polysynodie* on an efficient executive was in potential conflict with his contention that a group of men is more likely to discover the common interest than a single individual is. What is to prevent a forceful and efficient executive from substituting its own will for the general will, which is best arrived at by more democratic, less efficient methods? Precisely this problem would preoccupy Rousseau in Book III of the *Contrat social.*[5]

In the *Dédicace* and *Économie politique* he had been content for the most part to stress the need for an energetic executive, but now in his *Jugement sur la Polysynodie* he showed more concern with the problems that such an executive might create, although he continued to stress its importance. His increased awareness of the problematic nature of a strong executive was perhaps due to the fact that he was now dealing with a proposal to reform a monarchy, a situation in which his instinctive republicanism made him more skeptical of the good will of executives. And yet his concluding criticism of Saint-Pierre was not that he sought to give the monarch too much power but rather that he had failed to see that the system of the *Polysynodie* was fundamentally incompatible with a true monarchy where executive authority is vested in one person. Saint-Pierre's reform would achieve either too little or too much: too little if a strong monarch used the appearance of decentralized authority to accomplish his own purposes at the expense of the nation; too much if the reforms succeeded and effectively transferred sovereignty from the monarch to an administrative aristocracy. Since this latter possibility was the more likely consequence of Saint-Pierre's reforms, he was unwittingly calling for nothing less than a revolution that would set in motion the masses of France and lead to unpredictable but probably undesirable consequences.

Monarchical and republican institutions do not mix; one must choose for one of the other. And since the French monarchy had proved its worth by enduring for some 1300 years, it was better to make do with it as it was than to institute republican reforms for which the French people were not prepared. Patriotism, love of the public good, the desire for true glory: these were virtues that had disappeared from all but a few small republics, and without these virtues republican institutions would probably do more harm than good.[6]

At the same time that Rousseau immersed himself in the writings of the Abbé de Saint-Pierre, he began a project of a very different order that was eventually published in 1761 as *Julie, ou La Nouvelle Héloïse*. The pastoral setting of the Hermitage brought out the romantic that pervades all his writings but is nowhere more evident than in this, his only novel. *La Nouvelle Héloïse* has received considerable attention in recent years not only from those whose primary interest in Rousseau is literary but also from students of his political thought.[7] If *La Nouvelle Héloïse* was neglected by students of Rousseau's political thought in past years, it was probably because its political significance is embedded in a work of fiction and must therefore often be extracted. This is certainly true for anyone seeking a better understanding of Rousseau's view of political institutions, all the more so because the institution about which the novel centers is the family, not government. Still, the work does offer important insights even in this area of his political thought.[8] It includes one well-known account of a society whose institutions provide a distinctly different model from any discussed thus far, a model that is fittingly placed in the context of a novel but that reappears on several occasions in his later political writings. These institutions are those of the Haut-Valais, and they are described for the most part in a single letter from Saint-Preux (Rousseau) to Julie.[9]

Rousseau's interest in the Valais dated back at least to 1744, when he passed through the region on the way from Venice to Geneva.[10] During his stay in Geneva in 1754 he contemplated writing a history of the Valais, although the project never went beyond the stage of a few notes.[11] His friend Gauffecourt explained in a letter to the French chargé d'affaires at Sion, whom Rousseau had met in 1744, that Rousseau spoke enthusiastically of the Republic of the Valais and had planned to spend some time there to see what distinguished its government from other governments but gave up the idea because of bad health and the opposition of his friends in Paris.[12]

What Rousseau saw in the Valais—or more precisely, the Haut-Valais, since the Bas-Valais was already corrupted to some extent by outside influences—was a society so permeated by the spirit of liberty, patriotism, and equality that it realized spontaneously in its daily life what other societies could achieve only through carefully designed political institutions, if at all. Rousseau was deeply impressed by the simplicity of their way of life, their disinterested humanity, the rarity of money and hence of luxury among them. Children who had attained the age of reason were treated as the equals of their fathers, and domestics sat at the same tables with their masters. The same liberty that reigned in their homes reigned in the republic, for the family was the very image of the state.[13] The social and political life of the Haut-Valais were in fact one and the same. Although Rousseau says nothing about the institutions by which the Valaisans governed themselves, the Haut-Valais was in reality a direct democracy, at least at the local level.[14] Only a very few people in very special circumstances were still capable of attaining this idyllic existence, and even they were rapidly succumbing to the corrupting influences of modern civilization, which was typified by the French influence in Switzerland generally and in Geneva in particular. The differences between the Haut- and Bas-Valais exemplified the early stages of this process of corruption.[15]

The way of life of the Haut-Valais provided one standard by which moderns, even Genevans, could measure themselves, but it was not a model that Rousseau thought could be realized by more than a tiny minority of mankind. In the *Contrat social* he would provide a model with a much broader, potentially universal application, although factors such as size, climate, history, and relations with other societies would affect the way in which it could be applied and the extent to which the ideal could be realized. He was not optimistic about the prospects of realizing the model of the *Contrat social,* but whatever its chances of realization, it differed from the model of the Haut-Valais in that it was at least designed for modern man, not for imaginary human beings or for the very few who lived in the exceptional circumstances of the Haut-Valais and who could virtually dispense with political institutions. It is precisely because political institutions are indispensable to modern man that they are of decisive importance in the *Contrat social* but not in the Haut-Valais, where the very way of life makes virtue possible.[16]

The sharp contrast that Saint-Preux perceived between the artificial life of great cities like Paris and the simple, natural life of remote regions like the Haut-Valais constitutes one of the central themes of *La Nouvelle Héloïse*. The same letter in which he described the life of the Valaisans also develops a second, related theme of the novel, the exaltation of the life of solitude, which, together with Rousseau's celebration of the simple life, was perhaps the very essence of "Rousseauism" in the eighteenth century.[17] Rousseau expands on these themes in Saint-Preux's letters at the end of Part II in which he relates his first impressions of Paris,[18] in Claire's letter to Julie describing life in Geneva and the corrupting effects of French influence there,[19] and in his portrayal of the idyllic life at Clarens.[20] The same themes reappear in his *Lettre à d'Alembert*, which he wrote after the first four parts of *La Nouvelle Héloïse* but before completing the fifth and sixth parts. In the *Lettre à d'Alembert* he gives a more detailed account of the life of the *montagnons* who lived in the vicinity of Neuchâtel and whose simple but rich life contrasted so sharply with the life of the "big-city monkeys" of Paris.[21]

Rousseau had spent the winter of 1730–1731 at Neuchâtel,[22] and although he had forgotten much of what he experienced there as a youth, he still vividly recalled the favorable impression its inhabitants had made on him. As he describes it in his *Lettre à d'Alembert*, the mountaineers around Neuchâtel were remarkably autonomous, each family living on its own plot of land roughly equal to that of its neighbors and producing not only every necessity of life but many amenities as well, including items such as clocks and watches, which were sold abroad.[23] He does not discuss the political institutions of Neuchâtel, which at that time was a principality of Prussia, although relatively autonomous with respect to domestic affairs, and governed by institutions quite similar to those of Geneva, including a Petit Conseil and a Conseil Général.[24]

Rousseau included this account of the life of the *montagnons* of Neuchâtel primarily to show how the introduction of a theater would destroy it. The central argument of his *Lettre à d'Alembert* was of course that the introduction of a theater in Geneva, which d'Alembert had suggested in his article "Genève," published in the *Encyclopédie* in the fall of 1757, would have devastating consequences for the moral and political health of his native city. For some two months after learning of d'Alembert's article he was uncertain how to respond, but once he had decided on a course of action he worked with feverish intensity and completed his reply in early March 1758. In his *Confessions* he claimed that it was the first of his works that he had taken any delight in writing,[25] and on one occasion he declared the *Lettre à d'Alembert* to be his favorite work. Whether or not these claims are exaggerated, there is no doubt that the *Lettre à d'Alembert* is one of his most thoroughly Genevan works, both in inspiration and in the information he provides about Genevan life and institutions.[26]

The theater was an issue not only in Geneva but throughout Europe. In France the debate over the theater was essentially theological, at least in the beginning, but in Geneva it was social and political. Far from prohibiting the theater for doctrinal reasons, Calvin had used it as a vehicle to propagate the Reformed religion. Not until 1617, and then only over the strenuous objections of many of the aristocracy, did the sumptuary laws prohibit the theater in Geneva. Over the years this law led to increasingly bitter quarrels between the civil and religious authorities of the city, and in the eighteenth century this quarrel merged with that between the aristocracy and the bourgeoisie. A large body of Genevian opinion believed that only a pro-French and antirepublican upper class had any use for a theater and consequently considered it an act of patriotism to oppose it.[27]

In 1737, on the eve of the most violent uprising of the Genevan populace prior to the 1780s, the attorney general, Jean Du Pan, proposed the establishment of a theater, arguing before the Conseil des Deux Cents that it would serve the same function as the *panis et circensis* policy of the Greeks and Romans; that is, it would "turn the people away from criticism of the government."[28] Du Pan's proposal became reality later in the year as a direct result of French intervention, but within a few months the newly established theater was forced into bankruptcy. In the 1760s the aristocracy succeeded in reestablishing a theater, again with the help of their French allies, but as soon as the French left in 1768 the theater mysteriously burned to the ground. Not until a third French intervention in 1782 did the theater come to Geneva to stay.[29]

The bourgeoisie responded to Du Pan's proposal with an argument that Rousseau was to make the central thesis of his own reply to d'Alembert. De Luc used this same argument in April 1758, apparently unaware of what Rousseau had already written: a theater might be suitable for a great city like Paris, but not for little republican Geneva.[30] Rousseau elaborated on the same theme, adding that the reason a theater was good for Paris was that most Parisians were already corrupted and in need of relatively harmless distractions, whereas Genevans would see their life of virtue destroyed if they permitted a theater in their midst. He also agreed with the bourgeoisie that the theater would increase the inequality of fortunes because the poor would spend proportionately more on the theater than would the rich and thereby jeopardize the equilibrium between rich and poor that was the very foundation of Geneva's political system. A certain degree of inequality might offer some advantages, especially in a monarchy, but in a small republic severe inequality meant the end of democracy.[31]

As peculiar as Rousseau's view of the theater may appear today—and it struck many of the Encyclopedists as peculiar or worse even then—it was a prevalent view among the Genevan bourgeoisie. What Rousseau proposed in place of the theater was a revivification of several indigenous Genevan institutions, or more precisely, several institutions that were closely identified with life in the Saint-Gervais quarter of the city. One of these institutions, the *cercles*, was mentioned earlier in the context of the impact of Saint-Gervais on the early development of Rousseau's political thought. In his *Lettre à d'Alembert* Rousseau sketched a vivid portrait of the origin and nature of these *cercles*, which he compared to the clubs (*coteries*) of London before they degenerated into coffee houses and houses of prostitution. He traces the origins of the *cercles* to the many occasions—military exercises, festivals, awards of prizes, hunting parties—that brought the people of Saint-Gervais together, usually in taverns. These tumultuous gatherings, which were called *sociétés* when Rousseau was a youth, gave birth to the more serious and deliberative *cercles* during the civil unrest of the 1730s, when the bourgeoisie needed an organization in which to plan political strategy.[32] This, Rousseau observes, was a case of a fundamentally healthy institution arising from very unfortunate circumstances.

Each *cercle* was composed of some twelve to fifteen persons who rented quarters where they could meet during their free time and gamble, drink, smoke, read, talk politics, or whatnot. Women met in separate groups, a practice that Rousseau considered one of the main advantages of the *cercles* because it kept the sexes apart. What a welcome contrast to the salon society of the French capital, where "every woman at Paris gathers in her apartment a harem of men more womanish than she."[33] Although Rousseau acknowledged a few shortcomings in the *cercles*—malicious gossip among the women, excessive drinking among the men—he saw these as abuses of a basically sound institution whose advantages far outweighed its disadvantages. He summed up the case for the *cercles* as follows: "In a word, these decent and innocent institutions combine everything which can contribute to making friends, citizens, and soldiers out of the same men, and, in consequence, everything which is most appropriate to a free people."[34]

In addition to the *cercles*, which were limited to small groups of people, Rousseau encouraged a variety of public gatherings that would provide opportunities for the entire citizenry to assemble from time to time. To the already existing public festivals—reviews, awards, kings of the harquebus, cannon, and sailing—he proposed to add still others, including various sporting events and an annual ball to bring together the marriageable young. Anticipating criticism over this latter proposal, he urged that a magistrate preside over these annual dances to maintain a decent respect for the laws, morals, and propriety. He noted that this was already the custom with respect to the meetings of guilds and other public societies and considered it "one of the great bonds which unite the people to their leaders."[35] He lamented the declining role that these festivals played in Geneva:

> Ah! where are the games and festivals of my youth? Where is the concord of the citizens? Where is the public fraternity? Where is the pure joy and the real gaiety? Where are the peace, the liberty, the equity, the innocence? Let us go and seek out

63

all that again. My God! with the heart of a Genevan, with a city so cheerful, a land so charming, a government so just, pleasures so true and so pure and all that is needed to delight in them, what can prevent us all from adoring our country?[36]

If Genevans needed an example to follow, they could turn to Sparta, whose citizens were forever assembling for one public festival or another. Continuing on this Spartan theme, he recalled the profound emotion he had felt as a child when he witnessed the assembling of the regiments of Saint-Gervais. When the military exercises were concluded, soldiers and officers—in other words, bourgeoisie and patricians, since officers were invariably patricians—danced together around the public fountain, wives and children soon joined them, and all ended peaceably with the return of each to his family.[37]

Rousseau's praise of the *cercles* and of the civic and military public festivals could be interpreted as a critique of the ruling oligarchy, since it was these very institutions, especially the *cercles* and the regimental assemblies, that had made it possible for the bourgeoisie to successfully challenge the oligarchy's monopolization of political power in the 1730s.[38] Moreover, his approval of the *cercles* appears inconsistent with his usual denunciation of factions, for what were the *cercles* if not the rudimentary political organization of the bourgeoisie? The very fact that he singles out the institutions of Saint-Gervais as models and ignores those of the *haute ville* constitutes a form of criticism. And yet there are several indications that Rousseau rejected partisanship in his *Lettre à d'Alembert* just as he had rejected it in the *Dédicace* four years earlier. As he saw it, the *cercles* were not partisan organizations for furthering the political program of the bourgeoisie but rather civic associations in which one learned how to be a good citizen. There was nothing to prevent the aristocracy from following the healthy example set by the people of Saint-Gervais; nothing, that is, except their greater addiction to French culture in general and salon society in particular.

The public festivals were, if anything, even less given to partisanship than the *cercles*. For one thing they were public and therefore not a good breeding ground for partisan political movements.

Nor is there any indication that Rousseau saw them as a vehicle for mobilizing political forces. After all, he freely accepted the custom by which a magistrate appointed by the Petit Conseil presided over the festivals to maintain respect for law and order. Perhaps the closest he came to partisanship was his emotional account of the assembling of the militia of Saint-Gervais, for it was precisely these regiments that had temporarily seized power from the oligarchy in 1737. The *Règlement* of 1738 had discontinued this long-standing practice, so that it was no longer possible for the bourgeoisie to assemble the militia on its own initiative without appearing seditious.[39] On the other hand, Rousseau did not demand that the bourgeoisie be authorized to assemble the regiments, nor, for that matter, did he present the assembling of the regiments as a proposal of any kind but simply limited himself to a happy recollection. One of the sights that had deeply impressed him as a youth was that of soldiers and officers, bourgeoisie and patriciate, dancing together, which was another way of saying that he was moved by the mutual respect that prevailed between the people and its leaders.

In sum, while his celebration of the institutions of Saint-Gervais may indicate some disenchantment with the ruling aristocracy, he was as committed as ever to the ideal of a Geneva based on harmonious relations among all its citizens of whatever class. This harmony was breaking down as a result of French influence, which was particularly strong among the oligarchy but had also penetrated the ranks of the bourgeoisie. By calling for the restoration of Geneva's indigenous institutions, he was in effect calling on the aristocracy and bourgeoisie alike to return to an older and nobler way of life.

———

From the time that Rousseau first conceived the idea of writing the *Institutions politiques* in 1743 or 1744 until he began work on the *Contrat social* in the late 1750s, his thinking about political institutions evolved from an initial position similar to that of the Encyclopedists to one that was largely modeled on Genevan institutions. The extended polemics over the *Discours sur les sciences et les arts* forced him to reflect on ideas he had expressed hyperbolically and often paradoxically. The tentative nature of his political thought was still evident in his *Discours sur l'inégalité,* where he spoke of researches yet to be undertaken concerning the terms of the social contract. His deep respect for government, perhaps mixed with more than a little of the awe of an outsider, manifested itself in *Économie politique* as a call for government to minister to the public's needs. It was a thoroughly paternalistic image of political society. Wise leaders would of course recognize that they enhanced their power by respecting the persons and liberties of their people and by providing the necessities of life for their poor. Government was a trust, not an opportunity for self-aggrandizement. But wise leaders would make all the important decisions, take all the important initiatives, with a minimum of consultation with their people. Wise leaders could even determine the general will without assembling the people, who might not recognize the general will even if they saw it. There were of course certain occasions, generally involving the appropriation or expenditure of public funds, which required popular consent, but Rousseau seemed indifferent about whether this consent was given by primary assemblies or representative assemblies.

In the *Dédicace* Rousseau presented a significantly different conception of political institutions, one based on his own perception of Genevan institutions. This Genevan model was to remain the basic model of his thinking about political institutions throughout his life with few revisions or additions, although some of these were highly significant. The specific characteristics of this model can be properly understood only in the context of the political controversies that periodically shook Geneva in the first half of the eighteenth century. In the *Dédicace* Rousseau sought to remain above the partisan struggle, to reconcile opposing factions by pointing to the vision of a unified Geneva whose institutions made possible a harmonious relationship among all parties. He denounced those dissidents who demanded reforms that would have revived old and bitter controversies and would have set one party against another. He explicitly rejected demands that would have given the people, namely, the Conseil Général, the right to initiate legislation, and he ignored the system of nominations that made a mock-ery of the electoral process. Instead he urged his fellow citizens to respect their magistrates and be grateful for the many blessings that nature and their forefathers had bestowed on their native land. Rousseau was not alone in seeing Geneva as a harmonious, unified whole. The majority of the bourgeoisie, whose political views were most nearly his own, shared the illusions that blinded him and them from the unpleasant realities of Genevan political life.

He temporarily departed from the Genevan model in *La Nou-velle Héloïse* to portray an idyllic society that was almost apolitical, or, what amounted to the same, one in which the social and politi-cal were so thoroughly meshed as to be indistinguishable. The mountaineers of the Haut-Valais achieved spontaneously in their daily lives what most people could achieve, if at all, only with the aid of political institutions. In his *Lettre à d'Alembert* he drew a sim-ilar picture of the mountaineers in the vicinity of Neuchâtel. Rous-seau meant neither of these socieites as models for moderns to imi-tate. Isolated regions like the Haut-Valais and Neuchâtel were historical anomalies destined to succumb to modern civilization. They might serve as reminders of man's lost innocence, but they could not usefully serve as models for moderns, who had to con-struct with great care the institutions that were so essential to their well-being.

Rousseau returned to the Genevan model in his *Lettre à d'Alem-bert,* but this time he focused on the substructure, the social institu-tions that gave meaning to the political institutions and were in some respects even more important. A society with healthy social institutions like the *cercles* and public festivals could create what-ever political institutions it needed, but without these social insti-tutions even the best of political institutions would sooner or later degenerate into a sham. Geneva was in danger because its social in-stitutions had fallen into neglect. Worst of all, it was the patriciate that was setting the bad example by aping French manners, even to the point of trying to introduce a theater into Geneva's midst.

Although Rousseau continued to praise the magistracy and to urge unity among all classes, the very fact that all the institutions he sought to revive were unique to Saint-Gervais suggests his growing

67

disillusionment with the Genevan oligarchy. If a people's leaders fail them, the people must save themselves from their leaders. This meant a revival of institutions that unite the people, that bring them together in intimate *cercles* and public festivals to remind them of all they owe to each other. If this is a fair reading of the *Lettre à d'Alembert,* one can see in it the inklings of the changes that Rousseau would announce to the world in the *Contrat social,* which takes a dismal view of the tendency toward executive usurpation of sovereignty and which celebrates the virtues of popular assemblies as a corrective for this tendency. The *Institutions politiques,* which had originated in his recognition of the defects of the much-vaunted Republic of Venice, had now become primarily a means of rectifying the shortcomings of his beloved Republic of Geneva.

The Contrat Social

FOUR

The Principles of Political Right

THE *Contrat social* is undoubtedly the best known and most influential of Rousseau's political writings. It is in many respects the culmination and summation of his thinking on a number of key political concepts that have come to be closely associated with his name: the general will, the will of all, popular sovereignty, elective aristocracy, the lawgiver, civil religion, to name only some of the most prominent. It also reveals his mature thought on political institutions, their nature, their forms, and the manner in which they function in the ideal state as well as in less than ideal states.

And yet in other respects the *Contrat social* is atypical, an uncharacteristically rigid and extreme statement of views that he elsewhere modified or qualified for one reason or another. This exaggeration is nowhere more evident than in his insistence on popular assemblies as the basic political institution of all legitimate states. His uncompromising hostility toward representative government in the *Contrat social* is surprising in view of the lack of interest he had shown in the matter previously, and it is all the more surprising in view of his passive acceptance of representatives in *Économie politique.*

What accounts for the intransigent position he takes in the *Contrat social?* What had happened during the years since publication of *Économie politique* that led him to change his attitude toward representatives from passive acceptance to active hostility? These two questions constitute the primary focus of the following analysis of the *Contrat social,* but they cannot be answered until we have considered the chronology of the composition of the *Contrat* and the principal arguments that he makes against representatives.

It is rarely a simple matter to explain the evolution of someone's ideas, or even one's own ideas. The number of possible influences is almost infinite, and in any case the same influence affects people in different ways. In Rousseau's case the problem is complicated by his dogged insistence on the unity of all his ideas, a stance born out of the charges of inconsistency that contemporaries repeatedly brought against his writings, which led him either to ignore changes in his thought or to pretend that they did not exist. Most recent commentaries have properly stressed the unity of Rousseau's thought in opposition to the frequent charges of radical inconsistency that were once brought against Rousseau, but even these commentators disagree sharply about precisely what constitutes the unity of his thought.

The problem is that Rousseau was deeply ambivalent about the political capacities of ordinary citizens, and this ambivalence has given birth to almost innumerable contrasting and often conflicting interpretations. It is, of course, not enough to say simply that Rousseau was ambivalent, or that his ambivalence consisted in his equal commitment to the conflicting values of freedom and control, although it is a crucial first step to recognize this much. There are other ways of perceiving a unity of ideas in a person's thought, and one is to determine that influence or pattern of influences that shaped his thought and gave it some degree of unity. It seems to me that the most important of these influences, at least for purposes of understanding what was most distinctive about his political thought, was the common Genevan inspiration of his political writings. This also does not fully answer the question of what constitutes the unity of his thought, but it does provide a different perspective for understanding that unity, and one that also helps to explain the evolution of his thought, for the changes in his political thought, especially in his concept of political institutions, were closely related to his changing perception of Geneva and its institutions.

The problem of explaining the evolution of Rousseau's political thought is aggravated by the uncertainty that surrounds the dates of composition of the *Contrat social* in both its preliminary and final versions. Vaughan believes that the *Geneva Manuscript*, as the original version of the *Contrat social* is called, was written at about the same time as *Économie politique*, that is, 1754–1755.[1] Hubert notes that the *Geneva Manuscript* contains some elements that antedate publication of *Économie politique* and others that postdate it and concludes that it was completed by early 1756.[2] Derathé once agreed with Hubert that it was finished by 1756[3] but now thinks it was completed in its present form between 1758–1760, although some parts, notably the long chapter "De la société générale du genre humain," which was a refutation of Diderot's article "Droit naturel" in the *Encyclopédie,* were written earlier.[4]

In addition to the evidence Derathé cites in support of his contention that the *Geneva Manuscript* was written between 1758–1760, there are several indications in the text of the manuscript itself that it was written later than Vaughan and Hubert suggest. If one compares Rousseau's view of representatives in *Économie politique* with a number of passages in the *Geneva Manuscript,* it is difficult to believe that Rousseau could have written the two works at the same time, for it is in the *Geneva Manuscript* that his overt hostility toward representatives makes its first appearance. The manuscript does not contain, except perhaps by implication, the assertion that sovereignty cannot be represented, which Rousseau uses as his principal argument against representatives in the *Contrat social.*[5] On the other hand, Rousseau does state in the manuscript, and repeats in the *Contrat social,* that there is no basis for allowing a particular will to substitute for the general will since there is no way of guaranteeing that private wills will always correspond to the general will.[6] More explicitly, he contends that a particular will cannot represent the general will.[7]

Another sharp contrast with *Économie politique* appears in

Rousseau's view of the need for assembling the people to determine the general will. It will be recalled that in *Économie politique* he had given three reasons why it was not necessary to assemble the whole nation to determine the general will: first, there was no assurance that an assembly of the people would recognize the general will; second, it was impracticable in large states; and third, the executive could determine the general will on its own without reference to the people.[8] In the *Geneva Manuscript* he takes a diametrically opposed position on the same issue. He raises the issue in such a way that his answer is evident: "Will the People remain constantly assembled to declare it [i.e., the general will], or will they rely on individuals who are always ready to substitute their wills for the general will?"[9] He answers this question in subsequent chapters by declaring that the people are the sole judge of what constitutes the general will[10] and that the state must be small enough so that the people can be assembled whenever necessary.[11] This latter assertion is followed by an explicit rejection of representative government: "It will be seen later that assemblies by deputation can neither represent the body of the people nor receive from it power sufficient to legislate in its name as sovereign."[12]

The *Geneva Manuscript* breaks off incomplete at the beginning of Book III. The four paragraphs of this book are included virtually verbatim in the *Contrat social* III, 1. The last two sentences of the manuscript read as follows: "We have seen that the legislative power belongs to the people and can belong only to the people. By the same token, it is easy to see that the executive power cannot belong to the people."[13] The fact that the manuscript breaks off precisely at the point at which he begins to examine in detail the political institutions that accord with the general principles enunciated in Books I and II suggests that his thought on this subject was still in the process of development. In Book X of the *Confessions*, which covers the period 1758–1760, Rousseau says that he reviewed what he had written thus far of the *Institutions politiques*, realized that it would take several years to complete, decided that he did not have the stamina for such an undertaking, and abandoned the project, salvaging what he could and burning the rest. He continued working on both *Émile* and the *Contrat social* and completed the latter work in less than two years.[14] Since the *Contrat social* was completed in August 1761,[15] this indicates that it was the latter half of 1759 at the earliest when he abandoned the *Institutions politiques.*

This conclusion is corroborated by what is known of the composition of *Émile,* which contains an outline of the *Contrat social.*[16] In 1761 Rousseau added a footnote to this outline, citing the *Contrat social* as the source of most of the material included in it.[17] Significantly, the footnote was inserted at precisely the point at which the *Geneva Manuscript* breaks off, which suggests that the remainder of the outline in *Émile* contains either new material or perhaps a thorough revision of that portion of the *Institutions politiques* which he did not consider worth keeping.[18] The portion of the outline immediately following the footnote added in 1761 deals with the question of the legitimacy of representatives. Much of it is in the form of questions or tentative suggestions about the direction in which he will look for answers to these questions.[19] For example, the segment of the outline that corresponds to *Contrat social* III, 15, includes these comments on representatives:

> If the people cannot alienate its supreme right, can the people entrust it to others for a time? If the people cannot give itself a master, can it give itself representatives? This question is important and merits discussion.
> If the people can have neither sovereign nor representatives, we will examine how it can enact its own laws. . . .[20]

In sum, Rousseau's comments on representatives in the *Geneva Manuscript* and the outline of the *Contrat social* in *Émile* indicate that he had not yet fully developed the arguments against representatives that he would use in the final version of the *Contrat social,* although his view of representatives was already distinctly different from that of *Économie politique.* It was not until late 1759 at the earliest or possibly as late as early 1760 that he worked out the institutional arrangements that he presents in Book III of the *Contrat social* together with his final arguments against representative institutions. It follows that Rousseau's thinking about political institutions was among the last aspects of his political thought to mature and that he did not arrive at his well-known position of opposition to representatives until nearly a decade after he published the *Discours sur les sciences et les arts.*

If this, then, is the chronology of Rousseau's evolving view of political institutions in general and representative institutions in particular, what are his principal arguments against representatives in the *Contrat social?* Does his opposition to representative institutions necessarily follow from his conception of the nature of popular sovereignty; that is, is it the logical consequence of his basic theoretical premises?[21] Or is his opposition essentially practical; that is, does he favor popular over representative assemblies as a more effective means of achieving the goal of popular sovereignty? Rousseau argues against representation on both theoretical and practical grounds: his theoretical arguments are all based on his contention that will cannot be represented; his practical argument is that popular assemblies are more reliable than representative assemblies in preventing executive abuse of power, the main threat to popular sovereignty. My contention is that these two types of argument are logically independent of each other in that the validity or invalidity of one does not imply the validity or invalidity of the other; that he does not clearly distinguish between the two types of argument, which leads to serious confusion when he turns to the problem of devising political institutions for the legitimate state; and that, although he developed the two types of argument simultaneously, he devised a theoretical justification for his opposition to representatives only because he was already convinced on practical grounds that primary assemblies are to be preferred over representative assemblies.

As will be seen in the following analysis of Rousseau's arguments against representation, the significance that one attaches to the influence of the natural law school and Geneva on the development of Rousseau's political thought has a direct bearing on the significance of the two types of argument. In arguing for the primacy of practical considerations, I am at the same time arguing for the primacy of Geneva's influence. This is not to say that the natural law school did not exert an important influence on the development of Rousseau's political thought—Derathé has amply demonstrated that it did—but rather that Geneva provided both the initial inspiration for his political thought, especially his thinking about political institutions, and, at least in general outline, the solutions to what he saw as the fundamental problems of politics. While he might never have arrived at his fundamental political ideas without the help of the natural law school, he would never have turned to the jurisconsults for help unless he had been seeking the solution to a practical problem, namely, how to resolve the political and social conflict that plagued his native city, a problem that increasingly preoccupied him following his reinstatement as a citizen during his four-month stay there in 1754.[22] Nor is this to deny that other influences—for example, his admiration for the ancients or his dislike of feudalism—played a significant role in the development of his view of representatives, although I think it can be shown that these other influences were much less important for his distinctive view of representatives than were the combined influences of Geneva and the natural law school. The question of influences, or the sources of Rousseau's opposition to representative government, is examined in greater detail in chapter 7, but first it is important to analyze and evaluate his arguments against representatives in the *Contrat social*.

Rousseau opens the *Contrat* by refuting, or attempting to refute, various theories of the nature of the social bond. Grotius is the principal villain in the piece, with Hobbes a close second, but Aristotle is also singled out for criticism for his contention that some men are slaves by nature, and, among moderns, Filmer is clearly the target of Rousseau's ridicule of the theory of divine right monarchy in one of the rare moments of levity in the *Contrat social*. Rousseau's primary grievance against Grotius and Hobbes is that both accept voluntary servitude not only for individuals but for a whole nation. He contends that there is no possible *quid pro quo* that a people can receive in exchange for giving themselves to a master, that in fact to renounce one's freedom is equivalent to renouncing one's very humanity.[23] Montesquieu had used the very same argument in denying the legitimacy of slavery and had gone on to say that in a democracy the renunciation of one's freedom would be tantamount to renouncing part of the sovereignty since the freedom of each citizen in a democracy is a part of the public liberty.[24] Throughout the *Contrat* Rousseau tends to equate alienation of sovereignty with voluntary servitude and consequently sees most moderns as slaves.[25]

According to Rousseau, every legitimate political society must be based on a covenant, but not just any covenant. The problem is

"How to find a form of association which will defend the person and goods of each member with the collective force of all, and under which each individual, while uniting himself with the others, obeys no one but himself, and remains as free as before." This is the fundamental problem to which the social contract holds the solution.[26]

By posing the problem in these terms, Rousseau commits himself to sustaining an excessive thesis.[27] If each associate "obeys no one but himself," why should anyone be bound by the decision of the majority whenever that decision is contrary to his own? And yet Rousseau makes it clear that he does accept majority rule, that only the social contract itself requires unanimity.[28] It may be objected that Rousseau meant this phrase to apply only to the original contract, but if so, in what sense does each associate remain "as free as before"? Unless one defines freedom as some kind of higher law, an objective condition independent of one's own will,[29] what sense does it make to say that one remains "as free as before" except in those cases in which there is spontaneous and unanimous agreement on the general will? Certainly Rousseau's definition of freedom as "obedience to a law one prescribes to oneself"[30] is difficult to reconcile with his acceptance of majority rule, for a member of the minority may very well experience the decision of the majority as an imposition. Rousseau himself raises precisely this objection in Book IV, Chapter 2, of the *Contrat social*, as though he was having second thoughts about the way in which he had posed the fundamental problem and felt a need to clarify himself.

Yet it may be asked how a man can be at once free and forced to conform to wills which are not his own. How can the opposing minority be both free and subject to laws to which they have not consented?

I answer that the question is badly formulated. The citizen consents to all the laws, even to those that are passed against his will, and even to those which punish him when he dares to break any one of them. The constant will of all the members of the state is the general will; it is through it that they are citizens and free. When a law is proposed in the people's assembly, what is asked of them is not precisely whether they approve of the proposition or reject it, but whether it is in conformity with the general will which is theirs; each by giving his vote yields a declaration of the general will. When, therefore, the opinion contrary to my own prevails, this proves only that I have made a mistake, and that what I believed to be the general will was not so. If my particular opinion had prevailed against the general will, I should have done something other than what I had willed, and then I should not have been free.[31]

One might retort that it was Rousseau who formulated the question badly in the first place, but it is more fruitful to see his difficulty in defining the general will as the result of his attempt to reconcile the principle of majority rule with his contention that each "obeys no one but himself, and remains as free as before." The attempt failed, as even he seems to realize in the paragraph that follows the preceding quotation:

This presupposes, it is true, that all the characteristics of the general will are still to be found in the majority; when these cease to be there, no matter what position men adopt, there is no longer any freedom.[32]

This admission reduces the argument to a tautology: the majority determines the general will as long as the majority wills the general will. In other words, there is no way of guaranteeing that the majority will discern or express the general will insofar as the general will is perceived as an objective standard. Rousseau wants the general will conceived in this way to serve as a guide for the citizenry, but he also wants majority rule, and he is unable to choose for one or the other, although he is aware that the two may not always coincide.*

*This whole problem is closely related to the question of whether or not Rousseau accepted natural law, and if so, to what extent he equated natural law with the general will. Vaughan argues that Rousseau rejected natural law, and considers this one of Rousseau's greatest philosophical achievements (Vaughan, I, 16–18). Franz Haymann challenges, however, virtually every step of Vaughan's argument and concludes that Rousseau accepted natural law not only implicitly but explicitly and that he did so consistently from the *Discours sur l'inégalité* right through *Considérations sur*

Rousseau does not make these exaggerated claims in his summary of the terms of the contract: "Each one of us puts into the community his person and all his powers under the supreme direction of the general will; and as a body, we incorporate every

le gouvernement de Pologne (Haymann, "La loi naturelle dans la philosophie politique de J.-J. Rousseau," Annales de la Société Jean-Jacques Rousseau, 30 [1943–1945], pp. 65–110). Derathé relies heavily on Haymann's analysis in his discussion of natural law in Rousseau et la science politique, pp. 151–171.

Haymann equates the general will with natural law and the will of all with the will of the majority (pp. 96–97) and argues that Rousseau considered natural law binding on the popular assembly as well as on individual citizens (p. 101). By affirming unequivocally that Rousseau accepted natural law, Haymann suggests a solution to the problems I have raised, but it seems to me that Rousseau was much less clear about the relationship of natural law to the social contract and the general will than Haymann represents him to have been. The crucial question to which Haymann does not provide a satisfactory answer is who decides what is natural law (or the general will) and what is not. If each individual decides for himself, what obligation is there for a citizen to obey a decision (law) with which he disagrees? The only political system compatible with this solution is anarchy, which Haymann rightly dismisses as an implausible interpretation of the Contrat social (p. 66). But if the majority decides, then in what sense does each citizen remain "as free as before"? Haymann suggests that Rousseau meant by this phrase only "moral liberty"; that is, each citizen remains a morally free agent in the new society established by the social contract (p. 95). But surely Rousseau meant more than this, as his futile attempt to resolve this problem in Contrat social IV, 2, indicates.

Haymann convincingly argues that Rousseau accepted natural law and that the Contrat social presupposes and is based on natural law, and this acceptance explains why Rousseau was so reluctant to legitimate majority rule despite his commitment to popular sovereignty, but Haymann does not show how this acceptance of natural law can be reconciled with the conventional justice that results from majority rule. Nor does it follow, as Haymann interprets Rousseau to say, that popular assemblies are the only means of enacting laws in conformity with natural law (pp. 95–96). The best method for achieving this goal is a purely practical question. There is no logical reason why elected representatives or even a hereditary monarch cannot discover such laws as well as a popular assembly, and in any case the preponderant role that Rousseau attributes to government in making or discovering laws sharply reduces the significance of popular assemblies even in his own system. Rousseau himself treats this as an essentially practical problem once he has presented his questionable theoretical objections to representative government. The primary value of Haymann's analysis is its demonstration that Rousseau persistently attempted to construct a political system compatible with his understanding of natural law. Whether Rousseau succeeded or not seems to me far more problematical than Haymann suggests, but at least Haymann helps to explain why Rousseau had such difficulty in defining the general will and, more generally, in reconciling the highly voluntaristic political system of the Contrat social with his evident belief in the need for objective standards independent of human will.

member as an indivisible part of the whole."[33] The summary formulation makes it much clearer that entry into the contract involves an agreement to submit to other wills.[34] The difference between the more extreme and the more moderate formulations of the terms of the contract is significant for purposes of understanding his arguments against representation primarily because the persuasiveness of his arguments depends in part on acceptance of the more extreme formulation, which is itself questionable. If it is possible to create a society in which no one obeys anyone but himself, then it is perhaps not only possible but necessary that each member of that society speak for himself, that is, that he not permit anyone to represent him; but if creating a society necessarily entails that one submit to the direction of the general will, as the more moderate formulation puts it, then representation is not necessarily excluded, although one might still argue against it on other grounds, as Rousseau does. In other words, while the extreme formulation excludes not only representative government but all political systems except anarchy, the moderate formulation is compatible with both primary and representative assemblies, and hence a preference for one or the other must be based on something other than the nature or terms of the social contract.

If the social contract itself does not necessarily exclude representation, what then are Rousseau's theoretical grounds for opposing it? As has already been indicated, all of his theoretical arguments are ultimately based on a variation of his contention that will cannot be represented. He presents this argument on two separate occasions in the *Contrat*, the first being the paragraph in Book II, Chapter 1, which was apparently inserted after he had completed the *Geneva Manuscript:*

> My argument, then, is that sovereignty, being nothing other than the exercise of the general will, can never be alienated; and that the sovereign, which is simply a collective being, cannot be represented by anyone but itself—power may be delegated, but the will cannot be.[35]

The second statement of this argument, which is a more elaborate version of the first statement, appears in the chapter devoted to representatives in Book III:

Sovereignty cannot be represented, for the same reason that it cannot be alienated; its essence is the general will, and will cannot be represented—either it is the general will or it is something else; there is no intermediate possibility. Thus the people's deputies are not, and could not be, its representatives; they are merely its agents; and they cannot decide anything finally. Any law which the people has not ratified in person is void; it is not law at all.[36]

Since both statements are essentially summaries of a more elaborate argument, it is important to be clear about the concepts Rousseau employs here before proceeding to an analysis of his argument. Sovereignty is here defined on the one hand as "the exercise of the general will" and, on the other, as essentially the same thing as the general will. As Derathé observes, Rousseau provided a more precise definition of sovereignty in the *Geneva Manuscript*, which for some reason he eliminated from the final version.[37] After noting that "There is in the state a common force which sustains it" and "a general will which directs this force," he defined sovereignty as "the application of one to the other," that is, the application of the general will to the common force. The reason that only the general will may direct the power of the state is that "will always tends to the good of the being who wills," and since "the particular will always has private interest as its object, and the general will the common interest, it follows that the latter is or ought to be the only motive force of the social body."[38] Sovereignty, then, is the collective act of determining what use is to be made of the combined resources and powers of the body politic.

Rousseau contends that sovereignty cannot be alienated, because there is nothing that a people can receive in exchange for transferring sovereignty to another person or persons that justifies such an alienation.[39] For a people to alienate sovereignty is to surrender the right to determine what use shall be made of the collective powers of the state, which is to relinquish the very right on which the state is founded. Similarly, sovereignty cannot be represented, because this is equivalent to transferring to some other person or persons the right and power to decide how the collective power shall be used. It is no more legitimate to allow an individual citizen or group of citizens within the state to do this than it is to transfer this decision-making power to noncitizens. To summarize the argument in terms of the four basic concepts: sovereignty, or the exercise of the general will, can neither be alienated nor represented.

As it stands, the argument is thus far little more than assertion. The heart of the argument rests on Rousseau's concept of will in general and the general will in particular. Because each individual tends to give preference to his own interests rather than to those of the community to which he belongs,[40] the only way to ensure that the common interest prevails is to have the entire membership of the community participate in deciding how they are to govern themselves. When each participates, commitments are mutual, and this mutuality has two related consequences. The sovereign, namely, the citizens considered collectively, cannot impose any unnecessary burden on individual citizens, because no one can oblige any other member of the community to do or refrain from doing anything that he is not willing to do or refrain from doing himself.

On the other hand, no one can make the community serve his own interests without at the same time making it serve the interests of the other members of the community, so that there is a positive incentive to cooperate.[41] Will is either general or it is not; either it is the will of the whole body of citizens or it is not. This is what Rousseau means by the indivisibility of sovereignty.[42] The requirement of generality is purely formal; that is, each citizen must be able to participate in determining the general will, but decisions do not have to be unanimous to be binding.[43] To be truly general, the general will must not only come *from* the entire body of citizens but must also apply *to* the entire body of citizens. Lack of generality in either case deprives it of its natural rectitude.[44] Declarations of the general will that meet these two formal requirements are acts of sovereignty or laws.[45] By contrast, the decisions of individual citizens or groups of citizens authorized to act for the community not only do not derive from the entire body of citizens but may also not apply to the entire body of citizens; such decisions are called decrees or acts of the government.[46]

It is clear Rousseau considers that the requirement that the will come from all excludes determination of the general will by representatives authorized to act on behalf of the community. But on the assumption that these representatives are accountable to the community, is it not equally consistent with his definition of the general will for a community to determine that will indirectly through the use of representatives? Whatever practical objections there may be to the use of representatives, it remains true that representation is logically consistent with his concepts of sovereignty and the general will. What, then, is the meaning of his assertion that "will cannot be represented"? The answer appears to be, as Plamenatz has argued, that "Rousseau's dictum, that the will cannot be represented, is either a truism that has nothing to do with the conclusion he derives from it or else it is plainly false."[47] On the one hand, it is true that no one can will for another person in the sense of making up that person's mind, but this is hardly relevant to Rousseau's argument against representation. If this were all he meant, no citizen would have an obligation to obey the will of the majority if that will were contrary to his own, since this would mean that others were willing for him. On the other hand, as Plamenatz points out, it is simply not true that an individual cannot authorize another to will for him in the sense of making decisions on his behalf.[48] Granted that there are risks in doing so, that there are practical reasons for refusing to entrust others with this power, it is nevertheless important to distinguish these pragmatic objections from the fundamental principles of the legitimate state, and it appears that Rousseau failed to do so. The explanation for this failure, I suggest, is that he was already convinced that representatives tend to usurp popular sovereignty and was consequently led to stretch a point in order to provide a theoretical justification for this essentially pragmatic reason for opposing representatives.

Rousseau's concepts of the social contract, popular sovereignty, and the general will, then, do not in themselves necessarily exclude representation, notwithstanding his contention that will cannot be represented. As he proceeds to specify the conditions in which the general will is most likely to emerge and guide the life of the community, however, it becomes increasingly clear that popular assemblies are to be preferred over representative assemblies for other reasons. Unlike the *Dédicace*, the *Contrat social* does not contain a single list of the characteristics of the ideal state, partly because of the relativism of the latter work, but it is possible to piece together several basic characteristics that appear to be of primary importance, and not surprisingly these closely resemble those of the *Dédicace* and other earlier works.

Fundamental among the conditions necessary for the manifestation of the general will is that there be no partial societies, that is, factions, within the state, or, if this cannot be avoided, that there be a multiplicity of factions so that no one will be likely to dominate all the rest. That factions constitute a danger to the health of the state was a commonplace view, but Rousseau also saw a less obvious advantage in the absence of factions. Because he believed that private interests are less divisive than group interests, he believed that individuals unattached to any group would be more likely to appeal to the common interest in trying to resolve their differences than would citizens who had a group interest to uphold as well as their private interests. As a result, deliberations among unattached private citizens would be more likely to yield the general will.[49]

A second condition for realization of the general will is that the state be limited in territory and population.

> Just as nature has set bounds to the stature of a well-formed man, outside of which he is either a giant or a dwarf, in what concerns the best constitution for a state, there are limits to the size it can have if it is to be neither too large to be well-governed nor too small to maintain itself.[50]

His emphasis on the advantages of limited size suggests, however, that what he considered intermediate in size was in fact quite small, even by the standards of his own day. He speaks of the difficulties of governing large states, the heavier tax burden necessitated by the vast bureaucracies that accompany large states, and the inapplicability of the same laws to regions with different customs and traditions, but his most serious grievance against large states is their impersonality, for he believes that in large states "the people has less feeling for governors whom it never sees, for a homeland that seems as vast as the world, and for fellow-citizens who are mostly strangers." [51] Not only must the state be limited in size, but economic differences between citizens of even the small state must be minimized to prevent the kind of class differentiation that would make citizens of different classes feel like strangers to one another. He expresses this economic prerequisite in the well-known phrase "no citizen shall be rich enough to buy another and none so poor as to be forced to sell himself." [52]

Despite Rousseau's professed relativism in chapters 9 to 11 of Book II,[53] he appears to regard these conditions, and perhaps others as well,[54] as the necessary prerequisites for any people that seeks to govern itself in accordance with the general will. In the absence of these conditions the abstract requirements of the general will remain an empty formula. While these conditions are essential, however, they are insufficient to guarantee that the general will prevails. Only if, in addition to the formal requirements and the three conditions discussed thus far, a people is "properly informed" will the general will always result from its deliberations:

> . . . the general will is always rightful and always tends to the public good; but it does not follow that the decisions of the people are always equally right. We always want what is advantageous but we do not always discern it. The people is never corrupted, but it is often misled; and only then does it seem to will what is bad.[55]

It is a curious argument. On the one hand, Rousseau devotes considerable attention to demonstrating that certain conditions must obtain in order that the deliberations of the people result in the general will; on the other hand, he acknowledges that even these stringent conditions are not sufficient, for unless the people are "suffisamment informé" they may never discover the general will. The implication of his argument is that the general will is a standard independent of human will, and there is even the suggestion—particularly in view of his conception of the way in which popular assemblies actually function (which will be discussed in the following chapter)—that someone other than the people must first discern the general will and then present it to the people for their consideration. Rousseau appears genuinely unable to make up his mind about what constitutes the general will and how it comes to be. He cannot allow the people to determine the general will on their own, even if they satisfy all the formal requirements and the social conditions, because even then they might err, and Rousseau does not want to be bound by any decision with which he disagrees, for then it would no longer be true that he "obeys no one but himself, and remains as free as before." The general will must therefore be a standard that transcends human will, one that each citizen can invoke at his own discretion, if necessary as a minority of one.[56] True, the general will so conceived does not become legally binding unless a majority of the citizenry can be persuaded that it really is their will, but this is quite different from saying that the general will is the will of the people or a majority of the people.

Nor does it help matters to say that the general will is the *constant* will of the people as opposed to their will at any given moment, unless one is prepared to accept this constant will as definitive, and Rousseau makes it clear in the passage from *Contrat social* IV, 2, previously cited, that he is not prepared to do so. Rousseau wants to have it both ways. He wants the people to determine the general will and goes to great lengths to specify what conditions are necessary for them to do this, but at the same time he is unwilling to accept the people's decision as final because the people might err; that is, they might obligate him to obey their will rather than his own. This is not to say that Rousseau was intentionally vague on the subject, but rather that his attempt to reconcile two incompatible goals necessarily led to serious ambiguity. This ambiguity, I suggest, was the result of his profoundly ambivalent attitude toward "the people." There is perhaps no more radical theory of popular sovereignty than that set forth in the *Contrat social*, and such a theory is meaningless except on the basis of a deep respect for the good judgment of ordinary citizens. While there is no reason to doubt his sincerity in expounding this radical theory of popular sovereignty, it is nevertheless crucially important to recognize that he also harbored a deep distrust of the same people whose collective wisdom he often celebrated.

This distrust is painfully evident in his discussion of the need for a lawgiver. He begins by reaffirming the principle that a people should be the author of the laws to which it is subject, but when he turns to the question of how a people can exercise its lawmaking function, he takes a distinctly dim view of the people's capacities.

How can a blind multitude, which often does not know what it wants, because it seldom knows what is good for it, undertake by itself an enterprise as vast and difficult as a system of legislation? By themselves the people always will what is good, but by themselves they do not always discern it. The general will is always rightful, but the judgment which guides it is not always enlightened. It must be made to see things as they are, and sometimes as they should be seen; it must be shown the good path which it is seeking, and secured against seduction by the desires of individuals; it must be given a sense of situation and season, so as to weigh immediate and tangible advantages against distant and hidden evils. Individuals see the good and reject it; the public desires the good but does not see it. Both equally need guidance. Individuals must be obliged to subordinate their will to their reason; the public must be taught to recognize what it desires. Such public enlightenment would produce a union of understanding and will in the social body, bring the parts into perfect harmony and lift the whole to its fullest strength. Hence the necessity of a lawgiver.[57]

It might be objected that Rousseau is here speaking about the institution of a people, that he has more respect for the capacities of the "blind multitude" once they are members of a functioning political system. This may indeed account for some of the disparaging comments on "the people" in the chapters devoted to the lawgiver,[58] an almost godlike being whose superior nature contrasts so sharply with that of ordinary human beings, but it does not account for the essentially passive legislative role that he envisions for the people in the newly established polity. It will be recalled that in the *Dédicace* he not only accepted a passive role for the citizens of Geneva but also insisted on it by rejecting the demand for a popular legislative initiative. His position in the *Contrat social* is the same, notwithstanding his much more radical insistence on popular sovereignty and his revival of the age-old demand of the Genevan bourgeoisie for periodic popular assemblies. Will cannot be represented, no one can will for the people; but the people's role in formulating their will is much less than these ringing declarations might suggest.

FIVE

Political Institutions:
The Role of Government

THE MARKED CONTRAST in Rousseau's attitude toward the people when he enunciates the general principles of his political theory (the terms of the social contract, the inalienability and indivisibility of popular sovereignty, the nature of the general will) on the one hand, and when he speaks of the implementation of these principles through the aid of a lawgiver, on the other hand, reappears in Book III of the *Contrat social*, only now it is government that exercises the political initiative rather than the lawgiver. Rousseau opens Book III with an analogy intended to illustrate the proper relationship between the legislative power, namely, the popular assembly of all citizens, and the executive power, the government.

> Every free action has two causes which concur to produce it, one moral—the will which determines the act, the other physical—the strength which executes it. When I walk towards an object, it is necessary first that I should resolve to go that way and secondly that my feet should carry me. When a paralytic resolves to run and when a fit man resolves not to move,

both stay where they are. The body politic has the same two motive powers—and we can make the same distinction between will and strength, the former is *legislative power* and the latter *executive power*. Nothing can be, or should be, done in the body politic without the concurrence of both.[1]

The analogy underlines the separation between as well as the subordination of executive to legislative power, the former being the mere instrument or agent of the latter. But the analogy quickly breaks down, for Rousseau recognizes that the executive power, to function effectively, must have a will of its own. As the argument unfolds, it becomes clear that Rousseau does not adhere to this simplistic distinction between executive and legislative power, even though this distinction is essential to his argument against representative government. Not only does he attribute a will to the executive as well as the legislative power, but a very powerful will—one so powerful that it tends to nullify his original distinction between the two powers. He begins by defining government as the agent or minister of the legislative power, but as he proceeds with the argument, the emphasis is on government as an intermediate body, that is, a power that is intermediate between the people considered as sovereign and the people considered as subjects. He even expresses this relationship in terms of a geometrical proportion whereby government is the mean term and sovereign and subjects the extreme terms.[2] As long as government is seen as simply the agent of the people, the relationship between the two is simple, but once government is viewed as an intermediate body, this relationship becomes quite complicated, for government so conceived must be able to maintain a degree of independence vis-à-vis the people considered as subjects while at the same time remaining subordinate to the people considered as citizens.

[F]or the body of the government to have an existence, a real life distinct from the body of the state, and for all its members to be able to act in concert and serve the purpose for which the government has been set up, it must have a particular *ego*, a consciousness common to its members, a force, a will of its own tending to its preservation.[3]

But what if government substitutes its will for the will of the people? Will there not then be two sovereigns in effect, one *de jure* and one *de facto?*

> The difficulty is to find a method of ordering this subordinate whole within the greater whole, so that it does not weaken the general constitution while strengthening its own, and so that its private force, designed for its own preservation, shall always be distinct from the public force, designed for the preservation of the state; in short, so that it will always be ready to sacrifice the government to the people and not the people to the government.[4]

The difficulty is compounded by the tendency of the corporate will of government to dominate the general will of the people. As Rousseau sees it, the order of nature is just the reverse of the requirements of the social order. In the body politic the general will should prevail over the corporate will of government, and both should prevail over the individual will; in reality, the individual will usually take precedence over the corporate will, and both take precedence over the general will, which is the weakest of all.[5]

Rousseau's view of government in Book III of the *Contrat social* raises several questions about the general principles of his political theory set forth in Books I and II, and especially about his arguments against representation. If will cannot be represented, how can it be legitimate for the government, the elected representatives of the people, to will and act on their behalf? Is this not representation of the will? Rousseau's rejoinder to this objection, that "there cannot be representation of the people in the legislative power; but there may and should be such representation in the executive power, which is only the instrument for applying the law,"[6] is less than convincing. The difference, in Rousseau's view, is presumably that to give someone the right to will for us is to give up our very freedom, to alienate sovereignty, but to confide to someone else responsibility for executing our will is not only legitimate but a practical necessity, at least with regard to administration of the state. This presupposes, of course, that the people retain effective control over those who exercise executive power and are able to choose or depose those entrusted with this responsibility.

The argument is logically flawless and compelling as long as government is conceived as nothing more than the instrument that carries out the people's will, an agent that more or less mechanically executes the decisions the people have already made. But as soon as one sees the government as more than this, the argument ceases to be persuasive. Far from being the mere instrument of the people, government as Rousseau describes it in Book III is a semiindependent body possessed of a corporate will that tends to be more cohesive and therefore stronger than the general will whose servant it ostensibly is. It plays an active role in the life of the body politic, including a major role in legislation. If no law can be enacted without the direct approval of the people, neither can it be enacted unless it is proposed by the government.

Given the preponderant role of government, it is meaningless to reassert the principle that will cannot be represented or to claim that there is a radical difference between representation of the legislative and executive powers. Rousseau's real grievance was not against representation of the will but against executive abuse of power. He was less concerned with assuring the people an important, much less decisive, role in making law than he was with maintaining the supremacy of law in the face of the persistent efforts of government to bend the law to its own purposes. It is perhaps not too farfetched to say that he was prepared to grant such sweeping powers to the people in his accounts of the social contract, popular sovereignty, and the general will precisely because he did not expect the people to exercise these powers in the normal course of events.

At times Rousseau stresses the independence of government to such an extent that his concept of the inalienability and indivisibility of sovereignty, surely one of the most distinctive features of his political theory, is diluted to the point that it verges on Burlamaqui's concept of a separation and balance of powers. Thus his insistence in *Contrat social* III, 1, that the body politic can achieve nothing without the *concurrence* of the legislative and executive powers is not unlike Burlamaqui's contention that sovereignty in Geneva was divided among the Petit Conseil, the Grand Conseil, and the Conseil Général, no one of which could act without the concurrence of the other two orders. Rousseau would undoubtedly reject this interpretation, and rightly so insofar as he insists so strongly on the indivisibility of sovereignty.[7] And yet his willingness to grant government extremely broad discretionary powers, including what can fairly be called a dominant role in making law; his acceptance of a very active role for government in the life of the body politic, which he considered essential to the well-being of the community; and his expectation that the corporate will of government would normally prevail over the general will of the people—all describe a government that is not only relatively independent, a power in its own right, but that tends to be more than a match for a typically passive citizenry.

It is instructive to consider Rousseau's discussion of the various forms of government in the light of his deeply ambivalent attitude toward this institution he treats in Book III as both essential to the welfare of the community and a threat to its very existence.[8] At first glance, it might seem that direct democracy, namely, that system of government in which a majority of the citizens participate in the administration of the laws as well as in making the laws, would be the form of government most compatible with the fundamental principles of Books I and II. There is in fact one sense in which all legitimate government presupposes direct democracy, for no legitimate government can be instituted without first passing through a stage, however brief, of direct democracy.[9] There is also the vision at the beginning of Book IV of a group of peasants sitting beneath an oak tree and regulating all its affairs with ease.[10] It is perhaps partly for these reasons that so many commentators have misleadingly labeled his preferred form of government as direct democracy despite his repeated disclaimers. In a direct democracy there would be no problem of representation of the will either by the legislative or executive power, and Rousseau himself says that those who make the laws know better than anyone else how the laws should be interpreted and applied.[11]

Why, then, does he reject it? His objection to direct democracy is based on his concept of the relation between the general will and particular wills. The general will, it will be recalled, must derive from all and apply to all; it cannot deal with an individual case without by that very act ceasing to be general. The people, who alone can determine the general will, are ill suited to apply that will to individual cases because they inevitably confuse the general with the particular.[12] Hence it is better that a relatively small number of citizens be charged with the responsibility for applying the laws that the collectivity has enacted. This system is also open to abuses, especially the abuse of power by those who constitute the government, but Rousseau thinks it less dangerous to risk corruption of the executive power than to risk the corruption of the legislative power that he believes would result from confounding common and private interests. The people can deal with governmental corruption as long as the soul of the body politic remains healthy, but once the soul is corrupted, there is no hope. Rousseau appears to consider this objection decisive, but he nevertheless adds another that seems to eliminate direct democracy by definition, for he says that any people so virtuous that it could govern itself directly would not need to be governed.[13] In other words, if direct democracy were possible, it would be unnecessary.

He offers still another objection to direct democracy which appears to prove just the opposite of what he seeks to prove. This objection is that the conditions necessary for direct democracy are too severe, that they are beyond what can reasonably be expected of men. These conditions are indeed severe: (1) "a very small state, where the people may be readily assembled, and where each citizen may easily know all the others"; (2) "a great simplicity of manners and morals"; (3) "a large measure of equality in social rank and fortune"; and (4) "little or no luxury."[14] What is curious about these conditions is that each of them corresponds to one of the characteristics of the model he first presented in the *Dédicace,* a model that purported to be nothing more than a description of Geneva. Why should conditions that characterize Geneva be considered too demanding, and why should he list them as an argument against direct democracy? The explanation apparently is that it is a question of degree, for he goes on to say that these conditions should exist to some extent in every legitimate state, and, as will be seen, the conditions necessary for elective aristocracy, his preferred form of government, are little more than a slightly watered-down version of those necessary for direct democracy.

Rousseau thus opposes direct democracy for several reasons, but he does not mention, at least not explicitly, what is perhaps the most important reason, namely, his belief that the ordinary citizen, although capable of sound political judgment as a member of the sovereign assembly, lacks the sophistication needed to make good use of the broad discretionary powers that he believes magistrates should exercise. If this belief is only implicit in his discussion of direct democracy, it comes to the fore in his discussion of elective aristocracy. The principal advantage of elective aristocracy is that it permits the selection of the wisest and best as magistrates, and these are necessarily only a small number of the citizenry. Election has the same positive connotations for Rousseau that it had for aristocratic critics of Greek democracy, who contrasted election favorably to the use of the lot, the ultimate democratic device.

> Under popular government, all the citizens are born magistrates, while this other system [i.e., elective aristocracy] limits itself to a small number of magistrates, every one of whom is elected, a method which makes honesty, sagacity, experience and all the other grounds of popular preference and esteem ' r-ther guarantees of wise government.[15]

In addition, elective aristocracy facilitates the orderly and efficient conduct of public business, including the business of the popular assemblies, and enhances the international reputation of the state.

> In a word, it is the best and most natural arrangement for the wisest to govern the multitude, if we are sure that they will govern it for its advantage and not for their own. . . . But it must be noted that the corporate interest begins at this point to direct the national energies less strictly in accordance with the general will, and that a further inevitable tendency is for a part of the executive power to escape the domain of law.[16]

The "if" in the quote above only faintly suggests the gravity with which he views this problem, a problem that becomes his main preoccupation in the latter half of Book III. For the moment, however, it is worth considering some of the implications of his

95

conclusion that "it is the best and most natural arrangement for the wisest to govern the multitude." In what sense is it more natural than other forms of government? Surely not in the sense that it is the form of government most people have adopted, since it is clearly the historical exception rather than the norm. Nor would it seem to be the form of government appropriate to the condition of most men, or of most Europeans or civilized men, since the conditions necessary for elective aristocracy appear only slightly less demanding than those for direct democracy.[17] If elective aristocracy is the most natural form of government even in these atypically favorable circumstances, it can only be because Rousseau saw social and economic inequality so deeply rooted in human society that *de facto* political inequality was inevitable in even the best of political systems.

Rousseau's political philosophy has given birth to, or at least facilitated the birth of, various forms of radical democracy, and rightly so when one considers only his abstract principles and concepts. But Rousseau himself was far from being a radical democrat, and in his own writings he moderated the radicalism of his abstract theories by an acceptance of institutions that perpetuated the inequality that seemed to him an inevitable feature of the human condition. Others might legitimately draw radical conclusions from his theories; he was prevented from doing so by an ingrained social conservatism.

Even Rousseau's terminology is indicative of this conservatism. Vaughan suggests that Rousseau called his preferred form of government elective aristocracy rather than democracy either to conceal the radicalism of his political theory or to humor the Genevan authorities, or both.[18] This might help to explain the puzzling similarity between the conditions Rousseau listed as necessary for direct democracy and elective aristocracy, but it underestimates Rousseau's conviction that political society requires the kind of strong leadership suggested by the term *aristocracy*. Rousseau wants government by an elite, an aristocracy; but he wants that aristocracy to be accountable to the people it governs. It is a highly dynamic concept of government, both in the sense that he wants dynamic, activist leadership and, more importantly, in the sense that tension between the government and the people is built into the system.[19] He could hardly have found a more apt phrase than elective aristocracy to express this concept. Derathé, who cites Vaughan's observation with approval, also underrates Rousseau's sincerity in calling moderation the indispensable virtue of elective aristocracy. Derathé explains this as Rousseau's way of paying homage to Montesquieu, who held moderation to be the distinctive virtue of aristocratic government,[20] but there is no need to introduce Montesquieu's influence to account for Rousseau's attribution of moderation to elective aristocracy. However others may have interpreted the *Contrat social*, Rousseau saw himself as a political moderate. There is no better evidence for this than the fact that he consistently sided with the moderates among the Genevan bourgeoisie and just as consistently denounced Genevan radicals as dissidents and troublemakers.

If the *Contrat social* is not usually seen as the political philosophy of a moderate, it is because such moderation as the work displays is often only implicit. Rousseau can make sweeping claims for popular sovereignty only because he expects the practical consequences of these claims to be limited or moderated by the broad powers exercised by government. What appear to be two extreme views confronting one another, unlimited popular sovereignty on the one hand and a profound distrust of the people on the other, are reconciled, at least in Rousseau's mind, by implicit assumptions that moderate both views. There are, however, instances in which he takes a more obviously moderate position by preferring an intermediate position over either of two extremes, as he does in preferring elective aristocracy over both direct democracy and monarchy.

At times Rousseau seems to accept monarchy as a legitimate form of government,[21] and the chapter he devotes to monarchy is by far the longest of the three chapters in which he discusses alternative forms of government, but his criticism of monarchy is in fact at least as severe as his criticism of direct democracy. Even the principal advantage of monarchy, the identity of interest between the monarch and the government and the consequent unity of purpose that prevails in the administration of monarchies, is ultimately a disadvantage because the monarch's personal interests are rarely the same as those of the people he governs.[22] At one point he

97

declares monarchy inferior to republican government, even though elsewhere he claims that only republican government is legitimate.[23] Perhaps this is no more than a terminological inconsistency, but the overall impression of chapter 6 is that monarchy is at best only marginally legitimate and possibly beyond the pale. Strong leadership is essential, and the lack of it is one of the major weaknesses of direct democracy; but leadership in a monarchy tends to be so strong that it is indistinguishable in practice from absolutism, and this too is unacceptable.[24] Rousseau is much more concerned about the absolutist tendencies of monarchy in the *Contrat social* than he was in his *Jugement sur la Polysynodie*. In the earlier work he opposed Saint-Pierre's proposal to divide administrative authority among a number of councils on the grounds that this reform would weaken the monarchy, but in the *Contrat social* he favors this device as a means of keeping the executive subordinate to the legislative power.[25] Despite the relativism of the chapters that immediately follow his analysis of the various forms of government, then, it is apparent that he prefers elective aristocracy over the other forms of government except in extreme and highly improbable circumstances.[26]

––––––––––

Whatever the best form of government, and whatever the ideal social and natural conditions on which it is based, Rousseau is convinced that every state, no matter how well constituted or how well adapted to circumstances, tends to degenerate. Chapter 10 of Book III marks a distinctly new phase in the argument. In Books I and II he vigorously challenges traditional theories and sets forth his own general principles, and in the first half of Book III he presents a constructive analysis of government, but beginning with Chapter 10 this confident tone yields to a thoroughgoing pessimism.[27]

So complete is his pessimism that in several of the chapters on government the *Contrat social* becomes little more than "a clinical analysis of political deterioration."[28] "The body politic, no less than the body of a man, begins to die as soon as it is born, and bears within itself the causes of its own destruction."[29] The analogy suggests a period of growth and development before the process of degeneration becomes dominant, although elsewhere, for example, in his discussion of the institution of a republic by a lawgiver, he seems to envision a steady degeneration from an initial optimal point. In either case, he admits of no exceptions: "If Sparta and Rome perished, what state can hope to last forever?"[30] The reason for this degeneration, according to Rousseau, is the incessant effort of government, whatever its form, to usurp the power of legislation and thereby make itself sovereign. The government enjoys an advantage over the people because it has an *esprit de corps* that is usually lacking in the people.[31] Since degeneration of the body politic is as inevitable as degeneration of the human body, the most one can hope for is to prolong life by the best possible constitution. Once the people loses the power to make laws, the state dies. Again he offers an analogy: "The legislative power is the heart of the state, the executive power is the brain, which sets all the parts in motion. The brain may become paralyzed and the individual still live. A man can be an imbecile and survive, but as soon as his heart stops functioning, the creature is dead."[32]

The institutional problem is thus to prevent, or at least delay, the usurpation of legislative power by the government. Rousseau's solution is determined in part by the way he defines law: "since laws are nothing other than authentic acts of the general will, the sovereign can act only when the people is assembled."[33] Rousseau identifies law with will so completely that he regards respect for ancient laws as respect for the will that brought them into being. Silence implies consent, so that the original will that gave rise to a law is perpetually valid unless expressly revoked.[34] Laws are valid because men constantly will them to be valid, either actively or passively, overtly or tacitly.[35]

This identification of law and will leads Rousseau to see the problem of maintaining legislative sovereignty as essentially one of maintaining the vitality of the popular will, of maintaining a high degree of civic consciousness or public-spiritedness. Only a people devoted to the public interest can successfully resist the persistent efforts of the government to usurp the law-making power.[36] Such, Rousseau believes, were the peoples of Sparta and Rome. Why were Spartans and Romans so richly endowed with public-spiritedness?

Rousseau finds the answer in the active participation of every citizen of these ancient city-states in the law-making process. Regular popular assemblies were the key political institution that ensured the vigorous exercise of sovereignty and thereby the constitution and health of the body politic. For this reason regular popular assemblies have always been "the nightmare of rulers," "a brake on government." Rulers have resorted to every conceivable ruse and excuse to dispense with popular assemblies, for

> The moment the people is lawfully assembled as a sovereign body all jurisdiction of the government ceases; the executive power is suspended, and the person of the humblest citizen is as sacred and inviolable as that of the highest magistrate, for in the presence of the represented there is no longer any representation.[37]

At this point in the *Contrat social* Rousseau's theoretical argument against representation merges with his practical argument. The identification of law with will is closely linked with his contention that will cannot be represented, but the argument that participation in popular assemblies provides the most effective brake on government is an essentially practical argument whose validity does not depend on whether or not the will can be represented. Even if Rousseau were prepared to concede that it could be represented, which he is not, he would still be able to maintain just as forcefully that periodic popular assemblies are the most effective means of maintaining popular sovereignty. His real objection to representation is not the abstract notion that will cannot be represented but the conviction that the use of representatives dilutes the popular will and thus renders it impotent vis-à-vis the government.

That this is his main grievance against representation becomes clearer as he elaborates on the importance of periodic popular assemblies and participation in chapter 15, "Deputies or Representatives." He begins by portraying representatives as the political counterpart of mercenaries. Just as a people that values the private pursuit of money and the material comforts it makes possible more than the common good hires mercenaries to do its fighting, it pays representatives to carry out its political functions. By contrast, a truly public-spirited people does its own fighting and willingly participates in the public assemblies. Participation in the life of the community ought to be spontaneous and joyful, as is the case in well-governed states, but in badly governed states the people avoid public assemblies like the plague.[38] "The cooling-off of patriotism, the activity of private interest, the vastness of states, conquests, the abuse of government—all these have suggested the expedient of having deputies or representatives of the people in the assemblies of the nation."[39] Such a people is no longer free, or rather it is free only at those infrequent moments when it chooses new representatives. The English people, so celebrated for their love of liberty, are in fact slaves except during the election of members of Parliament.[40]

Rousseau's characterization of the English as slaves is clearly an example of literary overkill, but his use of the term leads him into a curious argument that reveals to what extent he is prepared to go to denounce representatives. After conceding that the Greeks may have been able to hold popular assemblies as often as they did only because they had slaves to do their work, he then asks plaintively

> What? Is freedom to be maintained only with the support of slavery? Perhaps. The two extremes meet. Everything outside nature has its disadvantages, civil society more than all the rest. There are some situations so unfortunate that one can preserve one's freedom only at the expense of the freedom of someone else; and the citizen can be perfectly free only if the slave is absolutely a slave. Such was the situation of Sparta.[41]

In response to this self-criticism, Rousseau lamely rejoins that moderns, who fancy themselves free because slavery has been abolished, are themselves slaves. Moderns have done away with slavery out of cowardice, not out of humanitarian considerations. He hastens to add that this does not prove that slavery is either necessary or legitimate; it only explains why moderns have representatives and the ancients did not. If Rousseau explains anything by this argument, it would seem to be that representative government is an advance over popular assemblies, at least insofar as popular assemblies presuppose slavery. Representation may compromise the principle of popular consent to legislation by making consent indirect, but slavery abolishes consent altogether. When Rousseau equates the two, as he does in his contention that "the moment a people adopts representatives it is no longer free; it no longer exists,"[42] he is showing more concern for rhetoric than for logic. Nor does it seem to occur to him that in a state based on popular assemblies the people are "free," according to the strict standards by which he condemns the English, only during the brief period that the assembly is in session and, like the English, are "slaves" the rest of the time. On the assumption that he had in mind the annual assemblies of Geneva, a free people, according to this logic, would be free only slightly more often than the English.

The use of representatives not only reflects a lack of public spirit, but it also contributes to the further deterioration of the body politic by fostering the habit of relying on others instead of participating in political life oneself. Representation and participation are in fact inversely related, two sides of the same coin. The more a people rely on representatives, the worse their situation becomes, while the more they participate in political life, the healthier the body politic. Rousseau sometimes sees political participation as having more than just an instrumental value, that is, the prevention of executive abuse of power, although this is his main emphasis in Book III. The citizen is by definition one who participates in the sovereign authority,[43] but the value of participation goes beyond the purely juridical function of voting in the assembly. Participation also serves the important psychological function of promoting closer identification with the community. Each citizen accepts the collective decisions taken by the assembly more willingly because he participates in making those decisions. Even when one is outvoted in the assembly, one is more likely to accept and obey the decision of the majority if he feels that the decision was reached justly, that the issue received a fair hearing even though his opinion was rejected.[44]

But participation in the assembly is only one form of participation in communal life, and, although decisive from a purely political point of view, not necessarily the most important form of participation. In his *Lettre à d'Alembert*, it will be recalled, Rousseau focused on the beneficial effects of participation in the *cercles*, public festivals, and other communal activities, and in *Contrat social* IV,

7, he refers back to this earlier work as an example of how a healthy public opinion can be created and serve as a guide for public morals, which are the basis of all political life.[45] In *Contrat social* II, 12, which classifies law into four categories—constitutional, civil, criminal, and moral—he describes the moral law written in the hearts of citizens as the most important of all, the cornerstone of the foundation on which the state rests.[46] In this sense, communal institutions, both political and social, are also educational institutions. It is not simply a matter of the government or other smaller associations educating the people, but rather a case of citizens educating one another through their common participation in these institutions.

This emphasis on the importance of participation has led some commentators to see Rousseau as a totalitarian. Even Chapman, who concludes that Rousseau cannot fairly be called a totalitarian for this reason, argues that Rousseau's "proposals for intensifying social sentiment" constitute one of the totalitarian aspects of his political theory. He refuses to label Rousseau a totalitarian only because he thinks this emphasis is inconsistent with Rousseau's basic political principles.[47] Other commentators go much further and argue that Rousseau's demand for "total participation" was essentially a technique for ensuring total obedience by a passive citizenry.[48] Crocker contends that Rousseau rejected representative government precisely because it "would nullify the total alienation and participation that Rousseau must have."[49] Talmon similarly argues that Rousseau opposed representative assemblies because he feared they would get in the way of the revolutionary vanguard of the people who sought to impose their particular version of dictatorship on the passive majority.[50]

Such criticisms seriously distort what Rousseau has to say on the subject. Talmon's thesis in particular is little more than a travesty of Rousseau's view of participation. As R. A. Leigh points out in an essay largely directed at Talmon's interpretation of Rousseau, Rousseau's ideal was to establish an equilibrium between the government and the people, between authority and liberty. Rousseau explicitly rejects direct democracy for many of the reasons that Talmon alleges that Rousseau used to argue for total participation.

Rousseau carefully stipulates that popular assemblies must conduct their business in an orderly fashion according to procedures previously agreed on, and he goes out of his way to provide for protection of individual rights, including the right to privacy, that is, the right not to participate.[51] Summarizing the limits of sovereign power in *Contrat social* II, 4, Rousseau makes this latter point quite clearly:

> From this it is clear that the sovereign power, wholly absolute, wholly sacred, wholly inviolable as it is, does not go beyond and cannot go beyond the limits of the general covenants; and thus that every man can do what he pleases with such goods and such freedom as is left to him by these covenants; and from this it follows that the sovereign has never any right to impose greater burdens on one subject than on another, for whenever that happens a private grievance is created and the sovereign's power is no longer competent.[52]

As much as Rousseau wants participation, he realizes that it must be voluntary or else it is meaningless. If his insistence on "intensifying social sentiment" is in any sense totalitarian, it is not because he favors compulsory methods to achieve it but rather because the principal means of political participation that he favors, participation in the popular assembly, is largely devoid of any content.

SIX

Political Institutions:
The People as Legislator

THE *Contrat social* is the first occasion on which Rousseau called for periodic popular assemblies, a demand that was notably absent from the *Dédicace,* even though it had been a major goal of Genevan dissidents ever since the days of Pierre Fatio. Despite Rouseau's evident reluctance to make this demand his own, however, the enthusiasm with which he now embraced periodic popular assemblies might reasonably lead one to expect that these assemblies would be the focal point of political activity in the ideal state. After all, one of his main purposes in *Contrat social* III, 12 through 18, was to show that well-attended popular asemblies are both a feasible and effective means of maintaining the sovereignty of the people. He also insists that attendance be regular. It is not enough that a people establish a constitution once and for all time; provision must be made for periodic assemblies at fixed times so that no government can dispense with the assemblies without its being clear that the government violates the constitution in doing so.[1]

But what about participation in the assembly itself? If the as-

105

semblies are to play the educative role that Rousseau seems to envision for them, does this not entail that citizens be encouraged to participate so that they can learn by doing? Above all, if citizens are to be truly the authors of their own laws and masters of their own fate, as the whole weight of the *Contrat social* argues that they should be, does this not require that they take an active part in the popular assembly, which alone can enact laws and oversee the work of the executive? Rousseau's answer to both questions, surprisingly, is "no." This can be seen from a comparison of the respective roles Rousseau expects ordinary citizens and the government to play in the assembly. Throughout the *Contrat social* he gives the impression that ordinary citizens play a decisive role in legislation, the most important function of the popular assemblies, but in fact this decisive role amounts to very little. As he summarizes it in the chapter on representatives, "Any law which the people has not ratified in person is void; it is not law at all."[2] The term *ratified* accurately describes the extent of popular participation in legislation: the role of the people is limited to approving or disapproving proposals submitted and debated by the government.

> I might say a great deal here about the simple right of voting in every act of sovereignty, a right of which nothing can deprive citizens, and also about the right of speaking, proposing, dividing and debating—a right which the government always takes great care to assign only to its own members—but this important subject would require a separate treatise, and I cannot put everything in this one.[3]

Rousseau seems to think that if each individual member of the assembly makes up his own mind, that is to say, if each decides for himself whether or not a given proposal conforms to the dictates of his own conscience, then the decision reached by the assembly is more likely to conform to the general will.

It is not entirely clear whether or not debate was permitted in the Conseil Général during the first three-quarters of the eighteenth century, and if so, under what conditions. There was lengthy and stormy debate in the series of meetings of the Conseil Général in May 1707 at which the syndic Chouet and Pierre Fatio presented their opposing conceptions of the meaning of the Conseil Général's sovereignty,[4] but these were extraordinary meetings during which the Conseil Général came close to realizing Fatio's dream of a "Conseil Général délibératif." The *Édits de la République de Genève* assembled and published in 1735 do not address the question of debate directly, but they repeatedly refer to the Petit Conseil and the Conseil des Deux Cents as "deliberating" bodies that, after deliberating, propose measures for the Conseil Général to either approve or reject.[5] The *Règlement* of 1738 uses similar language to describe the powers of the Conseil Général. It defines the legislative power as the power "d'agréer ou rejetter les Loix proposées, ou les changements a celles qui sont etablies," and all its other powers are similarly defined as the power "d'agréer ou rejetter" or "d'aprouver ou rejetter" candidates or proposals submitted to it.[6] Not until the *Edit de pacification de 1782* is there a clear statement on the matter of debate in the Conseil Général, and that statement makes it clear that the Conseil Général is not to be a deliberating body: "Le Conseil Général statuera sur les matières qui lui seront portées, en approuvant ou rejetant par billets & sans délibérer, les avis qui lui seront proposés par les Syndics Petit & Grand Conseils."[7]

It is reasonably clear, then, that the Conseil Général, although ostensibly a sovereign assembly of all citizens, did not normally function as a "deliberating" body, that is, one in which citizens debated the merits of candidates and proposals prior to voting on them, although on extraordinary occasions like the series of meetings in 1707 it temporarily functioned as a forum for debate among the citizenry. This of course does not necessarily imply that Rousseau preferred to exclude debate from his model assemblies, but in view of the other institutions and practices he borrowed from the Genevan constitution, this does make it more plausible that he did in fact intend to exclude debate. Nor is this as surprising as it might appear. The classical republican tradition that Rousseau so greatly admired included much more explicit justifications for limiting the right of debate to select groups within the state. James Harrington, who is perhaps the best-known spokesman for this view, declared that his model commonwealth consisted of "the senate proposing, the people resolving, and the magistracy executing."[8]

Rousseau does not provide for a popular legislative initiative in the *Contrat social* any more than he did in the *Dédicace*. The limited significance of the much-vaunted "droit législatif" is curious, but, as Derathé observes, it conformed to the practice of the Genevan constitution as Rousseau knew it.[9] And not only does Rousseau fail to provide for a popular legislative initiative in the assembly, but he also specifically prohibits the people from calling a meeting of the assembly on their own initiative. He acknowledges the need for extraordinary meetings of the assembly in times of emergency, but he says that only the government may summon such a meeting. Spontaneous meetings of the assembly have no validity.[10] The sentiment behind this prohibition is not unlike that behind his denunciation in the *Dédicace* of dissidents who seek to arouse the people against their leaders.

Even more surprising than Rousseau's opposition to a popular legislative initiative is his acceptance of the Genevan practice whereby nomination of candidates for public office was controlled by the government, in other words, by the Petit and Grand Conseils. It will be recalled that in the *Dédicace* Rousseau remained silent on the question of nominations. In the *Contrat social* he breaks this silence, not to criticize Genevan practice, as one might expect, but to approve it. That he does so is all the more surprising in that he voices his approval immediately after insisting, in *Contrat social* III, 16, that government is not instituted by a contract between the people and itself but is rather wholly subordinate to the sovereign people.[11] In the following chapter he explains that government is properly instituted by two separate acts, one legislative and the other executive.

> By the first, the sovereign enacts that there shall be a body of government established with such or such form; and it is clear that this act is a law.
> By the second, the people names the magistrates who are to be invested with the government thus established. Since this nomination is a particular act, it is not a second law, but simply a sequel to the first and a function of government.[12]

Note that, although "the people names the magistrates," the people in this case, which is clearly an extraordinary situation, are exercising a function that normally belongs to government alone.

This is necessarily the case since the act of nominating involves the naming of specific individuals, and the general will cannot properly deal with specific cases. How, then, does it happen that the people can sometimes act as magistrates?

> Now it is here once more that the body politic reveals one of the astonishing properties by which it reconciles operations that seem to be contradictory. For this operation is accomplished by the sudden transformation of the sovereignty into democracy in such a way that without undergoing any visible change, and simply through a new relation of all to all, the citizens become magistrates and pass from general acts to particular acts, and from the law to its execution.[13]

To prove that this peculiar operation is not just a trick of the imagination, Rousseau cites the example of the English House of Commons, which daily transforms itself into a committee of the whole to expedite business and then reports back to itself in its capacity as sovereign. He then concludes this short but vitally important chapter by explaining how the provisional government thus established either proceeds to function as the regular government or else yields to the government decided on by the sovereign.

> It is the advantage peculiar to democratic government that it can be established in fact by a single act of the general will. After this, the provisional government remains in office if such is the form adopted, or there is established in the name of the sovereign whatever government is prescribed by the law; and everything is then in order. It is not possible to institute the government in any other legitimate manner, without abandoning the principles established in earlier chapters.[14]

Nomination of magistrates is thus always a function of government, not an act of sovereignty. Only in the special case of the institution of a new government do the people, acting in their extraordinary joint capacity as legislative and executive power, nominate as well as elect their magistrates. Rousseau makes it clear that this is his meaning when he returns to the subject in *Contrat social* IV, 3, in which he discusses in greater detail the various modes of electing magistrates. He there refers back to *Contrat social* III, 17, recalling that "the election of chiefs is a function of government and not of sovereignty."[15] The term *election* must here be understood in the sense of "choice" or "selection" and hence of nomination, for just as proposals of the government must have the approval of the people before they can become laws, so too the nominees of the government must receive popular approval before they can become magistrates. The term *election* does, ironically, convey quite accurately the reality of Genevan practice. Rousseau would soon become thoroughly disillusioned with this reality and adopt a distinctly hostile view of the Petit Conseil, but he was not of this opinion when he wrote the *Contrat social*. In fact he must surely have had the Genevan government in mind when he added that "In an aristocracy the prince chooses the prince, the government perpetuates itself by its own actions; and then election by choice is appropriate."[16] Since he had just argued that election by lot is appropriate to a democracy, meaning a democratic government in his special sense of the term, it is evident that he was here speaking of an aristocratic government, that is, an elective aristocracy, and hence finds the practice of a self-perpetuating government acceptable, provided, of course, that the people retain the right to confirm the nominees of the government.

As if to drive home the point that he is modeling his preferred method of choosing magistrates on Genevan practice, he compares the systems of election in Venice and Geneva. He likens the Genevan Conseil Général to the Venetian Great Council, the Genevan bourgeoisie to the Venetian patriciate, the *natifs* and *habitants* to the townsmen and people of Venice, and the peasants of Geneva to the Venetian subjects on the mainland. His purpose in all this is to show that the Venetian government is no more aristocratic than Geneva's.[17] It is tempting to conclude that Rousseau is here being sarcastic, that he is indirectly criticizing the Genevan political system by likening it to one of the most celebrated oligarchies in Europe,[18] but there is no need to resort to this kind of interpretation, which relies on divining a hidden meaning in Rousseau's not altogether clear remarks, because his approval of Genevan practice, despite the apparent discrepancy between his basic principles and that practice, follows a consistent pattern that appears again and again in the *Contrat social*: seemingly unlimited claims for popular sovereignty, on the one hand, but balanced by an exceedingly cautious interpretation of the practical meaning of those claims.

There is thus every reason to believe that Rousseau was quite sincere in declaring the nomination of candidates to be a function of government, even though he realized that this would normally mean that government would be self-perpetuating.[19] It does not follow, however, that he intended to reduce the people to impotence vis-à-vis the executive, especially since he considered the tendency toward executive usurpation of sovereignty as the main threat to the body politic. What he does, in effect, is to regularize the extraordinary situation he describes in *Contrat social* III, 17, by returning the body politic to the stage of primitive democracy at the opening of each periodic assembly. He gives back with one hand what he takes away with the other. For if government *normally* possesses extraordinary powers, the people *periodically* repossesses these powers, indeed all legitimate political powers, and the government is at least temporarily reduced to the simple minister of the people that the general principles of the *Contrat social* declare it to be. This is accomplished by putting two questions to the people at the beginning of each assembly:

> The first: "Does it please the sovereign to maintain the present form of government?"
> The second: "Does it please the people to leave the administration to those at present charged with it?"[20]

The people thus retains the residual right not only to dismiss or replace individual magistrates but to completely alter the form of government.

It is safe to say that Rousseau did not expect that the people would often choose to exercise either of these powers, especially the power to alter the form of government. He considered radical changes in government, either in personnel or in form, to be dangerous: "one should never touch an established government unless it has become incompatible with the public welfare." But, he adds, "such circumspection is a precept of politics and not a rule of law; and the state is no more bound to leave civil authority to its magistrates than military authority to its generals."[21] The real importance of the periodic assemblies is thus preventive, that is, to deter government from abusing its power by holding over its head the constant reminder that it will have to render an account of its behavior to the whole people on specified occasions.[22] It is these periodic assemblies, then, that give substance to Rousseau's claim that

> the holders of the executive power are not the people's masters but its officers; and . . . the people can appoint them and dismiss them as it pleases; and . . . there is no question of their contracting, but of obeying; and . . . in discharging the functions which the state imposes on them, they are only doing their duty as citizens, without having any sort of right to argue terms.[23]

And at this point he does seem to have Geneva in mind when he says that even a hereditary government, including one based on an aristocratic class of citizens, is only a provisional form of government which the people can change at any periodic assembly.[24] It was in fact precisely this chapter that the Genevan authorities singled out when they condemned the *Contrat social* as seditious.[25]

Rousseau attempts to clarify further the nature and purpose of popular assemblies by examining in considerable detail how the Roman assemblies functioned. His principal reason for devoting so much attention to Roman political institutions—five chapters of Book IV comprising nearly one-fourth of the entire *Contrat social*—is to demonstrate the practicability of his proposed political institutions. He obviously anticipated objections to the *Contrat social* on this score, quite rightly as it turned out, and believed he could remove some of the sting from these objections by citing the example of a great republic that functioned quite well with institutions not unlike those called for in the *Contrat social*. As he puts it in *Contrat social* III, 12, "it seems to me good logic to reason from the actual to the possible."[26] If an assembly of 200,000 was able to conduct business in the Roman republic, surely his proposal for making periodic popular assemblies the centerpiece of his own political institutions cannot easily be dismissed as utopian.[27] The idea that the whole citizenry can be assembled on a regular basis may seem chimerical today, he says, but it was not so 2000 years ago. "The boundaries of the possible in the moral realm are less narrow than we think; it is our own weaknesses, our vices and our prejudices that limit them."[28] The Roman Republic had more than 400,000 citizens and the Empire more than 4 million and yet hardly a week passed without the people's being assembled.[29] At times the mass of humanity gathered in these assemblies was so great that citizens had to cast their votes from the rooftops, but even this was not enough to deter those patriots, for they were more concerned with justice and liberty than with convenience.[30]

The value of these chapters on Roman political institutions is a matter for debate. Vaughan dismisses them as a kind of appendix "barely relevant to the subject, and quite unworthy of the setting in which they stand."[31] Wright similarly regards them as trivial in importance,[32] and Derathé suggests that Rousseau included them only to pad the work and set the stage for the discussion of civil religion.[33] Masters notes their importance for understanding Rousseau's distinction between what Masters calls the principles of political right and the prudential maxims necessary to apply these principles[34] but otherwise makes little mention of them. Jean Cousin emphasizes their importance in revealing the Roman influence on Rousseau's political thought, but Cousin's main purpose is to demonstrate that Rousseau is not very reliable as a historian.[35] Launay concurs with Cousin's views but adds that Rousseau's unscientific approach to history does not at all detract from the importance of the chapters on Rome, since the true function of the image of Rome in Book IV is "to offer for reflection a middle term between the rules of right . . . and this reality which is never completely finished, which is still to be finished."[36] That is to say, Rousseau's cavalier treatment of the facts of Roman history does not prevent him from offering a model of political institutions that indicates how his general principles might look in practice. Of all these commentators, only Launay makes a serious effort to interpret the political theory and purpose of the *Contrat social* in the light of these chapters on Roman political institutions.

The problem with these chapters is not so much that they are out of place in the *Contrat social* as that it is difficult to determine with any certainty just what lessons Rousseau draws from the Roman example, and this uncertainty necessarily diminishes their value to anyone who seeks to use them as a key to understanding Rousseau's political thought. Launay is probably right in his contention that Rousseau saw Rome as a kind of middle term between the ideal and the real, but this does not answer the question of what facets of the Roman experience Rousseau saw as approaching the ideal and what facets he saw simply as concessions to human weakness or to the peculiar shortcomings of the Roman system of government. Launay's own view that Rousseau invokes the Roman experience largely as an example of the pitfalls that Genevans ought to avoid is highly questionable on a number of points. He is able to extract this meaning only by reading between the lines rather than by taking Rousseau's apparent meaning seriously. If there is any justification for proceeding in this way, it is that Rousseau's apparent meaning often seems contrary to both the letter and the spirit of much of what he says in Books I to III. In some cases it is more difficult to believe that he is serious in his praise of Rome than to believe that he is trying to conceal his true meaning for one reason or another. Reading between the lines remains a risky procedure, however, and Launay's particular reading appears to result as much from his attempt to portray Rousseau as a consistent spokesman for the Genevan dissidents as it does from what Rousseau says about Roman political institutions. Whatever Rousseau's meaning, the discrepancy between the radicalism of his basic principles and the conservative manner in which he applies these principles is a prominent feature of all his political writings, and this pattern suggests that caution is in order even when one is confronted by examples that seem to flagrantly contradict his basic principles.

Perhaps the clearest illustration of this type of discrepancy appears in Rousseau's discussion in *Contrat social* IV, 4, of voting methods in the assemblies. He describes a series of divisions of the voting population into tribes or classes and applauds the clever manner in which one of the divisions was carried out so as to ensure the domination of the rural tribes over the urban tribes, even though the population of the urban tribes was greater.[37] But this particular division appears as the very embodiment of justice compared to another, more important division attributed to Servius, who divided the population into six classes based on wealth, then subdivided these six classes into 193 centuries in such a way that the first and wealthiest class accounted for 98 centuries—that is, an absolute majority of the 193 centuries—while the sixth and poorest class, which contained an absolute majority of the population, was lumped together into one century. Since voting was by centuries, with a simple majority of each century determining the vote of that century, the wealthiest class invariably commanded a majority of the total vote as long as it was united. In fact, since the centuries normally voted according to rank, the centuries of the first class voting first and the one century of the sixth class voting last, only the votes of the first class needed to be counted to arrive at a decision, and the sixth class played virtually no role in the republic. Rousseau does not hesitate to draw the inevitable conclusion about this system of voting: "so it can be said that in the centuriate assemblies matters were decided by majorities of money rather than of votes."[38]

Although he refers to the "excessive power" of the wealthy minority in this arrangement and points out the ways in which its power was properly tempered, his overall opinion of the system of voting in the *comitia centuriata* is highly favorable. "There is no doubt that the whole majesty of the Roman people was to be seen in the *comitia centuriata;* this alone was a full assembly, for the *comitia curiata* excluded the rustic tribes and the *comitia tributa* excluded the Senate and patricians."[39] And despite what he says about the *de facto* exclusion of the majority of the population from participation in the fundamental act of voting, he nevertheless claims that "no citizen was excluded from the right to vote, and . . . the Roman people was truly sovereign, both in law and in fact."[40]

In the face of such an extravagant claim, such an obvious non sequitur when one considers only the evidence Rousseau himself presents, Launay's contention that Rousseau is in effect saying to his fellow Genevans that they should take care that their own patriciate does not manipulate them the way the Roman patriciate manipulated the Roman people acquires a certain plausibility. How else account for the jarring discrepancy between abstract principle

115

and concrete example, or between evidence and conclusion? Launay also discovers another instance of Rousseau's attempting to warn his fellow Genevans in his discussion of the tribunate.[41] According to Launay, Rousseau saw the Roman tribunate as a kind of middle term that could prevent either the government or the sovereign from dominating the state and may even have been suggesting that the Genevan attorney general play the role of mediator in the Genevan political system.[42]

Whatever the merits of Launay's specific interpretation of these passages, he does open up a promising line of inquiry with his suggestion that Rousseau sought to achieve a balance or equilibrium in the state. One of Rousseau's main goals in Book III was to establish an equilibrium between a strong and energetic executive and a popular assembly capable of maintaining the sovereignty of the people. Is it possible, then, that his puzzling praise of Roman institutions in Book IV can be explained as the result of his attempt to discover a similar type of equilibrium in the Roman system? Rousseau specifically mentions the tribunate as a balancing force in the state, and even the dictatorship and censorial tribunal can be seen as institutions that contribute to maintaining a proper balance.[43]

On the other hand, the "balance" that Rousseau praises in the Roman system is heavily weighted in favor of wealth. Not only does this weighting apply to the relationship between the government and the people—after all, Rousseau seems to think that elective aristocracy will usually mean that the wealthier class will hold most executive positions—but it also applies to relations within the assembly itself, and this type of imbalance tends to undermine much of what he says about the nature of the social contract and the general will. An assembly such as the *comitia centuriata* in which decisions are based on "majorities of money rather than of votes" lacks even the minimal conditions necessary for expressing the general will as Rousseau describes this process elsewhere in the *Contrat*. At most, the tribunate is a kind of makeshift device that partially compensates for the radical imbalance in the popular assembly, which in Book III was portrayed as the centerpiece of all political institutions in the state. The tribunate's power is essentially negative: "it can do nothing, it can prevent anything from being done."[44]

The power of the tribunate as Rousseau perceives it is in this respect typical of the Roman constitution as a whole, whose distinguishing characteristic, according to one authority, was "the superabundance of negative powers" mitigated mainly by a system of emergency institutions.[45] It is quite possible that this negativism was one of the features of the Roman system that most appealed to Rousseau. The principal virtue of the tribunate is the same as what Shklar believes Rousseau saw as the principal function of the primary assembly: both are essentially preventive institutions.[46] This similarity does not explain Rousseau's acceptance and even praise of the *comitia centuriata,* however, unless one is prepared to dismiss as meaningless much of what he says about the general will.

Even if one could accept the tribunate as a legitimate substitute for the popular assembly, a proper vehicle for the expression of the general will, this would not resolve the difficulties posed by Rousseau's praise of the Roman system, which in reality as well as in Rousseau's view was based on maintaining a balance of power among a number of independent or quasi-independent groups and institutions.[47] Just as Rousseau's stress in Book III on the independence of government tends toward a concept of separation and balance of powers similar to Burlamaqui's view of the Genevan constitution, so too his praise of the Roman constitution raises the question of whether he not only compromises but also perhaps even abandons the principle of the strict subordination of executive to legislative authority. It is one thing to concede that every political system requires some kind of *de facto* balance of power; perhaps Rousseau meant to say no more than this in his discussion of the relations between the government and the people in Book III. It is quite another matter to praise the very principle of a balance of power, as he does in his discussion of the tribunate.

––––––––––

Rousseau's analysis of Roman political institutions, which he says was intended "to demonstrate more forcefully all the principles that I might myself set forth,"[48] creates at least as many problems of interpretation as it solves. His examples often seem to prove just the opposite of what he attempts to prove elsewhere in the *Contrat*. If the role of the people in the *comitia centuriata* is a fair example of what popular sovereignty means in practice, what could a people possibly lose by electing representatives to legislate for them? Surely the risk of losing control over elected representatives is worth taking if the alternative is a popular assembly in which the great majority of citizens have no effective voice whatever. The question therefore arises whether Rome is a happy choice to illustrate the institutions described in Book III, whether the Roman example proves the practicability of popular assemblies, whether, in fact, Rome is not in many respects a counterexample of what Rousseau seeks to illustrate. In particular, the very size of the Roman assemblies, which Rousseau no doubt stresses in order to make his insistence on popular assemblies seem more realistic, may have prevented them from functioning in conformity with the general principles enunciated in the *Contrat social*. If this is the case, perhaps it is better to take seriously his melancholy remark at the conclusion of the chapter on representatives in which he acknowledges that size is an important limitation.

> All things carefully considered, I do not see how it will be possible henceforth among people like us for the sovereign to maintain the exercise of its rights unless the republic is very small.[49]

The phrase "henceforth among people like us" presumably exempts the gigantic Roman assemblies from this limitation, this in keeping with Rousseau's assumption that the more virtuous Romans could cope with problems far beyond the abilities of depraved moderns. Since Rousseau's own more detailed analysis of Roman assemblies makes one wonder whether his confidence in the superior virtue of the ancients was not misplaced, however, it is worthwhile to consider small assemblies as an alternative to the Roman example and to explore some of the implications of limiting the size of the body politic.

It will be recalled that in *Contrat social* II, 9, Rousseau contends that the body politic has a natural size just as the human body does. The ideal state is "neither too large to be well-governed nor too small to maintain itself."[50] The question is what is natural? How large or how small should the state be? Rousseau does not, to his credit, suggest a precise population figure such as the 5040 citizens or heads of families that Plato recommends in the *Laws*,[51] nor does he rely on the formula of Aristotle, who says that the optimum population is "the greatest surveyable number required for achieving a life of self-sufficiency."[52] He does, however, follow Aristotle's discussion of this problem quite closely, and it is not unlikely that the two basically agree on the optimum size, even though Rousseau does not specify the criteria for this optimum as succinctly as Aristotle does. The problem for both Aristotle and Rousseau is that there is no single, optimal size, not even if one agrees with one or the other on the remaining characteristics of the ideal state. This is clearly demonstrated by Robert A. Dahl and Edward R. Tufte in a recent study of the relationship between size and democracy. For some 2000 years the small city-state was considered optimal for democracy, while during the past 200 years the great nation-state has been considered optimal. In reality neither is optimal, for people live in a multiplicity of political, social, and economic units, and the optimal size of these units varies according to their various purposes and other factors.[53]

Although Rousseau was not entirely unaware of this problem, and was certainly more aware of it than either Plato or Aristotle, much of what he says about the appropriate size of the body politic suffers from his neglect of it. This is true, for example, of his attempt to show that democratic government suits small states; aristocratic government, intermediate-sized states; and monarchy, large states.[54] While he offers evidence to support this position, his arguments are for the most part simply a reiteration of the classical view that continued to prevail throughout most of the eighteenth century.[55] At one point he does introduce an argument that appears to be, if not original, at least based on his own experience rather than on traditional authority. Addressing himself to the relationship between population and territory, he notes that governments can more easily suppress popular revolts when the population is scattered over a large territory than when it is concentrated in a small territory.

> [T]he more a numerous people is packed together, the less easily can the government infringe on the sovereign; popular leaders deliberate as securely in their private rooms as the prince in his council, and the crowd gathers as swiftly in the public squares as the troops in their barracks. . . .
>
> The strength of the people . . . is effective only if it is concentrated; it evaporates and is lost when it is dispersed, just as gunpowder scattered on the ground ignites only grain by grain.[56]

Was he perhaps recalling his own experience when he wrote these lines, those violent days of August 1737 when the call to arms was sounded and the bourgeois militia assembled its regiments within a matter of hours and temporarily seized power from the Petit Conseil? And does he perhaps draw his image of popular leaders deliberating in the privacy of their rooms from the *cercles* he praises so highly in the *Lettre à d'Alembert?* The point he makes is interesting, not only because of its evident Genevan inspiration, but also because it suggests that popular assemblies might function better in city-states like Geneva than in less densely populated agricultural states. It is one of the few occasions in his political writings when Rousseau can be suspected of a pro-urban bias. The bias is genuine, however, and he makes it explicit in *Contrat social* III, 13, where he contends that periodic popular assemblies are uniquely suited to states consisting of just one city, namely, city-states.[57] States with more than one city present serious problems, for the natural tendency in such cases is for one capital city to dominate all the rest, which destroys the significance of citizenship. The remedy he proposes for these unfortunate states is "to have no fixed capital, but to move the seat of government from one place to another and to assemble the estates of the country in each in turn." To those who object that this is an unduly cumbersome arrangement, he responds "It is no use complaining about the evils of a large state to someone who wants only small ones."[58]

But does he really want only small states? The answer, as he recognizes, is not so simple as this "don't blame me" response suggests. The problem is that small states might find themselves at the mercy of their larger neighbors.

> But how are small states to be given enough strength to resist large states, as the Greek cities once resisted a great king and as, more recently, Holland and Switzerland resisted the House of Austria?[59]

Or, as he poses the question at the end of *Contrat social* III, 15:

> But if it [i.e., the republic] is very small, will it not be subjugated? No. I shall show later how the external strength of a large people can be combined with the free government and good order of a small state.[60]

In a footnote added to this passage in 1762 he explains that he planned to discuss this problem in the context of foreign relations, specifically under the subject of confederations, a subject that "is entirely new, and its principles have yet to be established."[61] Unfortunately, as he indicates in both the foreword and the conclusion to the *Contrat social*, he never completed the projected work on international relations.[62] Even more unfortunately, he apparently did write a fragment of some sixteen chapters on confederation, which he gave to the Comte d'Antraigues to use as the latter saw fit, but in 1789 the count destroyed it for fear that its publication would further the cause of the radicals among the French revolutionaries.[63]

The best single indication of what this fragment contained, if indeed it ever existed, is probably the brief sketch in Book V of *Émile* of what he planned to say about confederations. He there poses anew the dilemma of the democratic state, which must be small to be truly democratic but whose very size exposes it to the threat of foreign domination, the worst form of tyranny.

> Finally we will examine the type of remedies to these inconveniencies that have been sought in leagues and confederations, which, leaving each state its own master internally, arm it against every unjust aggressor. We will investigate how one can establish a good federative association, what can render it durable, and how far one can extend the right of the confederation without infringing on that of sovereignty.

The abbé de Saint-Pierre had proposed an association of all the states of Europe to maintain perpetual peace among them. Is this association practicable, and supposing that it had been established, would it have lasted? These investigations lead us directly to all the questions of *droit public* which can help to clarify those of *droit politique*. [64]

As this reference to Saint-Pierre's proposal for perpetual peace indicates, Rousseau intended to use the Abbé's proposal as the basis for his own discussion of confederation, although not without making significant changes. [65] In the *Extrait du Projet de paix perpétuelle* Saint-Pierre cites several of the leagues of the ancients as examples of how the advantages of large and small states can be combined, but he adds that none of these ancient confederations approaches the wisdom of three modern confederations, the Germanic Body, the Helvetic League, and the Estates General of the United Provinces. [66]

What Rousseau objects to in Saint-Pierre's proposal is not the Abbé's conception of confederation per se but rather his simplistic notion of how this proposal might be implemented. Short of a great statesman like Henry IV or Sully, Rousseau argues, confederations can be established only by revolution, and it is difficult to say whether the evils of revolution will not outweigh the benefits of the peace that confederation would make possible. [67] What Rousseau approves of in the Abbé's proposal, how his conception of confederation differs from that of the Abbé, is less clear.

The most extensive attempt to construct—or reconstruct, if Rousseau did write the sixteen chapters on confederation as d'Antraigues claimed—Rousseau's concept of confederation is that of J.-L. Windenberger in his *La république confédérative des petits états*. [68] Windenberger argues that the *Contrat social* must be supplemented by a *Contrat international* that protects the citizen from external threats just as the social contract protects him from internal threats. [69] As it stands, the *Contrat social* is incomplete because it does not show how the small state can uphold the social contract in a world dominated by large states. Windenberger therefore treats the *contrat international* as the logical extension of the principles of the *Contrat social*. He distinguishes between three forms that such an international contract might take—a simple military alliance, a federal state, and confederation—and contends that Rousseau favors a confederation, that is, an intermediate form which is more than a mere agreement for member states to come to one another's aid in case of aggression, but which at the same time strictly limits the powers of the central government to those functions absolutely essential to the common defense of the confederates. This means not only that member states will choose representatives to form a multinational legislative assembly, but also that these representatives will be no more than the *mandataires* of the member states. While a simple military alliance is too fragile an association to ensure the defense of each member state, a truly federal state with broad powers concentrated in the central government smacks too much of representative government. Confederation, which Windenberger defines as an association of sovereign states, promises the advantages of both forms without their accompanying disadvantages.[70]

Windenberger's thesis does appear consistent with the principles set forth in the *Contrat social* and with Rousseau's scattered remarks on confederation,[71] but he seriously underestimates the difficulties involved in the practical application of these principles when he claims that the "details" of administration are altogether secondary considerations.[72] How and where does one draw the line between a federal state and a confederation, or between those functions which properly belong to a central government and those which belong to each member of the association? How does one give sufficient powers to the central government to act in the common interest of all states without transforming *mandataires* into representatives? Rousseau takes these practical questions quite seriously but has difficulty reconciling his solutions with his basic political principles; Windenberger succeeds in reconciling the general principles of the *contrat international* with the practical application of these principles, but only by minimizing the importance of these practical problems.

Whatever the merits of Windenberger's reconstruction of Rousseau's view of confederation, it does draw attention to a problem that confronts anyone who seeks to make popular sovereignty the basis of any political system larger than a small city-state, namely, the problem of representation. Windenberger may be correct in saying that the central government of the confederate states would be composed of representatives of each state rather than of the individual citizens of each state. His further contention that Rousseau would have the magistrates of each state either serve as representatives or choose those who were to serve as representatives on the central governing body is also plausible in view of Rousseau's preference for leaving the conduct of foreign affairs in the hands of the executive.[73] But if so, if Rousseau was prepared to accept representatives for these purposes, what is one to make of his sweeping denunciation of representative government in the *Contrat social*, especially the several variations of his argument that will cannot be represented? Is it possible that he did not publish the fragment on confederation because he would have been compelled to accept representative government not only as a practical expedient but also as a matter of principle if he had done so? If his discussion of confederation had followed immediately the chapter on representatives, as the 1762 note to the *Contrat social* III, 15, suggests, the discrepancy would have been particularly glaring. These speculations on what Rousseau would have written are reinforced by what he did write when he was requested to devise a constitution for Poland, a state too large in both territory and population to function with the city-state institutions of the *Contrat social*. His attitude toward representation in *Considérations sur le gouvernement de Pologne* will be examined in more detail in the final chapter, but it is opportune to point out now that, in terms of the distinctions made by Windenberger, the political system Rousseau proposed for Poland might be more accurately described as a federation than as a confederation.

SEVEN

The Sources of
Rousseau's View of Representation

IF IT IS true that Rousseau's theoretical arguments against representation are not convincing; that even he does not take these arguments seriously when he turns to the problem of establishing an effective system of government; that he in fact favors a government
that not only exercises wide discretion in administrative decisions
but also plays a dominant role in the legislative process that renders
meaningless the distinction between executive and legislative representation; and that his views on confederation, although very
fragmentary, suggest that he would have favored some form of representative government as the only means of ensuring the survival
of the small city-states based on primary assemblies that he values
so highly—if all this is true, why was he so intensely opposed to
representative government in the *Contrat social?* What accounts for
the marked change in his view of representatives between the writing of *Économie politique* and the *Contrat?* Rousseau's hostility toward representative government has been attributed to a variety of
influences—his admiration for the ancients, his dislike of feudal-

ism, his intensive study of the writings of the natural law school, his attachment to Geneva—each of which probably played some role in the development of his view. While no one of these influences fully accounts for the position he took in the *Contrat social*, it is possible to show that certain of these influences were more important than others, and, by doing so, to arrive at a more nearly satisfactory understanding of his reasons for preferring primary over representative assemblies.

One possible explanation for Rousseau's view of representation in the *Contrat social* is that his admiration for the ancient Greeks and Romans led him to reject representative assemblies, a modern institution, in favor of the primary assemblies of the ancient city-states. As Rousseau pointed out in *Contrat social* III, 15, the ancient Greeks did not even have a word for representatives.[1] The Latin term *repraesentare* from which the modern term *representation* derives was not used in the political sense of one person acting for another until the thirteenth century.[2] Athenian democracy was direct democracy in that citizens exercised political power themselves instead of delegating it to representatives. The basic political institution in Athens during the classical period was the assembly of all citizens, which not only approved or disapproved proposals submitted to it by the council but also amended these proposals and even initiated proposals of its own. In addition, the assembly exercised extensive powers in the field of foreign policy, reserved supreme judicial power for itself, and supervised the work of the executive. All magistrates except those few who were chosen for special skills, mainly military leaders, were selected by lot, which by the fifth century was regarded as the democratic procedure *par excellence* in contrast to election, which was generally considered an aristocratic method of selection.[3]

Rousseau's opinion of Athenian democracy was mixed. He shared the Athenian belief that the collective wisdom of the people is superior to that of experts, a belief that perhaps more than any other led Athenians to prefer direct over representative democracy.[4] On the other hand, he condemned the popular legislative initiative as one of "the dangerous innovations that finally ruined the Athenians" and reproached them for attempting to administer the laws themselves rather than leaving this to the magistrates and for refusing to give their magistrates sufficient authority to govern effectively.[5] If Rousseau had little good to say about Athens, it was because he tended to identify the political virtues of ancient Greece with Sparta, even when these virtues were common to both Sparta and Athens. Chief among these common virtues was public-spiritedness, a willingness, even eagerness, to participate in the political life of the community.

This concept of civic virtue was undoubtedly a major factor in Rousseau's dismal view of representative government, for he was convinced that civic virtue was doomed among a people who habitually limited their participation in communal life to the occasional election of representatives. If modern man were no longer capable of the kind of participation that characterized the Greek city-states, it was only because his moral and political vision was so narrow. While Rousseau sometimes identified civic virtue with "the ancient republics of Greece" or simply "the Greeks," he often identified it solely with Sparta.[6] Notwithstanding his high praise of the Spartan spirit, he had relatively little to say about Spartan political institutions. The Spartan assembly was a less vital and powerful institution than its Athenian counterpart. It is not clear whether the ephors or the senate had the right of legislative initiative, but it is clear that the Spartan assembly did not. The assembly's role in legislation was apparently limited to ratifying or rejecting, without amendment and possibly without debate, proposals submitted to it by the ephors or senate. And if the ephors or senate were dissatisfied with a decision of the assembly, they could declare a "crooked judgment" and withdraw the proposal in question.[7] Rousseau did not comment on these features of the Spartan political system, but in view of what he considered to be the excesses of Athenian democracy, it is unlikely that he would have objected to the more oligarchic Spartan constitution.

Sparta's chief rival among the ancients for Rousseau's esteem was Rome, which he frequently mentioned together with Sparta as an example of an excellent political system[8] but occasionally singled out as "the best government which ever existed."[9] Perhaps this was only the exaggeration of a classical republican carried away by enthusiasm for his ideal; in any case, as his own analysis of Roman political institutions in Book IV of the *Contrat social* shows, there are important discrepancies between the institutional model presented in Book III of the *Contrat* and the institutions of the Roman republic.

One feature of the Roman system that he clearly admired was Rome's dogged adherence to primary assemblies long after its citizen population had become so great that holding these assemblies presented serious practical difficulties. Others might contend, as Montesquieu and most of the Encyclopedists did, that the example of the Roman assemblies was largely irrelevant to moderns, but Rousseau cited these same assemblies as proof of their feasibility. He agreed that depraved moderns are incapable of recapturing the full glory of the ancients, but he did not believe that their primary assemblies were beyond the reach of moderns. Yet precisely because admiration of the ancients and their political institutions was widespread among the Encyclopedists, Rousseau's own admiration for the ancients fails to explain his insistence on primary assemblies. He may have experienced this fascination more intensely than most of his contemporaries did, but this alone hardly accounts for his break with the Encyclopedists on the issue of representation. Had he not been a proud member of Geneva's primary assembly, the Conseil Général, his love affair with Sparta and Rome would most likely have ended as it did with most of his fellow Encyclopedists, who thought primary assemblies fine for the ancients but ill suited for moderns. In addition, Rousseau's admiration for the ancients fails to explain the evolution of his views on representation, for his praise of the ancients resounds just as loudly in his earliest political work, the *Discours sur les sciences et les arts,* as it does in his final political work, the *Considérations sur le gouvernement de Pologne.*

It is often said that Rousseau's hostility toward representation grew out of his dislike for feudalism. Cobban, for example, says that Rousseau was sufficiently a man of his century to condemn representative government simply because it was a feudal institution.[10] Gierke made the same point many years earlier, adding that the fact that representative government had matured in aristocratic

England was further cause for Rousseau to oppose it.[11] Shklar goes so far as to claim that "Rousseau's hostility to representative institutions arose *entirely* from his contempt for these remnants of feudal 'barbarism.' "[12] There is little doubt that the feudal origins of representation did nothing to endear it to Rousseau, for whom feudalism meant "that iniquitous and absurd system under which the human race is degraded and which dishonours the name of man."[13]

Precisely what it was about feudalism that Rousseau objected to is not entirely clear. When he called it degrading, he seems to have had in mind the system of personal dependencies on which feudalism was based. He believed that feudalism had originated in the barbarian conquests of the former Roman Empire and that it had split society into two distinct groups, the conquerors and the conquered, degrading both in the process.[14] One of Rousseau's greatest personal fears was dependence on the will of another person. The *Contrat social* itself may be seen as an attempt to construct a political system in which dependence on the law takes the place of personal dependence. It was this desire to avoid personal dependence that led him to seek a form of association in which each member "obeys no one but himself, and remains as free as before," and to define freedom as "obedience to a law one prescribes to oneself." The very purpose of civil law was to ensure "that each citizen shall be at the same time perfectly independent of all his fellow citizens and excessively dependent on the republic."[15] Rousseau thus saw common subjection to the impersonal law as the alternative to the system of personal dependencies among members of the body politic that characterized feudalism.

If this is what Rousseau meant when he called feudalism degrading, his characterization of it as absurd apparently referred above all to the legal inequality of the feudal system. Feudalism had originated with one law for the conqueror, another for the conquered, and traces of this original inequality still persisted in the form of special privileges extended to nobles who claimed descent from the original conquerors. Each estate of the *ancien régime* was in effect a state within a state with its own privileges and obligations, and a multiplicity of corporations prided themselves on their special status before the law. Again, the *Contrat social* can be seen as an attempt to found a state on equality before the law, and in fact treats legal equality as the means of achieving freedom from personal dependence. If all are equal before the law, all depend on the law, not on the personal will of this or that individual or group. In Rousseau's eyes, representation violated the principle of legal equality and thereby opened the way for a new system of personal dependence, for representatives were not the people's agents but their self-appointed masters, and as such, above the law.

Whether or not Rousseau was justified in linking representation with personal dependence, it was a much more plausible view in the eighteenth century, when many representatives held their positions by birth, than it is in the twentieth century, when representative government has become synonymous with democratically elected assemblies.[16] The whole eighteenth-century corporate structure was based on legal as well as social and economic inequality, and Rousseau was convinced that representative bodies, which typified this structure, would naturally pursue their own interests rather than the popular interest. They would, in short, become hereditary aristocracies, the worst of all forms of sovereignty. The only reliable way to prevent this was to have the entire people participate in the law-making process in primary assemblies.

While Rousseau's attitude toward feudalism undoubtedly influenced his view of representatives, it does not fully account for his intense opposition to representatives any more than does his admiration for the ancients. Just as the Encyclopedists shared Rousseau's admiration for the ancients, they also shared his contempt for feudalism and its eighteenth-century remnants. Diderot's opinion of feudalism, for example, was hardly less severe than Rousseau's. On one occasion Diderot declared that what was good about feudal government could be summarized in ten pages, while it would take a thousand to state what was wrong with it. Even the Gothic style in architecture offended the sensibilities of the Encyclopedists, who rarely expressed a favorable judgment about anything associated with the Middle Ages.[17] If the Encyclopedists could attack feudalism and the corporate system of representation without rejecting the principle of representation *per se*, why could not Rousseau do the same? Rousseau's dislike of fedualism thus leaves unexplained why he alone among the Encyclopedists arrived at his distinctly hostile view of representatives. And, like his admiration for the ancients, his contempt for feudalism is a constant theme of all his political writings and thus similarly fails to account for the evolution of his view of representatives.

A more promising explanation than either of these two is that Rousseau came to oppose the use of representatives as a result of his detailed study, in the course of the mid-1750s, of the major jurisconsults and political theorists of the school of natural law. By far the best known and most persuasive statement of this thesis is Derathé's *Jean-Jacques Rousseau et la science politique de son temps*. While Derathé does not directly attribute Rousseau's view of representatives in the *Contrat social* to his encounter with the natural law school, he does argue that Rousseau developed the theory of popular sovereignty on which he based his theoretical rejection of representation largely through the systematic critique of the jurisconsults.

One key point on which Rousseau differed with the jurisconsults was the alienability of sovereignty: the jurisconsults unanimously agreed that a people could alienate its sovereignty; Rousseau rejected the alienability of sovereignty for the same reason that he rejected slavery, arguing that it was just as illegitimate for a people to give itself a master as it was for an individual to do so. In any case, it would be absurd for a people to voluntarily surrender its sovereignty, since there would be no possible way for it to gain in exchange anything of equal value. Moreover, in Rousseau's view, it was no more legitimate for a people to alienate sovereignty in favor of a representative assembly than to alienate it in favor of an absolute monarch, for there was no guarantee that either one or the other would always express the will of the people.[18]

There is abundant evidence that Rousseau was well acquainted with the writings of the natural law school as a whole, although he may not have been well informed about some members of this school. Grotius, who figures prominently as Rousseau's chief adversary in the early chapters of the *Contrat social*,[19] was among the first, if not the very first, of the jurisconsults whose writings Rousseau came to know. In the *Dédicace* he recalled seeing the works of Grotius, together with those of Tacitus and Plutarch, intermingled with the tools in his father's workshop.[20] Despite this early introduction to Grotius, however, Rousseau rarely wrote anything favorable about him.[21] He ridiculed this reputed master of the jurisconsults as a mere child, and a child of bad faith at that, in the yet-to-be-born science of *droit politique*.[22] He objected above all to what he saw as Grotius's support of absolutism, even to the point of being a court flatterer.[23] Grotius paid lip service to the doctrine of popular sovereignty only to provide an additional rationalization for absolutist regimes by legitimating the unconditional transfer of sovereignty from the people to their rulers in a pact of submission.[24]

Pufendorf figures much less prominently in Rousseau's political writings than Grotius but may have exerted a greater influence on the development of Rousseau's theory of popular sovereignty. In the *Discours sur l'inégalité* Rousseau criticized Pufendorf for allowing an individual to divest himself of his liberty in the same way that he divests himself of his property,[25] which is similar to the criticism made of Grotius in the *Contrat social*.[26] This was Rousseau's only explicit criticism of Pufendorf; on three other occasions when Pufendorf is cited by name, he is invoked as an authority.[27] While Pufendorf agreed with Grotius that a people can legitimately transfer sovereignty to its rulers, he was less hostile to democracy than Grotius was in that he regarded popular or democratic sovereignty as no less legitimate than the sovereignty of rulers. Rousseau made use of Pufendorf's arguments for democratic sovereignty but went beyond him by declaring the sovereignty of the people inalienable under any circumstances.

Rousseau's attacks on Grotius were equaled in severity only by his criticism of Hobbes, who served as the *bête noire* for a number of eighteenth-century writers. Although it is not certain that Rousseau read any of Hobbes's works, it is probable that he not only read Hobbes but read him quite carefully. The only work of Hobbes that he specifically cited was *De Cive*,[28] which he probably read in French translation but may have known only through citations to Hobbes's works translated in the works of Pufendorf. It is less certain whether he was familiar with *Leviathan,* which was difficult to obtain in the eighteenth century, but if he did read it, he probably read the Latin edition because of his poor knowledge of English. Derathé is convinced that Rousseau carefully reread Hobbes during the 1750s after having severely attacked him in the *Discours sur l'inégalité,* and that Rousseau used Hobbes to criticize several key concepts of the natural law school and to develop his own theory of popular sovereignty.[29] In the same passage from *Émile* in which he ridiculed Grotius as an amateur political theorist, Rousseau contended that the fundamental principles of Grotius and Hobbes were exactly alike, differing only in mode of expression and method.[30] Elsewhere, however, Rousseau revealed a fascination for Hobbes that he never showed for Grotius. In *L'État de guerre* he seemed puzzled that "one of the most beautiful geniuses who ever existed," meaning Hobbes, could have so thoroughly misunderstood human nature. He found the explanation in Hobbes's desire to justify absolutism, for if people were as evil by nature as Hobbes said they were, they would more readily tolerate the absolutist regime desired by Hobbes.[31] Whether or not Rousseau's critique of Hobbes's view of human nature was justified, it was a common eighteenth-century conception of Hobbes. Diderot accepted it in his *Encyclopédie* article "Hobbisme" and singled out Hobbes's pessimistic view of human nature and Rousseau's optimistic view as the fundamental difference between the two philosophers.[32]

What Rousseau objected to in the political theories of Hobbes and Grotius was thus their defense of absolutism. Strictly speaking, Hobbes allowed sovereignty to rest with the whole body of the people as well as with an aristocracy or a single person, but he made it clear that his own preference was for absolute monarchy. Hobbes's formulation of sovereignty by institution in the *Elements of Law* and *De Cive* presupposed an original democracy that in turn would choose a council or individual to act as sovereign. As he described the process in *De Cive,* "Those who met together with intention to erect a city, were almost in the very act of meeting, a democracy."[33] Aristocracy, in turn, "receives its original from a democracy, which gives up its right unto it,"[34] and similarly "a *monarchy* is derived from the power of the *people,* transferring its right, that is, its authority on one man."[35] In *Leviathan*, however, Hobbes offered a different formulation of sovereignty by institution by introducing the concept of a representative that alone gives unity to the group.

> A multitude of men, are made *one person*, when they are by one man, or one person, represented; so that it be done with the consent of every one of that multitude in particular. For it is the *unity* of the represener, not the *unity* of the represented, that maketh the person *one*. [36]

A people is thus not truly a people until it is represented; prior to that time it is only a multitude of isolated individuals who could become a people only by transferring sovereignty to a representative. Hobbes's very insistence on the transfer of absolute power to a representative may well have negatively influenced Rousseau's own view of representatives.[37]

The contention that Rousseau arrived at his peculiar view of representation largely through his reading and criticism of the natural law theorists at least offers an explanation for the evolution of his view, which is lacking in the explanations that cite his dislike of feudalism and his fascination with the ancients. If Rousseau still accepted representatives in *Économie politique*, it was because he had not yet really come to grips with the political theories of the natural law school. When he did so in the mid-1750s, he gradually came to the conclusion that not only the absolutism of Hobbes and the jurisconsults but also the limited monarchy and parliamentary system favored by Locke and most of the Encyclopedists were illegitimate.[38] The influence of the natural law theorists is particularly evident in Books I and II of the *Contrat social*, where one after another Rousseau passes in review and often challenges these theorists.

Still, there is an important element missing from this explanation, just as there is from those explanations that stress Rousseau's attitude toward the ancients or feudalism. For that matter, all three explanations together—and Derathé mentions these other influences along with the influence of the natural law school[39]—fail to account adequately for Rousseau's view of representatives. Even with the assumption that Rousseau was more intensely and seriously engaged in the study and criticism of the natural law school than his fellow Encyclopedists were, what was there in his experience that led him to question the legitimacy of representative assemblies and insist on popular assemblies? It seems to me that Genevan political institutions were decisive in this respect and accordingly must be stressed in any explanation of the development of Rousseau's view of political institutions in general and representative institutions in particular. This is not to deny the validity of Derathé's explanation or those explanations that stress Rousseau's view of the ancients or feudalism, but rather to suggest that these explanations are incomplete because they seriously understate the Genevan influence in the development of Rousseau's political thought.

Geneva's influence is evident throughout the *Contrat social*.[40] The most revealing direct reference to Geneva may be that which appears in the introduction to Book I:

> Born as I was the citizen of a free state and a member of its sovereign body, the very right to vote imposes on me the duty to instruct myself in public affairs, however little influence my voice may have in them. And whenever I reflect upon governments, I am happy to find that my studies always give me fresh reasons for admiring that of my own country.[41]

It is as though he is declaring at the outset that this is a book about Geneva written by a Genevan for his fellow Genevans. It is obviously more than this as well, however, as both the title and subtitle of the work imply. He does not limit himself to an exposition and analysis of Genevan political theory and practice but seeks to present a universally valid political system. Vallette is surely not far from the truth when he says that the *Contrat social* is a work written by a Genevan of the opposition who seeks to elevate the political institutions of his homeland into a universal ideal and does this by revising the reality of Geneva in the light of the criticism of his fellow oppositionists.[42]

The parallels between the *Contrat social* and the claims of the Genevan bourgeoisie are indeed striking. Rousseau's assertion of popular sovereignty, meaning the sovereignty of the Conseil Général in terms of Genevan institutions[43]; his insistence that government is, at least in principle, a purely subordinate body; his demand for periodic popular assemblies—all of these were typically bourgeois claims and all were perceived as potentially threatening by the patriciate, especially the demand for periodic assemblies. Rousseau also shared the shortsightedness of the bourgeoisie on several crucial issues. He seems to have believed, as did most of the bourgeoisie at that time, that the *droit de représentation* guaranteed by the *Règlement* of 1738 was an adequate substitute for the lack of a popular legislative initiative. Even more significantly, he approved the Genevan practice by which the Petit Conseil monopolized the right to nominate candidates for public office, a monopoly that it used to limit public office to members of the patriciate. Only his claim in *Contrat social* III, 18, that each periodic assembly retained a natural right, so to speak, to pass judgment on both the form and the personnel of the government prevented these concessions from completely undermining the bourgeoisie's ability to challenge successfully the legitimacy of the ruling patriciate.

Other features of the *Contrat social* are distinctively Genevan although not necessarily associated with any particular faction. The similarity between Rousseau's concept of elective aristocracy and the existing relationship between the government and people of Geneva has already been noted. In addition, his preference for small states, his antimonarchical republicanism, his praise of the simple life, and his emphasis on the need for a relative equality of wealth were widely shared Genevan values. His suggestion that small states can compensate for their weakness through confederation was clearly inspired in part by the Swiss practice of confederation, although Geneva was not at that time part of this confederation.[44]

The contradictions inherent in Rousseau's view of representation were also inherent in the Genevan constitution, at least as it was understood by the bourgeoisie. Both the *Contrat social* and the bourgeoisie proclaimed the sovereignty of the people and insisted that this sovereignty could be exercised only by the Conseil Général. Prior to the troubles of the 1730s even prominent patricians acknowledged this in principle. But Rousseau and the bourgeoisie also accepted the need for a strong and forceful executive and were accordingly quite willing, even eager, to grant extensive powers to the government to represent the people in their executive function. Vallette argues that Rousseau opposed representation because the

Petit Conseil had tried to act as the people's legislative representative by approving new taxes on its own instead of submitting them to the Conseil Général. The extremes to which Rousseau was prepared to go to denounce representation—Vallette apparently has in mind Rousseau's indirect defense of slavery in *Contrat social* III, 15—reflected the intensity of Genevan opinion on this issue.[45]

This may indeed have influenced Rousseau's view of representation, but it seems somewhat arbitrary on the part of Vallette to single out this particular abuse of power, especially since this was one of the few significant powers the Conseil Général had managed to retain in the face of persistent patrician efforts to dilute or dispense with it. Rousseau's view of representation was in reality far more ambiguous than Vallette is prepared to admit, and this ambiguity was a faithful reflection of the ambiguities inherent in the Genevan constitution. Viewed from this perspective, Rousseau's attempt to remain faithful to the Genevan model was perhaps partly responsible for his failure to achieve a truly universal and coherent statement of the *principes du droit politique* in the *Contrat social*. The similarities between Rousseau's views in the *Contrat*, on the one hand, and the reality and bourgeois interpretation of the Genevan constitution on the other, can hardly be attributed to coincidence, particularly when it is recalled that Rousseau, alone among the Encyclopedists in his opposition to representative government, was also alone in being a Genevan. Geneva, or his somewhat idealized picture of Geneva, therefore appears the most important source of his distinctive view of representation.

If the influence of Geneva is only implicit in the *Contrat social* itself, Rousseau makes this influence explicit in the sixth letter of *Lettres écrites de la montagne*. After summarizing the basic principles of the *Contrat*, he asks his Genevan audience

> What do you think, Sir, in reading this short and faithful analysis of my book? I can guess. You say to yourself, there is the history of the government of Geneva. This is what all those familiar with your constitution have said on reading the work.[46]

He points out the various features of the *Contrat social*—the establishment of the rule of law through a primitive contract, the institution of government and its subsequent encroachments on the people's sovereignty, the dissolution of the primary assemblies which were the basis of this sovereignty—that he thinks demonstrate that the *Contrat* is in fact a step-by-step account of the evolution of the Genevan constitution and then concludes with an explanation of the manner in which Genevan institutions served as a model for the *Contrat*:

> I thus took your constitution, which I found good, as a model of political institutions, and by recommending you as an example for Europe, far from seeking to destroy you I revealed the means of your preservation. This constitution, as good as it is, is not without defects; one could have prevented the alterations it has suffered and insured it against the danger that it faces today. I foresaw this danger, I made it known, I indicated how to guard against it; was it out of a wish to destroy it that I showed what must be done to maintain it? It was because of my attachment to it that I wished that nothing had altered it. This is the whole of my crime; I was wrong, perhaps; but if the love of my country blinded me on this point, was that reason to punish me? [47]

In short, Rousseau says that he used Genevan institutions as a model for *Contrat social* although he recognized that even Geneva was less than perfect. He adds that it was precisely because he had taken an existing government as his model that the *Contrat* could not be dismissed as a utopian tract along the lines of Plato's *Republic* or More's *Utopia*. What splendid irony, then, that the sole government to condemn the *Contrat* was the very government on which it had been modeled. Neither France nor Bern nor Holland, all of which had condemned *Émile* for its allegedly heretical religious views, had condemned the *Contrat*. [48]

Rousseau's explicit statement that Genevan institutions provided a model for the political institutions of the *Contrat social* might appear to settle once and for all the question of the Genevan inspiration of the work, but a number of students of his political thought have doubted the validity of Rousseau's claim. Spink's thesis in *Jean-Jacques Rousseau et Genève* has been particularly influential in this regard. Spink, it will be recalled, argues that Geneva's institutions not only were not but could not have been the model for the *Contrat social*, for the simple reason that Rousseau had no more than a superficial knowledge of Genevan institutions at the time he wrote the *Contrat*.[49] Moreover, to say that Rousseau took Geneva as his ideal and then to argue that he criticized Geneva on the basis of that ideal, as Vallette does, is to argue in a circle. Spink therefore concludes that Rousseau was mistaken when he claimed in the *Lettres écrites de la montagne* that the *Contrat social* was modeled on Genevan institutions, however sincere he may have been in making that claim. The real source of Rousseau's ideal or model must thus be sought elsewhere, and Spink suggests that it is to be found in the political theories of Pufendorf, Grotius, Hobbes, Locke, and Montesquieu.[50] Derathé's *Jean-Jacques Rousseau et la science politique de son temps* is in effect an elaborate attempt to document in detail Spink's suggestion that Rousseau derived his ideal not from Geneva but from the political theorists of the natural law school.

While Spink and Derathé do raise serious questions about the validity of Rousseau's claim, Rousseau's own unequivocal statement about a matter concerning the source of his views cannot be dismissed without carefully examining every plausible argument in support of that statement. To begin with, it is not at all clear that Spink is justified in his contention that Rousseau was fundamentally ignorant of Geneva's political institutions. Candaux, the Pléiade editor of the *Lettres écrites de la montagne,* argues that Rousseau was reasonably well informed about the Genevan constitution when he wrote the *Contrat social.* He points out that the bourgeois leader De Luc sent Rousseau a copy of Michel Roset's *Chroniques,* an important source of Genevan history, as early as March 1758; that in 1759 the Genevan pastor Jacob Vernes asked Rousseau to read the manuscript copy of a history of Geneva that he and a colleague, Jacques-Antoine Roustan, had written; and that Rousseau had long been familiar with Jacob Spon's *Histoire de Genève,* a standard if somewhat popularized work on the subject.[51] Quite apart from the internal evidence of the *Contrat social,* then, there is reason to believe that Rousseau was sufficiently acquainted with the literature on Geneva to model the institutions of the *Contrat* after the Genevan constitution even if his knowledge was inadequate for other purposes.

Even if one assumes that Rousseau was less well read than Candaux contends, there is abundant evidence that Rousseau had learned a great deal about Genevan politics from personal experience. As a precocious youth he was exposed to the highly politicized environment of the Saint-Gervais quarter and, more intimately, to the political discussions of his father and relatives and close friends of his father, many of whom were among the leaders of the bourgeoisie during this period.[52] During his many years in self-imposed exile he had kept abreast of Genevan political developments through personal contacts with Genevan oppositionists like Lenieps and through correspondence with a number of politically active Genevans, including the bourgeois leader De Luc. He had personally witnessed the bitter political and military struggles of the 1730s, which clearly made a lasting impression on him. And, perhaps most importantly, he had stayed several months in Geneva in 1754, much of which was spent in the company of De Luc and others who were no doubt eager to discuss Genevan politics with their fellow Genevan who had made a reputation for himself as a political philosopher of some note. Even if Rousseau had never read a word about Genevan history, the knowledge that he acquired from these personal experiences was more than adequate for purposes of using Geneva's institutions as a model for the *Contrat social*. At the very least he knew the general outlines of the Genevan constitution and the spirit in which the bourgeoisie interpreted that constitution. He did not need a minute knowledge of the various edicts that served as the Genevan constitution or a thorough understanding of the intricacies of the Genevan political system, for the *Contrat social* itself does not go into a detailed analysis of political institutions, at least not in Book III, where Rousseau presents his institutional ideal.

Spink and Derathé both invoke unreasonably high standards when they contend that Rousseau knew too little about the Genevan constitution to use it as a model for the *Contrat*. If Rousseau misunderstood and thus misrepresented some features of the Genevan constitution, he was only following in the footsteps of the leaders of the Genevan bourgeoisie who shared his misconceptions. Not until a series of confrontations in the 1760s precipitated by the condemnation of the *Contrat social* would the nature of the Genevan constitution become clearer to either Rousseau or the bourgeois leadership.

Rousseau's sincerity in claiming a Genevan inspiration is not in question. Not even Spink disputes it. Indeed, commenting on Rousseau's reaction to news of the condemnation of the *Contrat*, Spink remarks that it was "all the more painful for him because it was unexpected." Unable to believe that the very government on which he had modeled the political institutions of the *Contrat* could condemn his work, he attributed the condemnation to the machinations of Voltaire and the members of the patriciate who were under Voltaire's influence.[53] Guéhenno even suggests that the unexpected condemnation of the *Contrat* was a major factor in the growth of Rousseau's obsession with the notion that his enemies were plotting to undo him. How else account for the inexplicable hostility of the Genevan authorities?[54] Rousseau's statement in the *Lettres écrites de la montagne* thus cannot be dismissed as the contrived claim of one who, embittered by his sufferings of the previous two years, now sought to justify his righteous indignation by pretending that his sufferings had been inflicted by the very authorities he had treated so well in the *Contrat*. Only a little more than a month after Geneva's condemnation of the work on June 19, 1762, Rousseau expressed the same view to his Genevan friend Marcet de Mézières that he was to express some two years later in the *Lettres écrites de la montagne*. Perplexed by the action of the Genevan authorities, he declared, with his usual flair for the dramatic, that if he were the attorney general he would charge with treason any Genevan who condemned the principles of the *Contrat social* since the principles were the very ones on which Geneva's constitution was based.[55]

In addition to these considerations, one can raise the same objection to the thesis of Spink and Derathé that Spink raises against Vallette, namely, if Rousseau derived his ideal from the political theorists and jurisconsults, as Spink and Derathé claim, from what source did he derive the ideal by which he criticized the political theorists and the jurisconsults? Since Rousseau himself claims in effect that Geneva was this source, it is reasonable to take his claim seriously, even if one agrees with Spink and Derathé that Rousseau misrepresented Genevan institutions in the *Contrat social*. The evidence thus favors an explanation that lies somewhere between the interpretations of Vallette and others, who strongly emphasize Geneva's influence, on the one hand, and Spink and Derathé, who rightly object to some of the excessive claims made in behalf of Geneva's influence but who seriously underestimate that influence in the process of demonstrating other influences. Rousseau may have exaggerated Geneva's influence in the *Lettres écrites de la montagne* because this tended to heighten the irony of Geneva's condemnation of the *Contrat,* but the basic validity of his claim must be granted.

At the same time, neither the Genevan constitution nor the bourgeoisie's interpretation of that constitution fully accounts for the general principles enunciated in the *Contrat.* Rousseau transcended both Genevan institutions and bourgeois theory, and he did so largely with the help of the natural law theorists. The particular lessons that Rousseau learned from the natural law school, however, were determined in large measure by his point of departure, Geneva, which led him to approach these theorists critically and to derive different lessons from them than did most of his fellow Encyclopedists, whose starting point and inspiration were some political system other than Geneva. After all, it was *Genevan* political institutions that were being idealized, not those of England or France or any of the other political systems that served as working models for most of Rousseau's contemporaries. It was thus Rousseau's Genevan background that led him to react to his study of the natural law theorists, as well as the ancients and feudalism, in ways that differed markedly from those of most of the Encyclopedists, who also studied these same theorists, admired the ancients, and despised feudalism. Geneva was what made Rousseau's response to these other influences distinctive, and on no issue was he more distinctive than on that of representation.

The nature of the Genevan and natural law school influences on the *Contrat social* can be stated more precisely. While the Genevan inspiration of the *Contrat* is especially evident in Rousseau's discussion of political institutions in Book III, the influence of the natural law theorists is most evident in his discussion of basic political principles in Books I and II. If Spink and Derathé fail to perceive the Genevan inspiration of the *Contrat*, it is perhaps because they focus on the general principles of Books I and II and tend to treat Rousseau's institutional views in Book III as the logical consequence of his basic political concepts. Rousseau himself suggests that his institutional principles are simply the practical application of his basic concepts. As I have tried to demonstrate in the previous two chapters, however, the political institutions of Book III do not necessarily follow from the basic concepts set forth in the first two books and are even sharply discrepant with these concepts in important respects, often surprising the reader who has taken at face value Rousseau's seemingly radical claims of popular sovereignty and his equally sweeping claim that "will cannot be represented."

These discrepancies suggest that Rousseau derived his institutional ideal from some other source, and the most obvious alternative is Geneva. Quite apart from his unequivocal statement in the *Lettres écrites de la montagne* that he modeled the political institutions of the *Contrat* on Genevan institutions, the striking parallels between the institutions of the *Contrat* and Geneva on precisely those features that appear most discrepant with the basic concepts enunciated in Books I and II can hardly have been coincidental. Thus his opposition to a popular legislative initiative and his approval of a governmental monopoly of nominations are certainly not the kind of institutional proposals that his basic concepts would lead one to expect, but they were features of the Genevan constitution. Rousseau clearly envisioned the primary assembly described in Book III as the centerpiece of the institutions that would ensure popular sovereignty, and yet he deprived it of the very powers necessary to make that sovereignty a reality, assigning it an essentially passive and negative role in the life of the body politic. The Genevan Conseil Général was similarly sovereign in theory but essentially impotent in practice. Even Rousseau's major departure from the Genevan constitution, his demand for periodic meetings of the primary assembly, was clearly borrowed not from the natural law theorists but from the Genevan oppositionists.

There is therefore abundant evidence to support Rousseau's

contention that he used Genevan institutions as a model for the institutions of the *Contrat*. In fact, it is just as plausible to see the basic concepts of Books I and II as an elaborate attempt to justify the Genevan institutional ideal as it is to see his institutional ideal as the consequence of his basic concepts. If anything, the Genevan influence on the development not only of Rousseau's view of political institutions but also of his political thought in general appears to have been greater than the influence of the natural law theorists. True, the two influences are closely, perhaps inseparably, related. Undoubtedly he developed his views dialectically, criticizing the natural law theorists on the basis of his understanding of the Genevan constitution, but also criticizing Geneva on the basis of his new understanding of the natural law theorists, continuing this process until he reached the position he adopted in the *Contrat social*. The two influences complemented and reinforced one another in such a way that it is difficult to say which of the two was more important.

If Rousseau was able to transcend the boundaries that limited the vision of his contemporaries, it was perhaps because he experienced both influences with an intensity matched by few if any of the other Encyclopedists. While one can legitimately stress either of these influences for understanding different aspects of his political thought, however, it seems to me that Rousseau was right in stressing the Genevan inspiration of the *Contrat*. Geneva was both the starting point and the finishing point, the inspiration and the goal, of Rousseau's political thought at the time he wrote the *Contrat social*. He was genuinely concerned about what he perceived to be the political and moral deterioration of his native city, and he wrote the *Contrat* in part to restore Geneva to good health, or at least to prevent its further decline. This is not to say that the work does not have universal meaning, that it was written solely for Geneva or inspired solely by Geneva. Despite the universalism of its principles, however, it remains a work that was in very large measure Genevan in both purpose and inspiration.

Constitutional Writings

EIGHT

Genevan Expatriate:
Lettres Écrites de la Montagne

WHATEVER the nature and extent of Geneva's influence on the *Contrat Social*, there is no doubt about the Genevan inspiration of the *Lettres écrites de la montagne*. It is perhaps the most thoroughly and indisputably Genevan of all Rousseau's political writings,[1] both in the sense that the entire work is devoted to an analysis of Genevan controversies and also in the sense that Rousseau here identifies the Genevan origins of many of his political ideas. When he had first written about Geneva ten years earlier in the *Dédicace*, he had portrayed its constitution in glowing colors and had urged citizens to respect their deserving magistrates. In his *Lettre à d'Alembert* he continued to urge Genevans to respect their government, but he warned them not to abandon the social institutions that were the very foundation of Geneva's political system and indirectly reprimanded the ruling patriciate for aping the foppish manners of the French. This indirect criticism reappeared in the *Contrat social* in the form of a thinly disguised demand for restoration of periodic primary assemblies in Geneva, and in the *Lettres écrites de la mon-*

147

tagne his differences with the patriciate finally burst into the open.

In the first part (the first six) of the *Lettres*, Rousseau defends himself against the Petit Conseil's accusations that *Émile* and the *Contrat* were subversive of Geneva's religious and political institutions. In the second part, the last three letters, he joins in the ongoing political dispute between the patriciate and the bourgeoisie. This controversy had flared into open and sometimes violent conflict on several occasions in the first third of the century, but the *Règlement* of 1738 inaugurated nearly a quarter century of civil peace and economic prosperity that was not seriously disrupted until the condemnation of *Émile* and the *Contrat* on June 19, 1762. Even this dramatic attack on one of Geneva's most celebrated sons did not arouse any immediate protests by the bourgeoisie, many of whom were sufficiently persuaded by the Petit Conseil's charge of religious heresy not to wish to associate themselves with Rousseau even though they shared his political views. The leaders of the bourgeoisie lamented the condemnation in private but made no significant show of support for Rousseau.

The most outspoken opposition to the condemnation during the months that immediately followed came not from the bourgeoisie but from a member of the Conseil des Deux Cents, a colonel Charles Pictet, who was formally reprimanded in July 1762 for having called into question the motives of the Petit Conseil in condemning Rousseau's works. Pictet contended in a widely circulated open letter that his fellow patricians had condemned these writings only to please Voltaire and the French government, and he added that the Petit Conseil had acted without regard for Rousseau's procedural rights as a citizen of Geneva.[2] Whatever the truth about Pictet's charges concerning the influence of Voltaire and France,[3] there is general agreement that his accusation of procedural violations was at least partially justified.[4] Rousseau was accordingly profoundly disturbed that the bourgeoisie had not only deserted him in his hour of need but also had failed to uphold the rule of law by not making use of the legal channels available to them to protest the questionable means by which the Petit Conseil proceeded against a fellow citizen.

Toward the end of 1762 Rousseau wrote a lengthy defense of

his religious views to reassure the Genevan bourgeoisie that he remained a devout Christian even though he differed from the orthodoxies of both French Catholicism and Genevan Protestantism. This reaffirmation of religious faith, known as the *Lettre à Christophe de Beaumont* and published in March 1763,[5] apparently did convince many of the bourgeoisie and even some patricians that the authenticity of his religious beliefs was beyond doubt, but Rousseau was nonetheless disappointed that this reassurance did not lead to any formal protests on his behalf. It was not that he wished for demonstrations or mass rallies, much less for any kind of protest that might lead to violence. Quite the contrary, when he had first learned of the condemnation of *Émile* and the *Contrat*, he was very much concerned that the bourgeoisie would "turn Geneva upside down" in protest against such a blatantly unjust action by the government. To his amazement the bourgeoisie made no public protest of any kind at the time.[6] Again in March 1763 he was concerned about the possibility of violent demonstrations as a result of publication of the *Lettre à Christophe de Beaumont* but again discovered the bourgeoisie unwilling to act. What he had hoped for was a dignified, formal protest according to the procedures prescribed by law, but by the end of April 1763 he had abandoned all hope that the bourgeoisie would ever exercise its legal rights in this matter, and feared that even if it did, it would act rashly and bring to the fore the hostility that seethed beneath the seemingly calm surface of Genevan politics. Bitterly disillusioned with the republic he had loved and admired so deeply and so long, he publicly renounced his citizenship on May 12, 1763, in a moving letter to the first syndic.[7]

It was this dramatic step that finally provoked some forty members of the bourgeoisie to submit a *représentation* or formal grievance to the first syndic on June 18, 1763, accusing the Genevan authorities of proceeding illegally against Rousseau, Pictet, and a Genevan bookseller whose copies of *Émile* had been confiscated without compensation. The intransigence of the Petit Conseil, which flatly rejected all charges and contended that was the end of the matter, led to a second and more radical *représentation* on August 8 and a mass demonstration on August 20 in which the bourgeois leaders declared that the Conseil Général alone could determine whether or not the magistrates had misinterpreted and violated the laws of Geneva. The Petit Conseil responded to this claim by aserting its right, under Articles V and VI of the *Règlement* of 1738, to refuse to submit to the Conseil Général any *représentations* or other proposals that it considered unsound. It was this so-called *droit négatif* that earned the patriciate the title of *Négatifs* and the corresponding significance attached to the *droit de représentation* that earned the bourgeoisie the title of *Représentants*.

Although the *Représentants* remained almost painfully respectful of their magistrates throughout this summer of protests, the *Négatifs* became increasingly uneasy over their growing strength and determination. Then in late September and October the patriciate countered the claims of the *Représentants* with the serialized publication of a work written principally by the attorney general, Jean-Robert Tronchin, called *Lettres écrites de la campagne*. The effect on the *Représentants* was immediate and devastating. Even Rousseau praised the skill with which Tronchin, whom he described as "an enlightened and intelligent man, and well versed in the laws and government of the Republic," argued the case for the *Négatifs*.[8] The *Représentants*, crushed by this unexpected turn of events, appealed to Rousseau as the only person capable of refuting Tronchin and reestablishing the rule of law Rousseau held so dear. It was in these circumstances that Rousseau, provided by De Luc and other bourgeois leaders with a wealth of information on Geneva's history and constitution, undertook to write the *Lettres écrites de la montagne*.[9]

Unlike Rousseau's earlier political writings, which are for the most part highly speculative philosophical works, the *Lettres* is based on a thorough analysis of the best historical documentation available at the time to one who had no access to Genevan archives.[10] If Rousseau's knowledge of the Genevan political system was deficient at the time he wrote the *Contrat social*, he was exceedingly well informed when he wrote the *Lettres*. The bulk of the work, or at least the final version of it, appears to have been written between late October 1763, when he finally acceded to the pleas of De Luc and other bourgeois leaders to respond to Tronchin and requested the necessary documentation, and May 1764.[11] Rousseau arranged to have it published in mid-December 1764, just in time to have the maximum impact on the annual election of magistrates in January 1765.[12]

It is clear that Rousseau's views on several key issues changed significantly between the writing of the *Contrat social* and the writing of the *Lettres écrites de la montagne*. This is not surprising in view of all that had happened during the interim. Not only was he much better informed about Genevan political life when he wrote the *Lettres*, but he had experienced at first hand both the arbitrary exercise of political power by the patriciate and the impotence of the allegedly sovereign Conseil Général to do anything about it.

One issue on which Rousseau adopts a different point of view concerns the right of the people to exercise the political initiative. From the *Dédicace* through the *Contrat social* Rousseau consistently opposed the Athenian model of direct democracy because he believed it provided for an excessive popular role in initiating policy, including a popular legislative initiative. By contrast, he preferred an essentially passive role for the people. The primary assembly of all citizens must of course ratify proposals put forward by the government before these proposals could become legally binding, but he thought it quite proper that the political initiative remain in the hands of the government. In the *Lettres écrites de la montagne* he continues to oppose a popular legislative initiative, but he now argues strenuously for a type of nonlegislative popular initiative that he considers indispensable if the fundamental principle of popular sovereignty is to have any practical significance. He presents this argument in the course of interpreting the *droit de représentation*, the meaning of which had become the primary bone of contention between the patriciate and the bourgeoisie during the latter half of 1763.

Tronchin, speaking for the patriciate in the *Lettres écrites de la campagne,* claimed in the fifth and final letter that the *droit négatif,* that is, the right of the Petit Conseil to refuse to submit a *représentation* to the Conseil Général if there was no doubt in the minds of the members of the Petit Conseil about the interpretation of the law in question, was "the most reliable guarantee of our laws and our

Constitution."[13] If it were not for the *droit négatif*, Tronchin argued, there would be no means of preventing constant innovation in the laws, and Geneva would degenerate into anarchy. The bourgeoisie, on the other hand, contended in their *représentations* of 1763 that the *droit négatif* claimed by the Petit Conseil was illegitimate, that only the Conseil Général could determine whether or not a *représentation* was justified, that all *représentations* must therefore be submitted to the Conseil Général regardless of what the Petit Conseil thought of them. In current terms, the Petit Conseil considered the *droit de représentation* as nothing more than a right of petition, while the bourgeoisie envisioned it as a true initiative whereby citizens could demand a referendum on the meaning of an existing law and the manner in which the government was enforcing that law.[14] This was not a demand for a popular legislative initiative, as the bourgeoisie was quick to point out, for they too feared that frequent changes would undermine respect for the laws and threaten the very foundations of the political order.

Rousseau fully endorses the bourgeoisie's interpretation of the *droit de représentation* in the *Lettres écrites de la montagne* and even turns Tronchin's arguments about innovation against him by demonstrating that the *droit négatif* as conceived by the patriciate makes possible a more insidious form of innovation that is all the more dangerous because it is obscured from public view. The *droit négatif* is only a sophism by which the Petit Conseil attempts to conceal the fact that it alone is absolute master of the state; Tronchin and the patriciate stand reality on its head only to sow confusion among the bourgeoisie. The true innovator is thus the Petit Conseil; its so-called *droit négatif* is in reality very much a *droit positif*, whereas the *droit de représentation* as conceived by the bourgeoisie is the most effective means of preventing the executive from acting contrary to the laws.[15] Rousseau supports this contention with an article-by-article analysis of the *Règlement de l'illustre Médiation* of 1738. Although he expresses some reservations about the *Règlement*, he finds it a veritable godsend to Geneva and opposes even the slightest revision for fear that this would upset the delicate equilibrium established by the mediators.

If the *Règlement* is less than perfect, this is not for lack of good will on the part of the mediators but only because they were not altogether familiar with republican institutions.[16] He notes that Article I established five separate orders—the four syndics, the Petit Conseil, the Conseil des Soixante, the Conseil des Deux Cents, and the Conseil Général—and confirmed each of them in their rights[17] but contends that the article failed to specify the sovereign, the "Puissance constitutive" or "Puissance suprême," which logically must exist in every state. Not surprisingly, he remedies this oversight by locating sovereignty in the Conseil Général, the only body in which all of the separate orders participate. "The Conseil Général is not an order in the state, it is the state itself."[18] He acknowledges that Article III explicitly limited the powers of the Conseil Général[19] but argues that these limitations are inconsistent with the very notion of the sovereignty of the Conseil Général implied in Article I.[20] He then explains that the legislative power, which the *Règlement* listed as only one of the powers of the Conseil Général, in fact encompasses all of the powers of sovereignty.

> The legislative power consists of two things inseparably linked: to make the laws and to maintain them; that is to say, to supervise the executive power. There is no state in the world in which the sovereign does not have this power of supervision. Without it there is no relation, no subordination between the two powers, the one would not depend on the other; execution would have no necessary relation to the laws; "law" would be a mere word, and this word would signify nothing. The Conseil Général has always had this right to protect its own work, it has always exercised it. Nevertheless this article does not mention it, and if it were not supplied by another article, by this silence alone your state would be undone.[21]

The article that remedied this defect, Article VII, was the one that confirmed the citizens' *droit de représentation*. But before Rousseau examines this article in detail, he has to show that Articles V and VI did not in fact establish the *droit négatif* claimed by the Petit Conseil. Article V stipulated that only the syndics and members of the Petit and Grand Conseils could formally present proposals for consideration by the Conseil Général. Article VI further provided that no proposal could be considered by the Grand Conseil until it had been considered and approved by the Petit Conseil and that no proposal could be considered by the Conseil Général until it had first been considered and approved by the Grand Conseil.[22] Rousseau argues that the effect of these two articles appears to be to prevent a sovereign body, the Conseil Général, from acting on its own initiative, which is, to say the least, a peculiar kind of limitation to impose on a sovereign. It is all the more peculiar in that the interests of the two subordinate bodies, the Petit and Grand Conseils, are virtually identical. Taken literally, these two articles provide a justification for tyranny, not a republic. Although accurate as a description of political reality in Geneva, it cannot have been the intention of the mediators to legitimate tyranny.[23]

Rousseau finds confirmation for his belief that the mediators did not intend to grant such arbitrary power to the government in two separate articles. One of these, Article XLIV, provided that the Conseil Général "légitimement assemblé" could make such changes in the articles as it saw fit, which Rousseau sees as a clear indication that the mediators did not seek to limit the sovereignty of the Conseil Général.[24] What Rousseau omits to say, however, and what Article XLIV makes explicit, is that the Conseil Général can be legitimately assembled only by the Petit and Grand Conseils.[25] As Spink notes, Rousseau in this case reads into the *Règlement*, whether consciously or not, the principles of the *Contrat social* that he needs to find there in order to have legal support for his views.[26]

The legal basis for his argument against the patriciate would indeed be very weak if he rested it solely or even primarily on Article XLIV, which if anything contradicted rather than confirmed the point he seeks o make. He therefore focuses his attention instead on Article VII, which set forth the *droit de représentation:* "The citizens and bourgeois, in conformity with the Edict of 26 May 1707, will have the right to make such *représentations* that they judge suitable to the good of the state to Messieurs the Syndics or to the Procureur Général, under the express prohibition against committing any sort of violence, on pain of punishment according to the nature of the case."[27] It was undoubtedly this article that he had in mind when he referred earlier to the one essential article in the *Règlement* that compensated for the shortcomings of all the others and lent substance to the pretension of the Conseil Général to sovereignty. He now claims that this article alone makes the government of Geneva "the best that ever existed." Curiously enough, one of his reasons for describing Geneva's constitution in these superlative terms was that Article VII established a "perfect equilibrium" among all the parties.[28]

Candaux notes the similarity of this view to Burlamaqui's theory of a balance of powers but says this comparison is misleading since Rousseau was here speaking only about the constituent parts of government, not sovereignty.[29] Although it is possible that he was using the term *government* in the narrower sense of administration, the context suggests that he meant it in the broader sense of constitution or political system. Even though he repeatedly insists on the importance of distinguishing between government and sovereignty, and even reaffirms this several times in the *Lettres écrites de la montagne*, he did not consistently adhere to his distinction. It is more likely, then, that his use of the phrase "perfect equilibrium" is simply another indication of his willingness to accept an equilibrium between the government and the sovereign despite his insistence on the subordination of the former to the latter.

He begins his analysis of Article VII by citing Pufendorf's definition of a right as "a moral quality by which something is owed to us." A right, then, must be meaningful, not just a useless exercise or the kind of liberty granted to everyone indiscriminately, as for example the "right" to complain. Since Article VII is vague on the specific meaning of the *droit de représentation,* one must derive this meaning from an analysis of the article in the context of the *Règlement* as a whole, bearing in mind the probable intentions of the mediators. The Edict of 1707 that first established the *droit de représentation* makes it clear that a *représentation* is simply a declaration of the opinion of one of more citizens on a matter lying within their competence. But when those who make a *représentation* represent a large body of public opinion, action by the Conseil Général may be not only advisable but necessary.

Représentations may be of two kinds: (1) those that seek to bring about some change in the laws and (2) those that address themselves to an alleged transgression of the laws. Since changes in the laws tend to disrupt the body politic, especially in small republics, every obstacle should be placed in the path of those who seek to change the laws; hence it is quite proper that the Petit Conseil has the power to reject on its own authority *représentations* of the first type. Citizens should be content to let their magistrates decide whether or not such a change is warranted. Articles V and VI justly prohibit consideration by the Conseil Général of any legislative proposal that has not been previously approved by the Petit and Grand Conseils. This is the legitimate *droit négatif* of the two patrician councils.[30]

If Rousseau's opposition to a popular legislative initiative in the *Contrat social* was not altogether unambiguous, his opposition in *Lettres écrites de la montagne* is emphatic and unequivocal. Nor is his opposition simply a matter of political expediency, for he goes out of his way to oppose a popular legislative initiative as a matter of principle. The only serious question is not whether he opposes it but why.[31] Vaughan finds Rousseau's opposition contrary to the spirit if not the letter of the *Contrat social* because he considers the right of legislation meaningless unless accompanied by the right to initiate legislation. He suggests several possible explanations for Rousseau's opposition: a desire to narrow the debate with the patriciate as much as possible; an instinctive dread of hasty legislation and its potentially revolutionary consequences; and a deepseated caution born out of respect for tradition, which in turn reflected the growing influence of Montesquieu.[32]

Derathé is less certain than Vaughan that Rousseau's arguments in the *Lettres* run counter to either the spirit or the letter of the *Contrat*, but he agrees with Vaughan that lack of the initiative reduces the legislative power to impotence, and he further agrees that Rousseau's fear of innovation was largely responsible for his opposition.[33] The analysis of the *Contrat* in the preceding chapter supports Derathé's qualification of Vaughan's view. However incongruous it may be to assert that the legislative power is the linchpin of popular sovereignty and yet deny the people a legislative initiative, this is one issue on which Rousseau was painstakingly consistent in all his political writings. If the incongruity of his position is more striking in the *Lettres écrites de la montagne* than in other writings, it is because, in addition to spelling out his opposition in no uncertain terms, he adheres doggedly to this position despite all that had occurred since publication of the *Contrat social*. How could he fail to see the weakness of his position in the wake of his traumatic experiences during the preceding two and a half years? The answer appears to be that Rousseau was simply reflecting the position taken by the majority of the Genevan bourgeoisie, whose legalism and profound respect for constituted authority, even in the face of flagrant abuses of the law, were qualities Rousseau shared.[34]

Having rejected a popular legislative initiative, however, Rousseau insists all the more forcefully that the second type of *représentation*, those having to do with the interpretation and enforcement of existing laws rather than with changes in the laws, can be judged only by the Conseil Général, that the *droit négatif* does not apply in this case. The requirement of Article VI that all proposals be approved by the Petit Conseil before being submitted to the Conseil Général can only mean, with reference to this second type of *représentation*, that the Petit Conseil can determine the *form* in which to submit them but does not have the right to disallow them altogether.[35] In making this rather fine distinction, Rousseau was again following in the steps of the bourgeoisie, who had made the same distinction in their *représentations* of 1763. It may have been a distinction without a difference, for it still left the way open for the Petit Conseil, never lacking in imagination when it came to legalistic maneuvering, to obstruct the efforts of the *Représentants*. The exiled Lenieps pointed out the weakness of this position in October 1763. The requirement for approval of all proposals by the Petit Conseil, not just consideration, meant that Article VI negated all the rights of the Conseil Général. Rousseau rejected the advice of Lenieps in favor of the more moderate, although weaker, position of the bourgeoisie.[36]

Whatever the merits of this distinction between form and content, Rousseau was on much firmer ground in claiming that *représentations* alleging government misconduct could not be judged by the government, since this would be an obvious violation of the principle that one cannot be judge in his own cause. All questions concerning the interpretation of a law or the manner in which it was applied must therefore be submitted to the soveriegn for a determination. The *droit de représentation* so conceived "is intimately linked to your constitution: it is the only possible means of uniting liberty and subordination, and of keeping the magistrate dependent on the laws without altering his authority over the people." Because Geneva's constitution provides for such a *droit de représentation*, the general will reigns supreme, the people is sovereign.[37]

It is remarkable that Rousseau was thus able to persuade himself, even after an intensive study of the laws and institutions of Geneva, that the Genevan constitution embodied the fundamental principles of the *Contrat social*. That he was able to do so, however, is all the more reason to take seriously his claim in *Lettre* VI that Genevan institutions served as the model for the *Contrat*. If he could still extract the principles of the *Contrat* from a careful analysis of the *Règlement*, if after all he had suffered at the hands of the patriciate he was still unable to see the Genevan constitution for what it was, how much easier must it have been to discern those principles in the Genevan constitution prior to his condemnation. As Spink observes, what begins as a careful analysis of the *Règlement* intended to show that it was the basis of Geneva's liberties ends up as a critique of the *Règlement* on the basis of the principles of the *Contrat social*. Rousseau simply failed to understand that the *Règlement* was based on the concept of a separation and balance of powers and instead blamed its shortcomings on the inability of the mediators to understand republican institutions.[38] And because he saw the *Règlement* as fundamentally consistent with the principles of the *Contrat social*, he saw the *droit de représentation*, even in the limited sense of a device for bringing charges of maladministration against the government, as an effective means of ensuring popular sovereignty.

As the conflicts between the bourgeoisie and patriciate were to prove in the following decade, the most that the bourgeoisie could achieve by pursuing its constitutional rights to their logical conclusion was stalemate. A united bourgeoisie could prevent the patriciate from acting, it could bring the political process to an impasse, but it lacked the constitutional authority to establish its own sovereignty despite its overwhelming numerical superiority—and despite Rousseau's claims. The truth is that the *droit de repré-sentation* was pathetically inadequate for the purposes for which Rousseau wanted to use it. By legitimating the Petit Conseil's *droit négatif* with regard to legislative proposals, by condemning what he saw as the radical demand for a popular legislative initiative, Rousseau deprived the bourgeoisie of an effective constitutional basis for challenging the continued rule of the patriciate, whether it abused its power or not.

Just as Rousseau slightly modified his position on a popular political initiative in the *Lettres écrites de la montagne* but remained firm in his opposition to a popular legislative initiative, he similarly modified his position on the right of nomination. In contrast to the *Contrat*, where he approved what amounted to a governmental monopoly of nominations, in the *Lettres* he attacks this practice, even ridicules it, but never explicitly rejects it or proposes an alternative method of nomination. The only specific revision he suggests, and even this is only by implication, is that the government select nominees from among the people, namely the bourgeoisie, as well as from the patriciate. Article II of the *Règlement* provided that the four syndics must be chosen from members of the Petit Conseil and that members of the Petit Conseil must in turn be chosen from members of the Conseil des Deux Cents.[39] Rousseau sharply criticizes this article, pointing out that there was no significant difference between the authority of a syndic and that of a member of the Petit Conseil and that consequently those eligible for the office of syndic had no incentive to distinguish themselves in that office by serving the common interest. Moreover, since all members of the Petit Conseil shared the same interests and were motivated by the same *esprit de corps*, the people were presented with no real choice of candidates for this, the highest office in the republic. Election under these circumstances in not only meaningless but actually harmful since it gives the illusion of liberty without the substance. Such an election is only a ritual by which the Petit Conseil legitimates its domination of the republic.[40]

Rousseau contends that this was not always the case, that there was a time when election was a process by which the people freely chose the wisest and best among them to serve as syndics and councilors. Under the episcopate the people either nominated and elected members of the Petit Conseil directly or else left this choice to syndics, who in turn had been nominated and elected directly by the people. As long as the people had a free choice in the selection of members of the Petit Conseil, it was fitting that syndics be chosen from that body since it included only those most highly esteemed by their fellow citizens. Another change for the worse was in the councilors' terms of office. Originally elected or reelected annually, members of the Petit Conseil were now chosen for life, a practice that began in 1487 with one councilor and eventually encompassed all members of the Petit Conseil.[41]

In his *Histoire de Genève*, which Rousseau probably wrote in 1764 but which was not published until 1861, he elaborates on the nature of the magistracy under the episcopate. One consequence of the free election of syndics by the people was that the people willingly granted extensive power to their leaders, a practice that is characteristic of all truly free and democratic societies. The people could do this because they retained the right to depose syndics who abused their power, although this was rare and inevitably accompanied by violence.[42] The central thesis of the *Histoire de Genève* is that the institutions that assured the sovereignty and civil liberties of the people originated during the episcopate, weakened toward the end of the episcopate as government concentrated more and more power in its hands, and were rendered impotent following the establishment of the republic in the sixteenth century. Not only did the republic confirm the tendency toward a governmental monopoly of political power, but its creation placed Geneva at the mercy of a foreign power, France, and thereby planted the seeds of its own destruction at its very inception.

Although the manuscript breaks off incomplete at the point that Rousseau begins to discuss the institutions of the republic, it is reasonably clear that he considered popular sovereignty more real and more secure under the episcopate than under the republic, and he explicitly says that Genevans enjoyed greater freedom under the episcopate.[43] In the early days of the republic there was a law that required that two syndics be chosen from residents of the *ville du bas* and two from the *ville du haut* and thus ensured representation of the two major classes in Geneva. Unfortunately the Conseil Général agreed in 1603 to abolish this requirement and thus effectively eliminated representation of the *ville du bas* among the syndics.[44]

Despite this trenchant criticism of the Genevan system of electing magistrates, Rousseau never urges that the right of nomination be restored to the people. At one point he does suggest, very elliptically, that the Conseil Général assert itself by rejecting all candidates proposed by the Petit Conseil.[45] It was precisely this tactic that the bourgeoisie adopted in the syndical elections of January 1766 and brought the government to the impasse that led to the first foreign intervention since the mediation of 1738.[46] His resurrection of the long-buried provision of the Edict of 1543, which stipulated that two syndics be chosen from the *ville du bas*, can be interpreted as an implicit recommendation for restoration of this practice. But apart from these limited reforms, if indeed it was Rousseau's intention to present them as reform proposals, there is little indication that he sought a broader popuar initiative in the choice of magistrates.

It is of course possible to interpret his praise of the system of popular nomination and election of syndics under the episcopate as an implicit call for restoration of this radically democratic procedure, and at the least it is evidence that he did not reject popular nomination of candidates as a matter of principle in the way that he rejected a popular legislative initiative. But the tone of both the *Lettres écrites de la montagne* and the *Histoire de Genève* strongly suggests that he regarded this solely as a thing of the past. To make such a radical demand in 1764 would be tantamount to fomenting revolution. While radicals like Micheli du Crest might not hesitate to make such a demand, Rousseau was much too fearful of the consequences of revolution to make this demand himself. So deeply ingrained was this fear of violence that he even counseled the *Représentants* against persisting in their use of the *droit de représentation* lest they provoke an upheaval in Geneva. Better to suffer injustice in peace than to risk violence by asserting one's rights too vociferously. Granted that the opening of the first *Lettre*, in which he feigned complete disapproval of the *Représentants* for invoking the *droit de représentation* in his behalf, cannot be taken at face value—

privately be congratulated them on their initial *représentation* and also borrowed heavily from their argumentation in the later *représentations,* which he more or less formally condemned[47]—granted too that his arguments as well as his flamboyant criticism of patrician rule helped fuel a succession of upheavals for many years afterwards, his anxiety over provoking civil conflict was genuine. Nor was it just a matter of avoiding violence, for he consistenly drew less radical conclusions from the basic premises of his political philosophy than others derived with equal justification.

A third issue on which Rousseau's views in the *Lettres écrites de la montagne* differ from those of his earlier political writings is that of the nature and role of the popular assembly, which in Geneva meant the Conseil Général. For one thing, he was now far more keenly aware of the powerlessness of the Conseil Général than he was when he wrote the *Dédicace* or the *Contrat social,* although a direct comparison with the latter work is difficult since he had little to say there specifically about the Conseil Général. In the *Dédicace* he praised Geneva as a state in which the people were sovereign and everyone was subject to the law,[48] and in the *Contrat* he spoke with pride of having been born the citizen of a free state and a member of its sovereign body.[49]

By contrast, he now distinguishes between the *legitimate* state of Geneva, which he professes to see as the freest in the world, and the *actual* state, which he condemns as the most unfree. In theory the Conseil Général is sovereign, the cornerstone of the people's liberties; in reality, "The body charged with the execution of your laws is their interpreter and supreme arbiter; it makes them speak as it pleases; it can make them keep silent; it can even violate them without your being able to put them back in order; it is above the laws."[50] The theoretical sovereignty of the Conseil Général is paralyzed because it cannot act without the permission of the Petit Conseil. In short, "if you are Sovereign Lords in the assembly"—a reference to the title by which the Conseil Général was traditionally addressed: *Magnifiques, très honorés et souverains Seigneurs*—"you are nothing outside of it. Four hours a year subordinate sovereigns, you are subjects the rest of your lives and completely at the mercy and discretion of others."[51]

As a result of this more clear-sighted view of the reality of Genevan politics, Rousseau now sees a significantly different role for the popular assembly. According to the *Contrat social,* the primary function of the popular assembly was legislation, for sovereignty consists essentially in the exercise of legislative power. The actual role of the popular assembly in legislation may have been mainly passive—to prevent the passage of bad laws rather than to initiate good new laws—but still it is the role on which he focused in the *Contrat.* While he insisted that periodic assemblies review the work of the executive, most of what he said about the popular assembly related to its legislative role. In the *Lettres écrites de la montagne* this emphasis is reversed. The primary function of the popular assembly is no longer legislation but supervision of the executive. That he now defines the legislative power to include supervision as well as enactment of the laws does not alter the fact that he focuses on a new role for the primary assembly. If anything, the fact that he felt it necessary to redefine the legislative power in this way underlines the shift of emphasis. He now realizes, as apparently neither he nor the majority of the bourgeoisie did before, that the Conseil Général must have some means of initiating action or else all claims of popular sovereignty are mere verbiage. What kind of sovereign body is it that cannot even assemble, much less act, on its own initiative? [52]

His principled opposition to a popular legislative initiative prevents him from resolving this problem by what might appear to be the most obvious method, and so he focuses instead almost exclusively on transforming the *droit de représentation* into an effective means of supervising the work of the executive. When he renews the demand for periodic assemblies in the *Lettres,* therefore, he declares their sole purpose to be that of considering *représentations* alleging maladministration, not legislation. Convinced that his demand for periodic *legislative* assemblies in the *Contrat social* was too radical for Geneva in its present circumstances, he now moderates his demand by urging that periodic assemblies be held for the more limited purpose of hearing grievances brought during the intervals between assemblies. He even ventures the opinion that this was the way Conseils Généraux functioned in the sixteenth century and that their decline was due to the infrequency of grievances at that time. The patriciate's argument that periodic assemblies would lead to constant innovation, an argument that would be persuasive to Rousseau and his bourgeois friends if valid, was thus unfounded. The patriciate's real purpose in doing away with the periodic assemblies agreed to in 1707 was its fear of being forced to obey the law.[53]

Rousseau realized that the patriciate would not tolerate periodic assemblies in 1764 any more than it had tolerated them half a century earlier, even for this more limited purpose. He therefore proposed as an alternative periodic assemblies by companies of the militia to be held at different times and places to avoid even the appearance of an attempt by the bourgeoisie to intimidate the government. He was only slightly more optimistic about the prospects for this proposal. Article XXV of the *Règlement* prohibited "attroupemens par Compagnie" because these companies had served as the political as well as military organization of the bourgeoisie during the upheavals of 1734–1737.[54] Still he thought it worthwhile to point out the essentially peaceful and constructive purposes of these assemblies.

By allowing the bourgeoisie to deliberate among themselves in smaller groups and making available a means by which deputies could present *représentations* on behalf of larger numbers of citizens, the government could ensure a more orderly method of exercising the *droit de représentation* than the present chaotic system of having each citizen speak for himself. Oddly enough, Rousseau here uses one of the arguments put forward by advocates of representative government, namely, that it offers a more rational method of conveying popular opinion on issues of general concern. He even suggests that these deputies, presumably one for each of the sixteen companies, be empowered to speak for a plurality of voters in their respective companies.[55] While he undoubtedly intended these deputies to be no more than the *mandataires* of those they represented, his willingness to consider this type of representative machinery marks a major departure from his ridicule of representative institutions in the *Contrat social*.

That this changed attitude toward representation was no fluke, that it was more than just a sop thrown out to make his proposal of assemblies by company more palatable to the patriciate, is clear from his lengthy comparison of the English Parliament and the Genevan Conseil Général. Rousseau was following English politics very closely at the time. He was especially intrigued by the affair of John Wilkes, which he cited as evidence that the liberties of Englishmen were far more secure than those of Genevans. Rousseau relates how Wilkes published a violent satire attacking not only ministers of the government but the king himself, yet neither he nor his publishers were punished, because there was no law specifically authorizing their arrest.[56]

His view of the Wilkes affair reflects a significantly different view of the English political system than that typical of works written both before and after the *Lettres écrites de la montagne*. In *Contrat social* III, 15, he had ridiculed the celebrated liberties of Englishmen, declaring that the English were free only during the election of members of Parliament.[57] Nor did his visit to England in 1766 change this bleak opinion. In the *Confessions*, which he began writing during his stay in England, he bluntly declares "I have never liked England nor the English."[58] Still later, in his *Considérations sur le gouvernement de Pologne*, he would deride the English for their childish attempt to legislate for every conceivable eventuality and thus create an impossibly complex system of laws that unnecessarily tied the hands of magistrates.[59]

His much more positive view of the English and their political institutions in the *Lettres écrites de la montagne* was no doubt partly due to the polemical nature of the work; that is, he praised England as a way of getting back at those who had unjustly condemned and rejected the tribute he had offered in good faith to his homeland. If, however, he was motivated by such lowly considerations to reexamine English institutions, much of his praise appears genuine, the result of a new insight into the virtues of these institutions. This is particularly true of his praise of the English Parliament vis-à-vis the Genevan Conseil Général.*

* While Rousseau was not alone among the philosophes in his generally unfavorable view of English politics, he seems to have been the only one who attacked the principle of representation on which Parliament, the centerpiece of English political institutions, was based. One of the most widely publicized critiques of English politics in the mid-eighteenth century was John Brown's *An Estimate of the Manners and*

What Parliament and the Conseil Général have in common is
that each is the legitimate sovereign in its own country; the fun-

Principles of the Times, first published in 1757 and immediately translated into
French. Brown's bugaboo was corruption, which he believed permeated English
social and political life, including Parliament. See Harold J. Laski, *Political Thought in
England: Locke to Bentham* (London: Oxford University Press, 1961), pp. 113–115. Although Brown's sweeping criticisms are often exaggerated and somewhat theatrical,
his basic charge of Parliamentary corruption is substantiated by recent histories that
describe the techniques by which a small oligarchy maintained control of Parliament.
See the works of Christopher Hill (*Reformation to Industrial Revolution*) and J. H.
Plumb (*England in the Eighteenth Century*), previously cited.

French opinion of the English constitution during the eighteenth century has been
examined in depth by Joseph Dedieu, whose *Montesquieu et la tradition politique
anglaise en France* (Paris: Librairie Victor Lecoffre, 1909) focuses on Montesquieu's
role in introducing English political thought to his fellow countrymen, and Gabriel
Bonno, whose *La constitution britannique devant l'opinion française de Montesquieu à
Bonaparte* (Paris: Librairie Ancienne Honoré Champion, 1931) picks up the story
where Dedieu leaves off and examines French opinion of the English constitution
during the latter half of the century. Both agree that "l'anglomanie," or French enthusiasm for British ideas and institutions, was at its peak in France around midcen-
tury but that a strong reaction set in within a decade—Dedieu suggests a date of
1760; Bonno insists on 1756, which marked the outset of the Seven Years' War—and
English political institutions came in for heavy criticism even among many of their
greatest admirers. Bonno further contends, in disagreement with Dedieu, that a second period of Anglomania began with the conclusion of the war in 1763 and lasted
until the outbreak of the American Revolution. For Dedieu's views, see pp. 1–7 and
356–385; for Bonno's criticism and revision of Dedieu's thesis, see especially
pp. 19–21, 37–43, 131–150, and 273.

Bonno's thesis is particularly intriguing because the ups and downs of French
opinion of the British constitution as he describes them correspond quite closely to
Rousseau's own fluctuating opinion of British institutions. Thus *Économie politique*,
written during the first period of Anglomania, reflects a strong Lockean influence
and appears to accept representative government; the *Contrat social*, written when
Anglophobia was at its peak, is decidedly hostile to the principle of representative
government and to Parliament in particular; the *Lettres écrites de la montagne* and the
constitutional proposals for Corsica and Poland, all three written during the second
period of Anglomania, also take a more favorable view of representative government, even if they remain critical of particular features of Parliament. While these
correlations do not prove that Rousseau's ideas changed as public opinion changed,
they may help to account for his distinctly more favorable view of Parliament in the
Lettres écrites de la montagne.

For a view that stresses Rousseau's affinities with a group of Anglophobes that in-
cluded Diderot, d'Holbach, and Mably, and the differences between this group and
Anglophiles like Voltaire, see Frances Acomb, *Anglophobia in France, 1763–1789: an
Essay in the History of Constitutionalism and Nationalism* (Durham: Duke University
Press, 1950), especially Chapter 3, "French Criticism of English Institutions,
1763–1778: the Liberals," pp. 30–50.

damental difference between them is that Parliament is a representative body; that is, it exercises sovereignty only by deputation, while the Conseil Général is sovereign in its own right: "it is the living and fundamental law which gives life and force to all the rest, and which knows no other rights but its own."[60] The two sovereign bodies are also comparable in size. Rousseau insists on this point because he wants to show that the Conseil Général is not too large a body to effectively supervise the work of the executive, as some patrician spokesmen contended. The membership of the Conseil Général may be as much as 1,400 to 1,500, but it is rare that more than 800 or 900 attend a given meeting. He adds that there were no more than 700 present at the meeting in 1754 in which he personally participated. Nor has the size of the Conseil Général significantly increased over the centuries, for even its earliest meetings, for example, the one held in 1420, consisted of at least 500 to 600 members.[61] Parliament, which includes more than 700 members, is thus practically the same size as the Conseil Général, and yet no one questions the efficiency and effectiveness of Parliament. That this great assemblage of men is able to conduct its business so expeditiously is all the more remarkable when one considers that it must cope with the complex legislation and other matters that go hand in hand with governing a great nation, that it is filled with a multiplicity of competing interests and intriguing factions, and that it grants each member the right to speak. How much easier it should be for the Conseil Général to cope with the business of a much smaller and more homogeneous state.[62]

Not only is Parliament more efficient than the Conseil Général, it also maintains a more effective control over the chief executive. In the *Lettres écrites de la campagne* Tronchin invoked the example of the English constitution to show that the *droit négatif* of the Petit Conseil was just as essential as the king's power to restrain Parliament. Rousseau refutes Tronchin's claim in *Lettre* IX by showing, through a systematic comparison of the English and Genevan constitutions, that the king's powers are in reality far more limited than those of the Petit Conseil. True, the English king is invested with great power, as it is fitting that an executive should be, but such is the nature of the English political system that he can use this power only to uphold the laws, not to break them. The king is as strictly bound to obey the laws as is the lowliest citizen, and Parliament makes the laws.[63] The *"droit négatif"* of the king consists in his power to convoke and dissolve Parliament and to veto legislation passed by Parliament, but both these powers are tempered by countervailing powers of Parliament. In the first place, Parliament is convened periodically—now every seven years, a regrettable change from the earlier requirement that it convene every three years—with or without the king's permission. Secondly, as a practical matter the king is obliged to convoke Parliament at least once a year since funds to operate the government are voted only one year at a time. Rousseau probably owed this insight to his friend Lenieps, who had pointed out to him in October 1763 that annual meetings of Parliament were effectively guaranteed by this requirement.[64] Finally, each house of Parliament has full authority over itself once assembled to propose, debate, and revise the laws as well as to supervise the work of the king and his ministers. In short, the English constitution gives the king a great deal of power to do good but no power to do evil.[65]

By contrast, the *droit négatif* claimed and exercised by the Petit Conseil gives it virtually absolute power. Since there is no provision in the Genevan constitution for periodic assemblies, the Conseil Général cannot assemble except when summoned by the Petit Conseil, and even when it does assemble it can deal only with those matters brought before it by the Petit Conseil. The requirement for Conseil Général approval of new taxes is not a serious limitation on the Petit Conseil, because taxes already in existence are sufficient for the ordinary needs of government. Nor does the Conseil Général have any effective means of supervising the work of the Petit Conseil or compelling it to obey the laws. On the contrary, as his own experience shows, the Petit Conseil can violate the laws with impunity, even to the point of depriving a fellow citizen of his rights when he has violated no laws.[66]

The contrast between the power of Parliament and that of the Conseil Général could hardly be more sharply drawn. Rousseau clearly recognizes that the best known contemporary example of a representative institution is superior in crucial respects to the popular assembly on which he modeled the institutions of the *Contrat social*. Parliament is a more efficient legislative body than the Conseil Général, it maintains a much more effective control over the executive, and it guarantees the civil liberties of those it represents far more effectively than members of the Conseil Général are able to protect their own liberties.

And yet despite this recognition that a representative legislative body may be more effective than a popular assembly in achieving some of the most basic goals of the *Contrat social*, Rousseau is unwilling to abandon his opposition to the principle of representation. Nor, despite his awareness that the legislative initiative is a key element in Parliament's power vis-à-vis the executive, is he willing to demand the same initiative for the Conseil Général. The whole purpose of the contrast is not to demonstrate the superiority of representative institutions but rather to underscore the weakness of the Conseil Général and deflate any remaining illusions about its actual role in Genevan political life.

If his hostility toward representation in the *Contrat social* was in part the result of his ignorance of representative institutions, this explanation cannot account for his position in the *Lettres écrites de la montagne*. Despite his new-found understanding, he continues to extol the superiority, in principle, of the primary assembly. He even accepts, although grudgingly, many of the crippling limitations that had been imposed on the Conseil Général over the centuries, preferring to stake everything on the debatable *droit de représentation* rather than risk violence by insisting on more radical reforms. In all these respects he was at one with the majority of the bourgeoisie, but in the years ahead even the bourgeoisie would, out of sheer necessity, move beyond the demands made by Rousseau, now withdrawn from the struggle. If Rousseau continued to be their spokesman, or to be treated as their spokesman, it was as much *malgré lui* as it was the fundamental radicalism of his political philosophy.

The most dramatic and clearcut difference between the *Lettres écrites de la montagne* and all Rousseau's previous writings on Geneva is his vehement, often scathing denunciation of the patriciate. Rousseau's change of heart did not come about all at once. In both

La Nouvelle Héloïse and the *Lettre à d'Alembert* he criticized the Genevan aristocracy for succumbing to the allures of French civilization, and parts of the *Contrat social*, most notably Book III, Chapter 18, appear to be thinly disguised attacks on the patriciate's attempt to monopolize political power.

But if he had long ago disabused himself of the kind of eulogy of the magistracy that appeared in the *Dédicace*, he was still far from being completely disillusioned with the Genevan ruling class at the time that *Émile* and the *Contrat* were condemned. Even in the immediate aftermath of this condemnation he continued to profess his everlasting respect for Geneva's magistrates, who, he was convinced, would soon realize their tragic error and set matters straight. But as the months passed and it became unmistakably clear that he could expect no justice from the Genevan authorities and no significant public support from the intimidated bourgeoisie, his attitude toward the patriciate became progressively embittered. In both his *Histoire de Genève* and in the *Lettres écrites de la montagne* he details the story of how Geneva's governing class, originally the servant of the people, gradually degenerated into a tightly knit aristocracy and ultimately into an oligarchy that ruled over the people as a master over subjects.[67] *Lettre* VII, the whole of which is a sustained attack on the patriciate, climaxes in a ringing denunciation of the Petit Conseil, whose twenty-five members he now likens to the thirty tyrants at Athens,[68] and the final *Lettre* concludes with a call to the bourgeoisie to unite against these tyrants. One senses that only his horror of violence prevents him from calling for their overthrow. As it is, he refrains from counseling the bourgeoisie on a specific course of action beyond working together and emphatically warns against listening to the advice of the radicals among them. Unity should be achieved rather by heeding those citizens whose "honest mediocrity secures them against the seductions of ambition and poverty" alike. He even holds out a faint ray of hope that the patriciate may yet see the light and reform itself. He believes that the present membership of the Petit Conseil is not entirely devoid of virtue, and he seems to think that it is by appealing to this remnant of virtue that the rule of law can be restored to Geneva.[69]

All of the changes that took place in Rousseau's view of political institutions between the writing of the *Contrat social* and the *Lettres écrites de la montagne*—his attempt to make the *droit de représentation* an effective substitute for the popular legislative initiative that he continued to oppose; his belated recognition that a governmental monopoly on the right of nomination rendered elections meaningless; his search for alternative forms of primary assemblies that might be more acceptable to the patriciate than his earlier, more strident demand for periodic legislative assemblies; his much more balanced and less hostile view of representative assemblies, including the leading contemporary example he had once criticized so severely; and his dramatic change of attitude toward the Genevan magistrates—reflect his bitter disillusionment over the arbitrary manner in which Genevan authorities condemned the *Contrat* and *Émile* and the inability or unwillingness, or both, of the bourgeoisie to do anything about it. At long last circumstances compelled him to take a closer look at the Genevan model he had once touted so highly, and he discovered that it was not all that it should be or that he had imagined it to be. What is surprising about his reaction to this discovery is that his criticism of Geneva's constitution was not more radical than it was. Apart from his lifelong distrust of radical political programs and his fear of revolution, only his determination to see Geneva as the rough embodiment of the principles of the *Contrat social* enabled him to continue to see it as a fundamentally sound political system that had been partly corrupted by the inevitable tendency of every political system to degenerate through the progressive accumulation of power in the hands of the government.

NINE

Rousseau as Lawgiver:
Corsica and Poland

A FEW MONTHS prior to publication of the *Lettres écrites de la montagne*, in September 1764, Rousseau received a letter from a prominent Corsican, Matteo Buttafuoco, requesting him to outline a system of political institutions for the then independent island nation. Buttafuoco represented himself to be the emissary of Pasquale Paoli, head of the Corsican government, but it is probable that Buttafuoco was in fact acting on his own initiative. In either case, Rousseau could hardly refuse such a request since he had previously singled out Corsica in the *Contrat social* as the one nation in Europe still suitable for the work of a lawgiver,[1] and now he was in effect being asked to act as that lawgiver. Corsica was widely regarded by the *philosophes* as a symbol of resistance to tyranny.[2] In 1729 the Corsicans had rebelled against a particularly oppressive domination by Genoa and declared their independence. Although Genoa, assisted by French troops, temporarily reestablished its hold over the island, the Corsicans regained their independence in an uprising led by Paoli, who then undertook to create a republic and provide it with institutions that would ensure the survival of independence once his personal rule of the island came to an end.[3] The basis of this republic was a constitution along the lines of the British constitution, that is, an *ad hoc* body of legislation, not a formal document in the manner of the American constitution. What Rousseau was being asked to do, therefore, was to propose a formal constitution that would harmonize and systematize Corsican laws and institutions in keeping with the spirit and principles of the *Contrat social*.[4]

Rousseau apparently began work on the manuscript that has come to be known as the *Projet de constitution pour la Corse* in January 1765, within a month after publication of the *Lettres écrites de la montagne,* and discontinued writing in October 1765. At the time he agreed to Buttafuoco's request, he anticipated that he would need at least a year to thoroughly inform himself about Corsican history and institutions before submitting even his provisional proposals for a constitution, and another three years to complete the project. He even considered making a journey to Corsica to get a first-hand knowledge of the country and its people but decided against it when he heard of an imminent French invasion of the island. As it happened, the French not only sent troops, but after a sequence of diplomatic intrigues—in which, incidentally, Buttafuoco collaborated[5]—and a decisive military engagement, France annexed Corsica in 1768 and thus rendered meaningless the project Rousseau had set himself. In the meantime, Rousseau's personal problems became more and more acute as he was driven from one country to another, and continued work on the project was all but impossible. The *Projet de constitution pour la Corse* is consequently no more than a very rough draft, never completed or revised, and not published until nearly a century after it was written.[6] This fragmentary quality of the *Projet* limits its value with regard to Rousseau's institutional thought, especially since most of the work deals with the social and economic foundations for the projected constitution rather than with specifically political institutions.

Rousseau scrupulously deferred to Corsican traditions and institutions in his constitutional proposals, this in keeping with his assertion in the *Contrat social* that "the wise lawgiver begins not by laying down laws good in themselves, but by finding out whether the people for whom the laws are intended is able to support them."[7] Accordingly, he found it necessary to modify to some extent the institutional views of the *Contrat*. Corsica's size alone precluded the kind of popular assembly that he had treated as the foundation of the institutional structure of the *Contrat*. But although he recognized the impracticability of assembling the entire citizenry of Corsica, at least on a regular basis,[8] he was still reluctant to accept an assembly of representatives as a legitimate alternative, even though he knew that the Corsican republic was based on such a representative body, the Consulte Générale.[9] He therefore settled on a compromise solution that he termed "un Gouvernement mixte," something in between democracy and aristocracy.

> It would be impossible to bring together the whole people of an island like those of a city; and when the supreme authority is entrusted to delegates, the government changes and becomes aristocratic. What Corsica needs is a mixed government, where the people assemble by sections rather than as a whole, and where the repositories of its power are changed at frequent intervals.[10]

Precisely what Rousseau meant by this is unfortunately never made very clear. When he recommended that the people assemble "by sections" (*par parties*), he presumably had in mind the administrative districts inherited from Genoan rule that he urged the Corsicans to keep, since each of these districts was small enough to permit popular assemblies. Taken together with his recommendation that the Swiss mountain cantons should serve as the model for Corsica, one might conclude that Rousseau was proposing that Corsica be transformed into a confederation, each province exercising full sovereignty internally but associating with the other provinces for specified purposes. This institutional arrangement also appears most consistent with his institutional views in the *Contrat social* and therefore the arrangement one would expect him to adopt if he were using that work as a guide. However plausible this may seem, Rousseau explicitly ruled it out, arguing that a confederation of small states, at least in the case of Corsica, would be too complicated to function effectively. He therefore proposed a relatively strong central government for the entire island and even accepted the need for a permanent capital city, Corte, as much as he disliked and distrusted capitals.[11]

All in all, his fragmentary remarks suggest a federal system rather than a confederation. In either case, the role of the popular assemblies remains unclear. Presumably they were to serve as legislative bodies on purely local affairs and perhaps to elect magistrates to serve on the administrative bodies of the central government, but Rousseau gives little idea of how national legislation was to be enacted. For one who consistently identified sovereignty with the power of legislation, his ambiguity on this issue is puzzling. It seems unlikely that he favored a system in which proposals would have to be approved by each of the provinces in order to become law, since this would in effect mean the kind of confederation he explicitly rejects. On the other hand, his failure even to mention the national representative institution of Corsica (apart from his references to an estates general in the two fragments previously noted) indicates a great reluctance to allow this body to legislate for the entire nation. It appears rather that he favored a compromise between these two alternatives whereby the people would elect deputies empowered to legislate in their behalf as members of the Consulte Générale, but who would be held more strictly accountable to their constituents than was the practice in Paoli's republic. This solution is fully consistent with Rousseau's reluctance to tamper with existing political institutions, even if it is less consistent with the principles of the *Contrat social* than other alternatives.

Beginning in 1764, the Consulte Générale was composed of no more than one member from each *pieve* [12] elected annually by all citizens aged twenty-five or more. When assembled, usually twice each year, it temporarily exercised all the powers of sovereignty, executive as well as legislative. Its actual power was, however, much more limited. The principal executive body, the Conseil d'État, whose nine members were elected annually by the provincial assemblies, normally exercised the legislative initiative and held a suspensive veto over proposals initiated and passed by members of the Consulte Générale; that is, these proposals did not become law, but the government was obliged to resubmit them at the next meeting of the Consulte Générale. In addition, Paoli, as General for Life, was the permanent president of the Conseil d'État and dominated both the executive and legislative powers as well as the judicial process.[13]

Rousseau could accept these institutions with few reservations, for the people were in principle sovereign even if their government, led by a single individual who held office for life, normally dominated all phases of the political process at the national level. If anything, Paoli's constitution may have allotted the people more real political power vis-à-vis the government than the institutions of the *Contrat social* or Geneva did, for in Corsica the people could nominate as well as elect their magistrats and they possessed a qualified legislative initiative. What seems to have bothered Rousseau most was not the wide-ranging powers of the central government but the delegation of sovereignty to a representative body, and he accepted this arrangement only on condition that the people's deputies be changed frequently, presumably by limiting their eligibility for reelection, to prevent this body from becoming a permanent aristocracy. Ironically, the effect of this proposal, if adopted, would almost certainly have been a diminution of popular power vis-à-vis the government, which in practice already dominated the Consulte Générale and could have done so all the more easily if any additional limitations had been placed on the membership of that body.

To summarize, the *Projet de constitution pour la Corse* demonstrates that Rousseau was more than willing to modify the institutional views of the *Contrat social* to accommodate Paoli's constitution, but his remarks on Corsican political institutions are too fragmentary to permit a precise statement of what changes he would have made. Not surprisingly, he was most reluctant to accept delegation of popular sovereignty to a national representative legislature, but the evidence, imperfect though it is, suggests that he compromised even on this principle, which he had treated as fundamental in the *Contrat social*. Whether the lack of clarity reflects indecision on his part or is simply due to the failure to complete a project whose *raison d'être* had ceased to exist is not possible to say. If the *Projet* were the only work in which he attempted to apply the principles of the *Contrat social* to a nation whose dimensions were significantly larger than those of Geneva, his views would necessarily remain obscure. Fortunately, he was subsequently presented with a second opportunity—or third, if one includes the request of the Genevan *Représentants* to come to their aid—to act as a lawgiver, this time for Poland, a nation whose territory and population made even Corsica look quite small by comparison, and in his proposals for Poland he directly confronted the issue of representation that for one reason or another he did not confront in the *Projet*.

————

Rousseau began work on the *Considérations sur le gouvernement de Pologne* within a few months after reestablishing his residence in Paris in June 1770. The fact that he returned to live in Paris, a city that he had long associated with modern man's worst social ills, is something of a mystery. Why would he give up his retreat in the little mountain village of Monquin in the Dauphiné and settle down in the midst of the very conspirators who had supposedly been plotting against him all these years? And still more puzzling is the outgoing lifestyle he adopted immediately after returning to Paris, cutting a figure in the salons and other meeting places that he had frequented years earlier before his break with the Encyclopedists, behavior that was in sharp contrast to the misanthropic seclusion that characterized his brief stay at Monquin.

The facility with which he made his reentry into Parisian society has prompted speculation that he returned with the blessing if not the actual support of highly placed French officials. Jean Fabre, the Pléiade editor of the *Considérations,* even suggests that Choiseul, the French foreign minister whom Rousseau had once accused of directing the conspiracy against him, may have smoothed the way for Rousseau. Choiseul privately supported the cause of the Polish Confederates that Rousseau was soon to adopt as his own in the *Considérations*—it would have been undiplomatic for the foreign minister to support this rebellious faction publicly—and quite possibly it was Choiseul, working through the intermediary of Claude Carloman de Rulhière, a former French diplomat then at work on a major study of Poland that was to be published some forty years later as the *Histoire de l'anarchie de Pologne*, who encouraged Rousseau to write about Poland. In any event, it was in all probability Rulhière who introduced Michel Wielhorski, the Confederates' representative in Paris, to Rousseau, and it was in response to Wielhorski's request that Rousseau wrote the *Considérations*. [14]

Rousseau was not the only *philosophe* called upon to defend the Confederates in print—the abbé de Mably had been contacted earlier and was half finished with his work when Rousseau began his own—but Rousseau was by far the most illustrious of the *philosophes* whom Wielhorski could expect to be sympathetic to the cause of the Confederates. Voltaire, Grimm, and others among those Rousseau referred to disparagingly as the Holbachian clique were at that time vehemently denouncing the fanatical Catholicism and intolerance of the Confederates and supporting what they saw as the enlightened policies of the Empress Catherine of Russia, who feigned concern for the religious Dissidents in Poland, as the Protestant and Orthodox minorities were called, but who in reality was only pursuing a policy of divide and conquer. Not only were the Confederates widely perceived as religious fanatics, they were also seen as remnants of an anachronistic feudal system chiefly interested in maintaining their antiquated rights and privileges, at Poland's expense if necessary. These were certainly not qualities that endeared the Confederates to Rousseau any more than to the other Encyclopedists, but he discerned positive attributes that he felt outweighed these negative qualities in the dire circumstances in which Poland then found itself.

The Confederation of Bar had been organized in 1768 by a group of Polish nobles in protest against Polish King Stanislas-Auguste Poniatowski's submission to Russian demands to grant full civil and political rights to the Dissidents. Although genuinely sympathetic to the grievances of the Dissidents, Poniatowski, a reform-minded king elected in 1764 with Russian support, was more interested in political and economic reforms that could be realized, if at all, only with the support of the Catholic nobility. Catherine, by loudly espousing the cause of the Dissidents, endeared herself to intellectuals like Voltaire for whom the cause of the Dissidents had become a kind of crusade, and at the same time, by accentuating deep divisions within the Polish leadership, rendered Poland incapable of making the reforms that were necessary for its survival as a state.

Rousseau, by espousing the cause of the Confederates, was in effect subordinating all other reforms to the immediate need for Polish national unity in the face of Russian and Prussian threats to dismember the state, threats that soon became reality in a series of partitions between 1772 and 1795. Although Polish nationalism is the dominant theme of the *Considérations*, Rousseau recognized that national unity could not be achieved without some of the reforms favored by Voltaire and other *philosophes*. Rousseau differed with them in that he urged, for the moment at least, only those reforms that would ensure Poland's survival as a nation, treating Polish Catholicism as a kind of civic religion and relegating to the future those religious reforms that threatened to render all reform impossible if insisted on at the moment.

In this instance, at least, Rousseau was far more realistic than his former friends, who prided themselves on their hardheadedness and never tired of denouncing the supposedly utopian quality of Rousseau's political proposals.[15] During most of the time that Rousseau worked on the *Considérations*, from October 1770 to June 1771,[16] the fortunes of the Confederates were at a peak, and for a while it appeared that even Poniatowski might ally himself with the Confederates in opposition to the Russians. Not until the spring of 1771 did the Confederates begin to suffer the severe military setbacks that eventually doomed their movement and prepared the way for the first partition of Poland in the following year.[17]

If the *Considérations* is thus not a utopian tract, neither is it simply a polemical work. Rousseau was committed to the Confederate cause before he was approached by Wielhorski, and in his own mind he probably saw the *Considérations* above all as the application of the principles of the *Contrat social* to a specific country and people. He frequently referred back to that earlier work, even quoting chapter and verse to show how its principles were to be understood and applied. From this perspective, perhaps the most surprising feature of the *Considérations* is Rousseau's conservatism in applying the principles of the *Contrat*.

This disjunction between principle and practice, theory and

application, raises the question whether Rousseau's proposals in the *Considérations* can in any meaningful sense be regarded as the outcome of the principles of the *Contrat*. It is not enough to say, as Fabre does in Rousseau's defense,[18] that the same spirit pervades the two works if in reality some of Rousseau's most important specific proposals have little or nothing to do with the earlier work and on occasion even directly contradict fundamental principles set forth in that work. In the conclusion of the *Considérations* Rousseau claimed that he had proposed only the minimum changes necessary to correct the faults of Poland's constitution, and in several other passages he cautioned the Poles against attempting to achieve too many reforms too quickly.[19] Given this approach to his project, certainly legitimate in itself, concessions to circumstances are to be expected. The significant question, however, is not whether Rousseau made concessions, for this he explicitly acknowledged, but whether the kinds of concessions he made were consistent with the fundamental principles as well as the spirit of the *Contrat social*.

Perhaps the most dramatic concession that Rousseau made was his acceptance of representative government in Poland. His acceptance was reluctant, but in view of Poland's immense size he saw no alternative. He was as convinced as ever that small states, whether republics or monarchies, tend to prosper simply by virtue of being small. Ideally, he would like Poland to become a confederation of thirty-three small states (one for each of the existing palatines or districts), for such a confederation "would combine the power of a great monarchy with the freedom of a small republic." Even if Poland's size were reduced, either by its own initiative or by neighboring states, it would probably remain too large to govern properly unless it were subdivided into several smaller parts united in a federation or confederation. One of the chief disadvantages of a large state, whether federal or unitary in its organization, "is that the legislative power cannot manifest itself directly, and can act only by delegation"[20]; that is, the state must resort to some form of representative government.

That Rousseau was willing to accept representative government at all is somewhat surprising in view of his intense opposition in previous writings, but even more surprising was his acceptance of the existing Polish system whereby deputies to the national diet had the final say in legislation, an arrangement that appears directly contrary to his emphatic assertion in the *Contrat social*, III, 15, for example, that "the people's deputies are not, and could not be, its representatives; they are merely its agents; and they cannot decide anything finally. Any law which the people has not ratified in person is void; it is not law at all." [21] Rousseau seems to have been well aware that this constituted a significant departure from the principles of the *Contrat*, although he did not explicitly acknowledge as much. Speaking of the legislative process in Poland, he declared that laws were not binding on "anyone who has not voted for them in person, like the deputies, *or at least through representatives*, like the body of the nobility." [22] And he went out of his way to emphasize the finality of the diet's authority as legislator by denying the dietines the right even to protest decisions of the diet, much less to change or ignore them. [23]

It might appear that Rousseau's reluctance to tamper with traditional institutions explains his acceptance of a feature so contrary to his previously expressed views on political institutions, but on closer examination this explanation proves unsatisfactory. Granted that respect for tradition requires concessions on matters of principle, why make a concession on a matter that he had consistently treated as fundamental and yet at the same time propose radical innovations—for example, the gradual extension of the franchise to burghers and serfs—that not only were not treated as fundamental in previous writings but also were likely to antagonize the nobility and possibly jeopardize the whole project? [24]

Alternatively, if one takes Rousseau at his word and sees the *Considérations* as the application of the principles of the *Contrat social*, one might expect such concessions as circumstances dictated, for example, the necessity for representative government in a large and populous state, but not the kind of gratuitous concession he made by accepting and even insisting on the final authority of a representative body in legislation. It is as though, having decided that representative government was inevitable in Poland, he felt that he had to accept the existing system intact, even if this further violated his fundamental views on political institutions. Why should a concession on the one issue lead to concessions on related issues when circumstances did not necessitate additional concessions? If the principles of the *Contrat* were really his guide, why, having already conceded the necessity for representative government, would he not insist on reforming the Polish system of representation to make it as compatible as possible with the principles of the *Contrat*, especially since he could have done so without proposing changes as radical as the extension of the franchise? Simply by adding to the existing system the requirement that all measures passed by the diet be resubmitted to the dietines or to the people at large for final approval, he could have brought the Polish system into line with his own basic principles.

The point is, not to try to improve on Rousseau's own constitutional proposals, but rather to demonstrate that alternatives that could have satisfied the demands of the *Contrat* were readily available to him and yet for some reason he chose not to make use of them. Perhaps he thought that such an arrangement was too cumbersome, but this seems unlikely since he accepted and even insisted on several features of the existing system—notably imperative mandates and postdiet review of the conduct of deputies—that made the legislative process so cumbersome as to render it unworkable in the eyes of many would-be reformers.

In fact, by resubmitting the work of the diet to the dietines or to the people in a popular referendum, he might have eliminated or at least mitigated one of the chief shortcomings of a system of imperative mandates, a problem that he acknowledged but for which he found no satisfactory solution, namely, the difficulty of legislating without the freedom to consider issues not covered by the mandates. Referenda would have given the people the final voice in all legislation, including legislation concerning matters not foreseen by those who drafted the deputies' instructions, and such matters were likely to be fairly numerous in a large and diverse state. In view of all this, Rousseau's departure from one of the basic principles of the *Contrat*, far from having been dictated by circumstances, appears unwarranted and gratuitous.

His willingness to make such a concession suggests to Derathé that Rousseau finally accepted representation not only out of expediency but as a matter of principle.[25] If Derathé means by this no more than that Rousseau accepted, as a matter of principle, the necessity for representative government in a large state, then his interpretation is undoubtedly correct, for Rousseau himself said as much. But if Derathé means that Rousseau came to embrace the principle of representation in the same way that he had embraced the popular ratification of all laws in the *Contrat,* the interpretation is highly questionable.

Rousseau was still unhappy with representative government when he wrote the *Considérations,* and he accepted it only with the greatest reluctance, and even then only if very stringent conditions were imposed on the repesentatives. Basically these conditions, which were directed primarily at the problem of corruption of the deputies, were twofold: (1) frequent meetings of the diet and frequent election of new members to the diet and (2) a system of imperative mandates and postdiet review of the work of deputies to hold them accountable for their conduct at the diet. These conditions were the logical consequence of Rousseau's concept of the representative: "after all, it is not to express their own private sentiments, but to declare the will of the nation, that the nation sends deputies to the diet."[26]

Perhaps he believed that these features, both of which he adopted from the existing Polish system, rendered superfluous any provision for final approval of legislation by the dietines. Since he consistently underrated the difficulty and complexity of the legislative process—his ridicule of the English for trying to legislate for every possible eventuality typifies his simplistic view of legislation[27]—he could plausibly conclude that these conditions amounted to the rough equivalent of popular ratification of all legislation. The diet, on this view, would then do little more than formalize the popular ratification that had already taken place in the dietines.

The problem with this view is that the diet, for all its shortcomings, was not a mere formality but the very heart of the Polish political system, and Rousseau in his more clear-sighted moments recognized this and developed his proposals on the basis of this recognition. He was torn between conflicting goals, between the need for a strong and effective diet, on the one hand, and his deepseated distrust of representative government, on the other. Once he had conceded the necessity for representative government, he might logically have proceeded to make the diet into a dynamic and efficient political institution, perhaps adding some form of popular approval of its work to prevent its becoming too powerful and usurping sovereignty for itself, as he believed the English Parliament had done. This had been and still was his attitude toward the executive: it was an evil, but a necessary evil, and therefore should be made strong enough to cope with the weighty demands made of it, even at the risk of having it usurp the people's sovereignty. He did not adopt the same attitude toward the diet, because his acceptance of representation was at best halfhearted, and his obsession with the possibility that the diet might become a self-perpetuating aristocracy led him to place obstacles such as the imperative mandate—ironically, a preeminently feudal device now advocated by one who had always held the feudal system in contempt[28]—in the way of the efficient functioning of the diet. Instead of reforming Poland's constitution according to the principles of the *Contrat*, he attempted to discover virtues in Poland's political institutions that other reformers dismissed as feudal anachronisms.

Even with regard to the *liberum veto*, the one feature of the Polish constitution that many conservatives as well as reformers considered an anachronism and obstacle to national unity, Rousseau was unwilling to call for its outright abolition. By invoking the *liberum veto*, any individual member of the diet could not only prevent a measure from becoming law but also cause the dissolution of that diet and render void all its previous acts.[29] Rousseau agreed that the *liberum veto* should be abolished as far as administrative acts and ordinary acts of legislation were concerned, but he argued that it should be retained for all fundamental laws since these laws had properly required unanimity in the first place. As a further precaution against abuse of the *liberum veto* even for this more limited purpose, he did suggest that anyone who invoked it without justification should have to answer for it with his life if a properly constituted tribunal found this to be the case.[30] The effect of such a drastic limitation on its use might well have been the same as outright abolition of the *liberum veto*, but it is indicative of

Rousseau's approach to constitutional reform in Poland that he was so reluctant to modify even the most flagrantly abusive institutions if they had the weight of tradition behind them.

While Rousseau was thus deeply ambivalent about the role that the diet should play in the Polish political system, he was highly enthusiastic about the dietines, the regional primary assemblies of noblemen that he characterized as "the true palladium of liberty" in Poland. He was convinced that the Poles and their foreign supporters for the most part had failed to appreciate the historical importance of the dietines and their potential for rejuvenating political life if the constitution were revised to give them greater authority.[31] There were actually several types of dietine,[32] constituted in different ways and serving a variety of purposes, but Rousseau spoke as though the dietines were all regional primary assemblies that had as their principal functions the election and supervision of local officials, election and instruction of deputies to the national diet, and review of the conduct of deputies to the diet. In other words, for Rousseau the dietines were the counterparts of the Genevan Conseil Général, with the difference of course that the dietines were also part of a larger federation to which they sent representatives. The dietines were the only political institution in Poland in which all citizens could participate personally, and this alone would be sufficient reason for Rousseau to wish them to play a more prominent role in the Polish political system.[33] There is no indication, however, that Rousseau expected or wanted the nature or extent of participation in the dietines to be any different from that of citizen participation in the Genevan Conseil Général.

He had little to say about how the dietines should deal with purely local affairs, but his proposals concerning the manner of preparing instructions for the deputies elected to represent the dietines in the diet suggest that most citizens, whether technically "active" or "passive," would play no more than a passive role in the dietines. The instructions would be drafted by a popularly elected commission, then presented to the full dietine for discussion and approval.[34] The dietines would thus collectively exercise the initiative in the legislative process, but the manner in which they would do so indicates that Rousseau had not abandoned his long-standing opposition to a popular legislative initiative. Although the dietines would be the focal point of political life under the constitution envisaged by Rousseau, in all probability the political initiative, even with a citizenry composed solely of noblemen, would be confined to the few entrusted with this task by the great majority of citizens whose function would be primarily that of ratifying the decisions of this "elective aristocracy."

In one respect, however, Rousseau would have broadened participation in the political process far beyond anything he had advocated in the past. Although citizenship would initially be limited to the nobility, as under the existing system, he urged its gradual extension to burghers and eventually even to serfs. He dismissed as irrelevant the traditional threefold classification of Poles into the equestrian order, the senate, and the king, contending that all three orders were in fact part of the same order, the nobility. In reality, he argued, the three orders in Poland were "the nobles, who are everything; the burghers, who are nothing; and the peasants, who are less than nothing." [35]

Casting aside his customary respect for tradition, he launched into one of the most radically democratic proposals to be found in all his political writings. Whatever the ancient constitution of Poland might say on the subject, the burghers and peasants must be liberated and the way opened for them to achieve full political equality with the nobility. He justified this proposal by pointing out its advantages to Poland in terms of stimulating the growth of patriotism, strengthening national unity, and, not incidentally, providing a greatly enlarged citizenry to serve in the militia. This last advantage was closely related to the proposal he had previously outlined, which called for transformation of the regular army into a citizen's militia and reliance on guerilla warfare to make foreign occupation of Poland unbearably costly to any invader.

Quite apart from these very tangible benefits, however, he argued for extension of citizenship on the purely rationalistic grounds that the inherent worth of serfs as human beings entitled them to citizenship. He appealed to the nobility to "remember that your serfs are men like you, that they have in themselves the capacity to become all that you are." True, the process of emancipation must be gradual, for "Liberty is a food easy to eat, but hard to digest; it takes very strong stomachs to stand it,"[36] but however difficult the task, serfs must be made worthy of the liberty they have a right to enjoy.

He suggested two basic methods of promoting burghers and serfs to full citizens. The first was simply to reform the courts to ensure that all persons enjoyed equality before the laws. The second was to establish biennial assemblies in each province to review "a roster of those peasants who were distinguished for good conduct, education and morals, for their devotion to their families and for the proper fulfilment of all the duties of their station," and to emancipate a prescribed number of those who satisfied these requirements. It might even prove feasible to emancipate entire villages or provinces at one time. In addition, both free peasants and burghers should be eligible for "ennoblement," as Rousseau called it, or in other words promotion to full citizenship.[37]

One reason that Rousseau urged extension of the franchise was his conviction that Poland was depriving itself of a great deal of talent by excluding all but the nobility from public life. As a firm believer in the Enlightenment demand for "carrières ouvertes aux talents," he applied the principle of promotion according to merit not only to peasants and burghers but also to the nobility itself. Political and economic inequality within the Polish nobility was almost as severe as that between the nobility on the one hand and peasants and burghers on the other. One historian suggests that the nobility was effectively divided into two basic groups: the two or three dozen magnates possessing great fortunes, mainly in land, and exercising corresponding political power; and perhaps a million lesser noblemen who depended on the magnates for both economic and political favors. The increasingly numerous landless nobility had lost the right to participate in the election of deputies in 1630 and now more often than not acted as the political pawns of one or another magnate.[38]

Rousseau insisted that this severe inequality among noblemen be reduced[39] and suggested that the property requirement for full or "active" citizenship be eliminated. All noblemen, whether wealthy or poor, should have to pass a strict legal examination before being admitted to memberhsip in a dietine.[40] To ensure that all noblemen would compete on an equal basis, he proposed a system of public education with free scholarships provided by the state for the children of poor noblemen who could not otherwise afford to send their children to school.[41]

But beyond these measures to achieve equality within the nobility, Rousseau would extend the merit principle to include all public offices by creating a complicated three-class structure, each class being higher in prestige and importance, with promotions from one class to the next highest based solely on merit. Burghers and peasants would become eligible to compete for these offices on an equal basis once they had been liberated and ennobled.[42] The merit system would thus open the way for a much broader participation in the political life of Poland in addition to improving the quality of its public servants.

Despite this strong commitment to a greater role in public life for many who had up to then been excluded from participation, and despite his praise for the dietines, confederations, and other decentralizing institutions, Rousseau was no less committed to a strong executive than he had been in previous political writings. He acknowledged that Poland had managed to avoid the despotism that characterized most of Europe largely as a result of Poland's historically weak and divided executive, but he saw this same weakness as the principal cause of the anarchy that debilitated the state. Division within the executive power was a mixed blessing, and on balance the evil outweighed the good. Only a strong and unified executive could provide the kind of direction necessary to guarantee impartial application of the laws and thereby social harmony. What Poland needed was therefore a permanent, united, forceful executive, and the most obvious candidate for this role was the senate, which already commanded great respect in the nation through the prestige of its membership.[43] Under the existing Polish constitution, senators held office by virtue of their official status, which in turn derived from royal appointment.[44]

Rousseau preferred that senators be elected rather than appointed by the king, but he compromised to some extent and devised a complicated system whereby half of the senate would be elected by the diet for two-year terms, slightly less than half would be elected for life by the dietines, and the remainder, with one exception, would continue to be appointed by the king. While the senate would constitute the principal executive body, the king would continue to exercise important executive powers as chief of state. His appointive powers would be greatly reduced and confined largely to honorary positions, but he would still play a significant role in both domestic and foreign policy, especially in crisis situations.[45] In any case, the principle of elective monarchy must be retained, even though an occasional interregnum could be a serious threat to political stability.

Once again Rousseau displayed his gift for improvisation by devising a method of election that he contended would combine the advantages of election and inheritance: the king would be elected by the diet from a list of three candidates previously chosen by lot from the palatines, one of several types of senators-for-life.[46] All in all, Rousseau would make the king the symbol of national unity and give him considerable power to investigate and correct the shortcomings of executive officers but deny him any real executive power except in crises such as war or civil strife.

In his final three major political writings—*Lettres écrites de la montagne*, *Projet de constitution pour la Corse*, and *Considérations sur le gouvernement de Pologne*—Rousseau adopted a much more conciliatory view of representative government and even accepted it as a legitimate alternative for Poland and possibly Corsica, but in none of these works did he accept representative government with the same wholehearted enthusiasm with which he had embraced government based on primary assemblies of all citizens. In the *Lettres écrites de la montagne* he showed a much greater appreciation of the strengths of representative government and recognized that it might be more effective in realizing some of the most basic goals of the *Contrat social* than the Genevan system based on a primary assembly was, but despite this recognition he remained devoted to the primary assembly as the ideal and still held out the hope that this ideal could be restored in Geneva.

Corsica and Poland posed special problems for Rousseau because both were too large for primary assemblies. He had clearly given little thought to this problem when he boldly proclaimed in the *Contrat* that Corsica was the one country in Europe still fit for the work of a lawgiver. What impressed him at the time was what he as well as his fellow *philosophes* perceived to be Corsica's determination to be free. When actually confronted with the task of drafting a constitution for Corsica, he informed Buttafuoco that it would take several years to complete the project because of his ignorance of Corsican traditions and institutions. As it happened, events overtook Rousseau and the project was never completed, and it is not clear from the fragmentary manuscript what position he took or would have taken on the issue of primary versus representative assemblies.

Not until his final political work, the *Considérations sur le gouvernement de Pologne*, did he clearly accept representative government, and then only grudgingly. The result of this halfhearted acceptance was a curious mixture of restrictions such as the imperative mandate that would have severely hampered the efficient functioning of the Polish diet, on the one hand, but surprising concessions on the other, notably his willingness to give final legislative authority to the diet. And even in the *Considérations* he would have made the primary assemblies of the dietines the focal point of political life in Poland. Whether this combination of strong local government and a hamstrung national representative body could have unified Poland is doubtful. In any case it epitomizes Rousseau's ambivalence toward representative government, for he clearly recognized its advantages vis-à-vis primary assemblies and yet was unwilling to give representative assemblies the authority necessary to realize these advantages.

Rousseau's view of political participation underwent a similar evolution in his final three political writings. No one pointed out more graphically than he the hollowness of the bourgeoisie's claim that Geneva's primary assembly was sovereign. No one described more forcefully how the ruling patriciate had transformed Geneva into a self-perpetuating oligarchy. And yet he refused to sanction, much less demand, reforms that would have given substance to the theoretical sovereignty of the Conseil Général. He opposed more vehemently than ever the demand for a popular legislative initiative and acquiesced in the patriciate's monopoly of the process of nomination of candidates for public office, staking everything on a limited *droit de représentation* that had manifestly proved ineffective as a check on executive abuse of power. Despite his biting criticism of Geneva's political leaders, he was as convinced as ever of the need for strong executive leadership, which for him meant that the political initiative must remain in the hands of the few to whom the people, however indirectly, had entrusted it. The average citizen was simply not capable of the vision and discretion necessary for the wise conduct of government, and consequently his role should be essentially passive and negative, choosing from among those candidates and proposals put forward by the executive authority.

Only in the *Considérations* did he significantly change his view of political participation, and then only by extending the concept of citizenship to all classes of society. His recognition that even Polish serfs, widely regarded by the *philosophes* as among the lowest form of humanity, were potentially all that their masters were was a major departure from his previous refusal to condone broadening the franchise in Geneva.

And yet the political role of the average citizen in Poland, whether nobleman or burgher or former serf, would have remained essentially unchanged under his proposed constitution. Far from advocating mass dmocracy or even direct democracy as these terms are usually understood, he was horrified by the specter of the masses' seizing the political initiative, for this could only mean the kind of turmoil and revolution that had once plagued Athens and now plagued Geneva. He was deeply ambivalent about the capacities of the average citizen, insisting on the one hand that citizen participation was essential to the health of the body politic, but recoiling, on the other, from the potential breakdown between leaders and led and the corresponding decline in political stability that might result from an excessive stress on participation and on the equal status of all citizens. He was genuinely perplexed when forced to choose between the peace of Leviathan and the unlicensed freedom of the masses.

CONCLUSION

THE TENSION between Rousseau's sweeping concept of popular sovereignty, which appears to give virtually unlimited political power to the people, and his institutional ideal of elective aristocracy, which places severe restraints on the people's exercise of sovereignty, reveals a deep ambivalence in Rousseau's attitude toward "the people." It is difficult to imagine a more radical concept of democracy than that set forth in the general principles of the *Contrat social.* Not only are the people sovereign, but their sovereignty is indivisible and inalienable, which to Rousseau meant that the people themselves must exercise sovereignty, that they cannot delegate this crucial function to representatives. Even allowing for Rousseau's addiction to the use of flamboyant language, this is a radically democratic conception of democracy.

But if one turns from these general principles to a careful examination of how Rousseau intended the institutions of this democracy to function, it quickly becomes apparent that his concept of democracy was far less radical than these general principles might lead one to believe. The people exercise very little real power in the popular assemblies. Their role is essentially passive and negative; they react to the initiatives of an executive that, through its monopoly of the right to nominate candidates for public office and its

193

preponderant role in legislation, can fairly be described as a self-perpetuating aristocracy. If one takes Rousseau's concept of popular sovereignty seriously, these limitations on the exercise of sovereignty cannot help but be surprising, but they are less surprising if one also takes seriously his own claim in the *Lettres écrites de la montagne* that the political institutions of the *Contrat social* were modeled on those of Geneva.

Whatever the source of Rousseau's concept of sovereignty—and certainly the Genevan bourgeoisie as well as the natural law theorists exerted a major influence in this regard—his institutional ideal was closely modeled on Genevan institutions, at least on his perception of those institutions, and this perception in turn was based on a reasonably adequate understanding of the reality. Rousseau may have been critical of the Genevan partriciate when he wrote the *Contrat social*—his advocacy of periodic popular assemblies is evidence of that—but he was also deeply opposed to revolution and to any form of popular protest that might lead to a violent confrontation with the patriciate. Even after the patriciate's condemnation of the *Contrat social* and *Émile,* Rousseau could not bring himself to support the kind of popular political initiatives that were essential for the Genevan popular assembly to become sovereign in fact as well as in principle. His fear of mass violence by the bourgeoisie was just as great as his contempt for the oligarchic rule of the patriciate, and he abandoned Geneva rather than risk the first evil in order to overcome the second. There is perhaps no clearer indication of his ambivalence than his inability to support initiatives that would have given substance to his own claims of popular sovereignty because he did not trust even his fellow Genevan citizens sufficiently to accept them as true sovereigns.

Rousseau's ambivalence toward the people is especially evident if one focuses on his view of political institutions rather than on his basic political concepts. For Rousseau the key institution in any legitimate political system was the legislative body because he equated sovereignty with legislative power. In the *Contrat social* he vehemently opposed representative government insofar as this entailed the delegation of sovereignty to a representative body, but precisely because he opposed representation in this sense he insisted all the more forcefully that the people delegate all executive functions to representatives, and he included among these executive functions a dominant role in legislation. The people might always will the good, but without proper guidance the people could not always discern the good. The task of the executive was thus to prepare and submit proposals for popular enactment; the role of the popular assembly was to ratify or reject these proposals, possibly without the benefit of debate and definitely without the right to modify these proposals or substitute proposals of its own. Since the executive exercised the initiative at every step of the legislative process, Rousseau's distinction between legislative and executive representation tended to disappear, to become a distinction without a difference.

The earliest work in which Rousseau explicitly mentioned representatives in a political sense was *Économie politique*, which appears to accept representative assemblies as a legitimate alternative to popular assemblies, and which disparages the value of popular assemblies, declaring that the executive can usually determine the general will without assembling the citizenry. Although these references to representatives are not entirely clear, the context in which he made them suggests that in 1755 Rousseau, whose political thought at the time was still quite close to that of his fellow Encyclopedists, simply acquiesced in the prevailing Encyclopedist view that representative government is one of several forms of legitimate government.

Not until the *Contrat social*, published seven years later, did he adopt the hostile view of representation with which his political thought has come to be closely associated, and in none of his subsequent political writings did he condemn representation in the uncompromising terms of the *Contrat*. His principal theoretical argument against representation in the *Contrat* was based on his contention that will cannot be represented, but this argument, in addition to being of dubious validity, was clearly subordinate to his pragmatic objection to representation on the grounds that representative assemblies are less effective than popular assemblies in preventing executive usurpation of popular sovereignty. In the *Lettres écrites de la montagne*, published just two years after the *Contrat*, he showed a new appreciation for the effectiveness of representative institutions, but he continued to cling to the primary assembly as his institutional ideal.

It is not clear what kind of political institutions he envisaged for Corsica, but when he drafted a constitution for Poland in 1771 he directly confronted the issue of representation and reluctantly accepted a mandate system of representation, provided that there would be frequent elections of new representatives, frequent meetings of the representative assembly, and strict accounting of the conduct of representatives. He did make one concession that appears quite gratuitous in view of the options available to him. Instead of giving the final voice in legislation to the popular assemblies, or dietines, he insisted that the national representative assembly, the diet, must have this power, a concession that seems to fly in the face of his declaration in the *Contrat* that the people must personally approve every law. This went far beyond the kind of minimal concession that one might expect if he were simply adapting the principles of the *Contrat* to the circumstances of Poland. Even so, his acceptance of representation was at most half-hearted, and he placed a number of obstacles in the way of the efficient functioning of the diet that would probably have prevented it from becoming an effective institution. All of these changes in his view of representation point to an evolution from a position of passive acceptance in *Économie politique* to overt hostility in the *Contrat social* to qualified opposition in the *Lettres écrites de la montagne* to qualified acceptance in the *Considérations sur le gouvernement de Pologne*.

Rousseau's ambivalence about popular participation in the formal political process extended to his feelings about popular participation in a variety of activities that, although not strictly political, had an important political impact. Public festivals, games, and ceremonies were all perceived by Rousseau as means of reinforcing a feeling of identification with the community, instilling patriotism, and, in general, promoting public-spiritedness. In his *Lettre à d'Alembert*, where he wrote of the joy that the people of his own Saint-Gervais quarter of Geneva derived from participation in various public events, he even seemed to see participation as intrinsically worthwhile, not just as a means of strengthening the body politic. And yet for all his celebration of this form of participation, he was reluctant to channel the fellow feeling of these communal activities into effective popular political power. His emphasis was instead on social and political harmony, and in fact one of the chief purposes of these public activities was to reinforce mutual respect between leaders and led by bringing them together in a convivial social setting. The practical effect of encouraging this kind of ritualistic participation was to reinforce a status quo that was heavily weighted in favor of the aristocracy.

One of the most dramatic instances of Rousseau's ambivalence toward popular participation in politics was the manner in which he proposed to institute a state embodying the principles of the *Contrat*. For all practical purposes, the state would be created by a single extraordinary individual, the lawgiver. The people, whom Rousseau in this context variously characterized as "a blind multitude" and "the common herd," would participate in the creation of the state only to the extent of consenting to the political system proposed by the lawgiver. And since the lawgiver would not be able to convince the ignorant masses by reasoned arguments, he would have to resort to myths and other ruses to persuade them. It is true that Rousseau was here speaking about an amorphous mass of individuals, not the citizens of a free republic, but it is also true that his proposed method of institution was little more than a desperate attempt to achieve by superhuman means what he believed ordinary human beings incapable of achieving on their own. He lacked any notion of a *pouvoir constituant*, an assembly of ordinary people or their representatives who could themselves institute a new state. The American and French revolutions in which such assemblies played a crucial role in creating new states were still in the future when Rousseau wrote, but he did have the benefit of the example of the Genevan bourgeoisie, whose more radical members had long sought to transform the Conseil Général into a kind of *pouvoir constituant*, and he consistently opposed their demands because he believed that the bourgeoisie acting alone was incapable of anything more than turmoil. Just as the political initiative in an existing republic must come from the executive, the political initiative in the creation of a new republic must come from a semi-divine lawgiver, not from the people themselves.

Rousseau may have believed that men are potentially capable of a way of life that exceeds their fondest dreams, capable even of the exacting demands of the *Contrat social,* but he was deeply pessimistic about the human prospect in the short term, and this pessimism prevented him from translating his radical political concepts into the revolutionary demands that others would derive from them with equal validity.

The problem was that his radically democratic principles made sense only on the basis of a very optimistic view of human nature. When confronted with the opportunity to apply his radical principles, whether in the *Contrat* itself or in Geneva, Corsica, and Poland, his pessimism came to the fore, and he recoiled from the prospect of revolution and civil unrest that he associated with giving ordinary citizens the kind of real political power that his concept of sovereignty seems to imply.

NOTES

INTRODUCTION

1. Otto von Gierke, *The Development of Political Theory*, trans. by Bernard Freyd (New York: Norton, 1939), p. 247; Charles W. Hendel, *Jean-Jacques Rousseau: Moralist* (London: Oxford University Press, 1934), II, 169, 215; Ernest Barker, "Introduction" to *Social Contract: Essays by Locke, Hume, and Rousseau* (1947; rpt. New York: Oxford University Press, 1962), pp. xxxiii–xxxvi; John W. Chapman, *Rousseau—Totalitarian or Liberal?* (New York: Columbia University Press, 1956), pp. 53–54; George H. Sabine, *A History of Political Theory*, 3rd ed. (New York: Holt, Rinehart and Winston, 1961), p. 592; J. H. Broome, *Rousseau: A Study of His Thought* (London: Edward Arnold, 1963), p. 60; John Plamenatz, *Man and Society* (New York: McGraw-Hill, 1963), I, 399–403; Alfred Cobban, *Rousseau and the Modern State*, 2nd ed. (London: George Allen and Unwin, 1964), pp. 41–43; Lester G. Crocker, *Rousseau's Social Contract: An Interpretive Essay* (Cleveland: Case Western Reserve University Press, 1968), pp. 68–69; Judith N. Shklar, *Men and Citizens: A Study of Rousseau's Social Theory* (Cambridge, England: Cambridge University Press, 1969), pp. 94–95; Peter Gay, *The Enlightenment: An Interpretation* (New York: Knopf, 1969), II, 550; Ronald Grimsley, "Introduction" to *Du Contrat social* (Oxford, England: Clarendon Press, 1972), pp. 43–44; Allan Bloom, "Jean-Jacques Rousseau," in *History of Political Theory*, 2nd ed., edited by Leo Strauss and Joseph Cropsey (Chicago: Rand McNally, 1972), p. 543.

2. E.g., Cobban, pp. 42–43.

3. E.g., C. E. Vaughan, *The Political Writings of Jean-Jacques Rousseau* (1915; rpt. New York: Wiley, 1962), I, 266.

4. Robert Derathé, *Jean-Jacques Rousseau et la science politique de son temps*, 2nd ed. (Paris: Librairie Philosophique J. Vrin, 1970), pp. 279–280.

5. Roger D. Masters, *The Political Philosophy of Rousseau* (Princeton, N.J.: Princeton University Press, 1968), p. 402.

6. Hanna Fenichel Pitkin, *The Concept of Representation* (Berkeley: University of California Press, 1967).

7. Cobban, p. 43.

8. One of the most forceful recent statements of the thesis that Rousseau favored participatory democracy is that of Carole Pateman, *Participation and Democratic Theory* (Cambridge, England: Cambridge University Press, 1970), especially pp. 22–27. Among those who refer to Rousseau as an advocate of direct democracy are Sabine, p. 592; A. H. Birch, *Representation* (New York: Praeger, 1971), p. 34; and Olivier Krafft, *La politique de Jean-Jacques Rousseau: aspects méconnus* (Paris: Pichon et Durand-Auzias, 1958), pp. 72–85.

9. Cf. Rousseau's account in the *Confessions,* Book IX, in *Oeuvres complètes de Jean-Jacques Rousseau,* édition publiée sous la direction de Bernard Gagnebin et Marcel Raymond (Paris: Éditions Gallimard: Bibliothèque de la Pléiade, 1959), I, 404–405. This is now generally regarded as the standard edition of Rousseau's works. Four volumes have been published to date, including most of Rousseau's political writings with the exception of his *Lettre à d'Alembert* and his *Histoire de Genève.* Citations to this edition are indicated by O.C. followed by the volume and page number.

10. See especially the following articles published in *Études sur le Contrat social de Jean-Jacques Rousseau,* actes des journées d'étude organisées à Dijon pour la commémoration du 200e anniversaire du *Contrat social* (Paris: Société Les Belles Lettres, 1964): Jean Cousin, "J.-J. Rousseau interprète des institutions romaines dans le *Contrat social,*" pp. 13–34; Georges Davy, "Le corps politique selon le *Contrat social* de J.-J. Rousseau et ses antécédents chez Hobbes," pp. 65–93; Charles Eisenmann, "La cité de Jean-Jacques Rousseau," pp. 191–201; Jean-Jacques Chevallier, "Le mot et la notion de *gouvernement* chez Rousseau," pp. 291–313; and Paul Bastid, "Rousseau et la théorie des formes de gouvernement," pp. 315–327.

11. Bertrand de Jouvenel, "Théorie des formes de gouvernement chez Rousseau," *Le Contrat social,* 6, no. 6 (nov.–déc. 1962), 343–351; Robert Derathé, "Rousseau et le problème de la monarchie," *Le Contrat social,* 6, no. 3 (mai–juin 1962), 165–168.

12. E.g., Robert Derathé, "Les rapports de l'exécutif et du législatif chez J.-J. Rousseau," *Annales de la philosophie politique,* 5 (1965), 153–169. Shklar's *Men and Citizens* also discusses Rousseau's institutional thought in some detail.

13. Roger D. Masters notes the lack of attention given to this subject, and to Books III and IV of the *Contrat social* in which it is treated, in his "The Structure of Rousseau's Political Thought," in *Hobbes and Rousseau: A Collection of Critical Essays,* ed. by Maurice Cranston and Richard S. Peters (Garden City, N.Y.: Doubleday, 1972), pp. 414–415. The absence of a decent English translation of the *Lettres écrites de la montagne*—the only available English translation is a reprint of an eighteenth-century translation—is indicative of the neglect of Rousseau's institutional thought. It is odd that there are multiple English translations of his other two constitutional works on Corsica and Poland, even though these are less important for an understanding of Rousseau's political thought than his work on Geneva is.

14. Bertrand de Jouvenel stresses Rousseau's pessimism, his fascination for the ancients, and his reaction against modernizing trends in eighteenth-century society in "Essai sur la politique de Rousseau," in his edition of Rousseau's *Du Contrat social* (Genève: Les Éditions du Cheval Ailé, 1947), pp. 1–160. In a later essay, "Rousseau the Pessimistic Evolutionist," *Yale French Studies,* 28 (Fall–Winter 1961–1962), 83–96, Jouvenel continues to stress Rousseau's fundamentally pessimistic view of man but

nevertheless finds Rousseau's view of social evolution quite modern. Eric Weil, in a long bibliographic essay, "J.-J. Rousseau et sa politique," *Critique*, 8, no. 56 (Jan. 1952), 3–28, contends that Rousseau was essentially a pessimist and moralist whose main purpose was to preach to mankind rather than reform it. Judith Shklar pursues Weil's thesis in her *Men and Citizens* and, like Weil, stresses Rousseau's pessimism. Iring Fetscher portrays Rousseau as a determined opponent of emerging eighteenth-century liberal bourgeois economic and social thought in his *Rousseaus politische Philosophie: zur Geschichte des demokratischen Freiheitsbegriffs*, 2nd ed. (Neuwied am Rhein: Luchterhand, 1968) and paints a similar picture of Rousseau in his "Rousseau, auteur d'intention conservatrice et d'action révolutionnaire," in *Rousseau et la philosophie politique* (Paris: Press Universitaires de France, 1965), pp. 51–75.

15. Mario Einaudi reviews some of the literature on this theme in his *The Early Rousseau* (Ithaca, N.Y.: Cornell University Press, 1967), pp. 9–16, where he notes that what were once perceived simply as "contradictions" in Rousseau's thought are now seen as fruitful and illuminating tensions. An earlier but more detailed bibliographical essay that focuses on this approach to the interpretation of Rousseau is Peter Gay's "Reading About Rousseau," in *The Party of Humanity: Essays in the French Enlightenment* (1963; rpt. New York: Norton, 1971), pp. 211–261.

16. Paris: Gallimard, 1949.

17. See especially chapter 4, "Dualité d'idéals chez Rousseau," pp. 117–140.

18. In 2nd ed. (Paris: Gallimard, 1971). Originally published in 1957.

19. The psychological approach, although appropriate and potentially of great value in the study of Rousseau, is perhaps more easily abused than other approaches. Lester G. Crocker's two-volume psychobiography, *Jean-Jacques Rousseau: A New Interpretative Analysis of His Life and Works* (New York: Macmillan, 1968, 1973), e.g., treats the tensions in Rousseau's thought as indications of a schizoid personality and effectively reduces Rousseau's writings to the mutterings of a demented mind. For a critique of Crocker's work, see Jean Starobinski's "Rousseau & Modern Tyranny," *The New York Review of Books*, November 29, 1973, pp. 20–25.

20. In *The Wish to Be Free: Society, Psyche, and Value Change* (Berkeley: University of California Press, 1969), pp. 82–107. I am indebted to Prof. Isser Woloch for this reference.

21. For classical republicanism in the seventeenth century, see Zera S. Fink, *The Classical Republicans: An Essay in the Recovery of a Pattern of Thought in Seventeenth Century England* (Evanston, Ill.: Northwestern University Press, 1945). Caroline Robbins has demonstrated the persistence of this tradition in eighteenth-century England in her *The Eighteenth-Century Commonwealthman: Studies in the Transmission, Development and Circumstance of English Liberal Thought from the Restoration of Charles II Until the War with the Thirteen Colonies* (Cambridge, Mass.: Harvard University Press, 1959).

22. Cf. Starobinski's notes in *O.C.* III, 1353–1358; also *Lettres écrites de la montagne*, in *O.C.* III, 812.

23. Subtitled *Essai sur les idées politiques et religieuses de Rousseau dans leur relation avec la pensée genevoise au XVIIIe siècle* (Paris: Boivin, 1934). Spink reviews the work of earlier writers who stressed Geneva's influence in the conclusion to Part I, pp. 83–86.

24. See especially pp. 86–90.

ONE. CHILD OF THE ENLIGHTENMENT

1. Robert R. Palmer, *The Age of the Democratic Revolution: A Political History of Europe and America, 1760–1800* (Princeton, N.J.: Princeton University Press, 1959), I, 27–52.

2. J. R. Pole, *Political Representation in England and the Origins of the American Republic* (New York: St. Martin's, 1966), pp. 395–401. For a description of the various categories of the franchise in England, see *The Eighteenth-Century Constitution, 1688–1815: Documents and Commentary*, edited by E. Neville Williams (Cambridge, England: Cambridge University Press, 1960), pp. 152–154.

3. Palmer, I, 33–39.

4. Rousseau used this distinction throughout his political writings and defined it explicitly in *Contrat social* I, 6: "The public person thus formed by the union of all other persons was once called the *city*, and is now known as the *republic* or *body politic*. In its passive role it is called the *state*, when it plays an active role it is the *sovereign*; and when it is compared to others of its own kind, it is a *power*. Those who are associated in it take collectively the name of *a people*, and call themselves individually *citizens*, in so far as they share in the sovereign power, and *subjects*, in so far as they put themselves under the laws of the state." *O.C.* III, 361–362; Cranston trans., pp. 61–62.

5. Franklin L. Ford, *Robe and Sword: The Regrouping of the French Aristocracy after Louis XIV* (1953; rpt. New York: Harper and Row, 1965), pp. 193–197. Cf. Palmer, I, 41–42.

6. Christopher Hill, *Reformation to Industrial Revolution* (Baltimore: Penguin, 1969), pp. 217–218; J. H. Plumb, *England in the Eighteenth Century (1714–1815)* (Baltimore: Penguin, 1969), pp. 37–40.

7. Eberhard Schmitt, *Repräsentation und Revolution. Eine Untersuchung zur Genesis der kontinentalen Theorie und Praxis parlamentarischer Repräsentation aus der Herrschaftspraxis des Ancien régime in Frankreich (1760–1789)* (München: Verlag C. H. Beck, 1969), pp. 89–103.

8. Palmer, I, 31, 38–39.

9. Schmitt, pp. 103–113.

10. Franz Neumann, "Introduction" to *The Spirit of the Laws*, trans. by Thomas Nugent (New York: Hafner, 1949), I, xix–xxix.

11. Palmer, I, 96.

12. See especially *Contrat social* II, 8–10.

13. Vaughan heavily stresses Montesquieu's influence and sees in it the explanation for the somewhat incongruous relativism of sections of the *Contrat social* and later writings (Vaughan, I, 71–86). Derathé concurs with Vaughan's view in "Montesquieu et Jean-Jacques Rousseau," *Revue internationale de philosophie*, IX (1955), p. 377, but stresses more than Vaughan does the incompatibility of much of Rousseau's political thought with what he apparently borrowed from Montesquieu.

14. *Contrat social* III, 4, in *O.C.* III, 404–406.

15. Derathé, "Montesquieu et Jean-Jacques Rousseau," pp. 370–371.

16. *The Spirit of the Laws*, I, 154.

17. *Contrat social* III, 15, in *O.C.* III, 430.

18. *The Spirit of the Laws*, I, 154–155.

19. It is interesting that Montesquieu here favored the modern concept of the

representative and Rousseau the corporate concept with regard to the *mandat impéra-tif*. This is less surprising than it might appear. It is clear that Rousseau favored a mandate system because he wanted to prevent representatives from usurping the sovereignty of the citizen body as a whole. Montesquieu did not see this as a problem, because he envisoned a system of corporate representation in which all members of any given estate would naturally express more or less the same interest.

20. *The Spirit of the Laws,* I, 155.

21. *O.C.* III, 1002.

22. *The Spirit of the Laws,* I, 155.

23. Whereas for Montesquieu the nobility was the backbone of a stable political order, Rousseau compared nobles to a troop of valets. See Rousseau's *Fragments politiques* in *O.C.* III, 552–553.

24. Daniel Mornet, *Les origines intellectuelles de la Révolution française* (1715–1787), 5th ed. (Paris: Armand Colin, 1954), p. 32.

25. Henri Sée, *L'Évolution de la pensée politique en France au XVIIIe siècle* (Paris: Marcel Giard, 1925), p. 123.

26. Peter Gay, *Voltaire's Politics: The Poet as Realist* (New York: Vintage Books, 1965), pp. 329–330. Gay recounts Voltaire's involvement in the debate over the *thèse royale* and *thèse nobiliaire* in a section entitled "Voltaire Against the Nobility," pp. 87–116.

27. Theodore Besterman, *Voltaire* (New York: Harcourt, Brace and World, 1969), p. 306.

28. "Letter to M. le Marquis de Mirabeau, July 26, 1767," in *Citizen of Geneva: Selections from the Letters of Jean-Jacques Rousseau,* ed. by Charles W. Hendel (New York: Oxford University Press, 1937), pp. 350–353. Robert Derathé has noted that Rousseau's criticism of the phrase *despotisme légal* was probably misplaced since the Physiocrats distinguished between *despotisme arbitraire,* which is what the term *despotisme* meant to Rousseau, and their own *despotisme légal,* by which they meant absolute power limited by natural law. "Les philosophes et le despotisme," in *Utopie et institutions au XVIIIe siècle: le pragmatisme des Lumières,* ed. by Pierre Francastel (Paris, Mouton, 1963), pp. 72–75.

29. Georges Weulersee, *La physiocratie à la fin du règne de Louis XV* (1770–1774) (Paris: Presses Universitaires de France, 1959), pp. 97–100, 217–225.

30. John Lough, *The Encyclopédie* (London: Longman, 1971), pp. 274–275.

31. Arthur M. Wilson, *Diderot* (New York: Oxford University Press, 1972), pp. 480–485.

32. *Ibid.,* pp. 490–491. Paul Vernière, in his introduction to Diderot's *Oeuvres politiques* (Paris: Garnier, 1963), p. 26, also describes Diderot as an advocate of limited monarchy. Henri Sée, on the other hand, characterizes Diderot's political thought as "profoundly democratic," presumably because of Diderot's desire to reduce some of the more glaring social inequalities of the *ancien régime* (see, pp. 190–197).

33. Lough, *The Encyclopédie,* p. 312. Vernière includes the article "Représentants" in his edition of Diderot's *Oeuvres politiques* but notes that recently discovered evidence indicates that d'Holbach may have been the author. In any event, he sees the political views of d'Holbach and Diderot as very similar (Vernière, p. 25). Arthur M. Wilson agrees that d'Holbach was the author in "The Development and Scope of Diderot's Political Thought," *Studies on Voltaire and the Eighteenth Century,*

27 (1963), 1871–1900. Eberhard Weis identifies Diderot as the author of "Représentants" in his *Geschichtsschreibung und Staatsauffassung in der französischen Enzyklopädie* (Wiesbaden: Franz Steiner Verlag, 1956), pp. 47–49, and Schmitt, who relies heavily on Weis's analysis of the *Encylopédie*, also follows Weis in attributing authorship to Diderot rather than to d'Holbach (Schmitt, pp. 114–128). D'Holbach is not mentioned in Rousseau's political writings, but Rousseau made clear his distrust and dislike of this wealthy nobleman in his *Confessions* (*O.C.* I, 371, 381–387, 491–493), where he dubbed his former Encyclopedist friends as the Holbachian clique ("la coterie holbachique").

34. Lough, *The Encyclopédie*, p. 313.

35. *The Encyclopédie of Diderot and d'Alembert: Selected Articles*, ed. by John Lough (Cambridge: Cambridge University Press, 1954), p. 197.

36. *Ibid.*, pp. 198–199.

37. *Ibid.*, p. 200.

38. *Ibid.*, pp. 200–203.

39. *Contrat social* I, 4, in *O.C.* III, 357; III, 15, in *O.C.* III, 430.

40. *The Encyclopédie of Diderot and d'Alembert*, pp. 204–208.

41. *Ibid.*, pp. 208–209.

42. D'Holbach was somewhat more emphatic on this point in two treatises published after the article "Représentants." In his *Système sociale, ou Principes naturels de la morale et de la politique* (Londres: 1773), II, 52, he concluded a discussion of representatives by insisting that each estate instruct its deputies to the "Assemblée Nationale" or Estates General. He made this same point in his discussion of representatives in *La politique naturelle, ou Discours sur les vrais principes du gouvernement* (Londres: 1773), I, 177–182.

43. *The Encyclopédie of Diderot and d'Alembert*, p. 209.

44. Rousseau's account in the *Confessions* appears in *O.C.* I, 404–405. For a more detailed account of the *Institutions politiques*, cf. Derathé, *Rousseau et la science politique*, pp. 52–62.

45. *Préface à Narcisse*, in *O.C.* II, 962.

46. François Bouchardy argues that the experience of Vincennes was an important event in the evolution of Rousseau's thought because it brought together a set of ideas that had previously seemed unrelated. *O.C.* III, xxxi–xxxiii. For Rousseau's description of this event as a kind of divine revelation, see his *Confessions*, *O.C.* I, 350–351.

47. Bouchardy, in *O.C.* III, xxxiii. Havens argues that "Dans ce premier *Discours* se trouvent en germe presque toutes les idées caractéristiques de Rousseau: la vertu plus importante que le savoir, la réforme de l'éducation, l'hostilité envers le luxe et l'inégalité, l'amour des temps primitifs, les menaces de corruption et de ruine qui pèsent sur la société. Jean-Jacques n'avait pas tort de voir dans cet ouvrage le commencement de son 'grand système.' C'est ce qui explique en partie l'extraordinaire intérêt que, malgré ses faiblesses, nous y trouvons encore." George R. Havens, ed., *Discours sur les sciences et les arts* (New York: MLAA, 1946), p. 88. This somewhat exaggerates the importance of the work. If one considers what is omitted from Havens's list, especially the distinctively Rousseauist political ideas omitted from the list—and from the *Discours* as well—it quickly becomes apparent that many basic concepts of Rousseau's thought did not make their appearance in this initial effort. Sovereignty, the general will, the social contract, the importance of primary as-

semblies and other city-state institutions—none of these was dealt with, and there is little reason to believe that he had yet seriously confronted these issues. His use of the term *sovereign* (*souverain*) in the traditional sense of a monarch (*O.C.* III, 26) is just one example of the distance his political thought and terminology still had to travel.

48. Havens, pp. 60–61.

49. *O.C.* III, 43. The critic to whom Rousseau was responding was d'Alembert, who had challenged several of Rousseau's arguments or assertions in a firm but friendly manner in his *Discours préliminaire à l'Encyclopédie*.

50. *O.C.* III, 26.

51. *O.C.* III, 1. Bouchardy notes that Rousseau adopted the title "Citizen of Geneva" in his letter to Voltaire, January 30, 1750, to distinguish himself from Jean-Baptiste Rousseau of Paris and Pierre Rousseau of Toulouse but adds that he may also have wanted to identify himself with his native Geneva. *O.C.* III, 1239.

52. *O.C.* III, 7. Havens notes that it was quite natural for Rousseau to identify with France and the French since he had lived the greater part of his life outside Switzerland. Havens, p. 182.

53. *O.C.* III, 11. Cf. Bouchardy's notes, *O.C.* III, 1245.

54. *O.C.* III, 20. Rousseau commented on these indirect references to Switzerland in *Observations de Jean-Jacques Rousseau de Genève*, where he responded to the accusation that he had mentioned only ancient examples of virtue in the first *Discours*; Rousseau claimed he had been able to discover only one modern people that qualified for that honor. *O.C.* III, 42. Cf. Bouchardy's note, *O.C.* III, 1260.

55. Jean Starobinski, in *O.C.* III, xlii–xliii.

56. *O.C.* III, 184; *The First and Second Discourses*, edited, with introduction and notes by Roger D. Masters, trans. by Roger D. and Judith R. Masters (New York: St. Martin's, 1964), pp. 168–169.

57. Derathé distinguishes three phases in the development of Rousseau's thought regarding the *pacte de soumission:* the above-quoted passage from the *Discours sur l'inégalité* was the first phase, and Books I and III of the *Contrat social* were, respectively, the second and third phases. Only in Book III of the *Contrat social* did Rousseau formally reject the pact of submission (*Rousseau et la science politique*, pp. 222–223). Starobinski concurs in Derathé's explanation of the passage from the second *Discours* (*O.C.* III, 1355–1356).

58. *O.C.* III, 184–185; Masters trans., p. 169.

59. Masters, *The Political Philosophy of Rousseau*, pp. 189–191.

60. René Hubert, *Rousseau et l'Encyclopédie: essai sur la formation des idées politiques de Rousseau* (1742–1756) (Paris: Gamber, 1928), pp. 21–26, 51–66.

61. Jean Guéhenno suggests that Rousseau completed it in Geneva in the fall of 1754 (*Jean-Jacques Rousseau*, trans. by John and Doreen Weightman (New York: Columbia University Press, 1967), I, 310). Derathé admits that Hubert may be right in his dating of the work but seems to prefer the view that Rousseau wrote it after his return to Paris in October 1754 (*O.C.* III, lxxiii). Hendel insists on this later date, mainly because he sees abundant evidence of a close collaboration between Rousseau and Diderot that he thinks could have occurred only in Paris and only after Rousseau's trip to Geneva (*Jean-Jacques Rousseau: Moralist*, I, 92–98).

62. *O.C.* III, 247–254; *The Social Contract and Discourses*, trans. with an introduction by G. D. H. Cole (New York: Dutton, 1950), pp. 294–301.

63. Saint-Lambert's article "Législateur" is summarized and quoted at length in Lough, *The Encyclopédie*, pp. 304–309.

64. Rousseau presents his tax policies in *O.C.* III, 258–259, 262–278. For the Encyclopedist view on taxation, including a summary of Jaucourt's article "Impôts," see Lough, *The Encyclopédie*, pp. 371–382. Lough surveys Encyclopedist opinion on social inequality and poverty on pp. 382–387.

65. *O.C.* III, 258; Cole trans., p. 305.

66. Merle L. Perkins sees this emphasis on the role of government as the most distinctive feature of *Économie politique* and accordingly entitles the chapter in which he discusses this work "The Enlightened Prince." *Jean-Jacques Rousseau on the Individual and Society* (Lexington: University of Kentucky Press, 1974), Chapter 4, pp. 115–147.

67. *O.C.* III, 250–251.

68. Cf. Derathé's note, *O.C.* III, 1396. Hubert observes that Rousseau's attitude toward primary assemblies in *Économie politique* is just one more indication of the continuing influence of the Encyclopedists (pp. 110–111).

69. *O.C.* III, 265; Cole trans., p. 314.

70. *O.C.* III, 270; Cole trans., p. 320.

71. *Two Treatises of Government*, ed. by Peter Laslett. Rev. ed. (New York: Cambridge University Press, 1963), Chapter 11, paragraph 134, p. 401. Derathé quotes the same passage from the French translation of the treatise, *Essai sur le gouvernement civil*, which Rousseau probably used (*O.C.* III, 1406).

72. *O.C.* III, 269–270; Cole trans., p. 320. Elsewhere in *Économie politique* Rousseau declared that "the right of property is the most sacred of all the rights of citizens, and more important in certain respects than liberty itself." *O.C.* III, 262–263; Cole trans., p. 311. This thoroughly Lockean conception of property does not fit well with Rousseau's usual view, discussed above, that private property is definitely subordinate to the needs of the state, which, moreover, should assume an active role in reducing excessive inequalities in property. Cf. Derathé's comments, *O.C.* III, 1402–1403.

73. *Two Treatises of Government*, Chapter 11, paragraph 138, p. 406.

74. *Ibid.*, Chapter 11, paragraph 140, p. 408. Derathé quotes this passage from the French translation in *O.C.* III, 1406.

74. *O.C.* III, 270; Cole trans., p. 320.

76. *O.C.* III, 1406.

77. See Rousseau's *Oeuvres complètes*, introduction, présentation et notes de Michel Launay (Paris: Éditions du Seuil, 1971), II, 303–304. The Lockean influence of this passage was pointed out long ago by Vaughan, who observed that "Rousseau, still under the influence of Locke, does not here reject the representative system as he does in the *Contrat social* (III.XV.)" (Vaughan, I, 266). Derathé agrees with Vaughan's comment regarding Rousseau's acceptance of representative government, although he differs with other aspects of Vaughan's interpretation of this passage (*Rousseau et la science politique*, pp. 115–116).

78. *O.C.* III, 277–278; Cole trans., pp. 329–330.

79. To give an idea of what he meant by luxury items, he proposed that "Heavy taxes should be laid on servants in livery, on equipages, rich furniture, fine clothes, on spacious courts and gardens, on public entertainments of all kinds, on useless professions, such as dancers, singers, players, and in a word, on all that multiplicity

of objects of luxury, amusement, and idleness, which strike the eyes of all, and can the less be hidden, as their whole purpose is to be seen, without which they would be useless." *O.C.* III, 276; Cole trans., p. 328.
80. *O.C.* III, 278.

Two. Reborn Genevan

1. Guglielmo Ferrero, "Genève et le Contrat social," *Annales de la Société Jean-Jacques Rousseau*, 23 (1934), 137–152; Palmer, I, 36; Gay, *Voltaire's Politics*, p. 190. Michel Launay cites recent studies of Geneva's population in the eighteenth century, which suggest somewhat higher figures for the number of *citoyens* and *bourgeois*, ranging from a high of 4,000 to a low of 1,500. Launay notes that if the higher figure is accurate, *citoyens* and *bourgeois* together with their families constituted a majority of the total population of Geneva. Even the lower figure of 1,500, when taken as 1,500 heads of families, suggests that *citoyens* and *bourgeois* were at least a substantial minority of the total population. *Jean-Jacques Rousseau écrivain politique (1712–1762)* (Cannes; C.E.L.; Grenoble: A.C.E.R., 1971), pp. 34–36.

2. Spink, *Jean-Jacques Rousseau et Genève*, pp. 9–11. Launay suggests a similar threefold class division that differs in terminology and to some extent in substance: (1) the upper class (*la classe du haut*), composed of the great, the rich, and the politically powerful, and including, according to Rousseau, nearly all priests, pastors, and writers; (2) the middle class (*la classe du milieu*), composed of artisans, especially watch and clock makers, and constituting, again according to Rousseau, the political, economic, and moral backbone of Geneva; (3) the lower class (*l'état du bas, la populace, la canaille*), composed of manual workers, mercenaries, poor peasants, valets and lackeys, apprentices and journeymen who were not the inheritors of a master artisan, beggars, the unemployed, and, in general, the Lumpenproletariat (Launay, *Rousseau écrivain politique*, pp. 29–30).

3. E. William Monter, *Calvin's Geneva* (New York: Wiley, 1967), pp. 29–63; Edouard Favre and Paul-F. Geisendorf, "Les combourgeoisies avec Fribourg et Berne," in *Histoire de Genève des origines à 1789* (Genève: Jullien, 1951), pp. 171–186; Henri Naef, "L'émancipation politique et la Réforme," in *Histoire de Genève des origines à 1789, pp.* 187–217.

4. Henry Fazy, *Les constitutions de la République de Genève* (Paris: Librairie Fischbacher, 1890), pp. 42–60; also Monter, pp. 64–92.

5. This account is based on Fazy, pp. 1–97, and on the relevant chapters of the *Histoire de Genève des origines à 1789*, pp. 402–412; Fazy, pp. 98–107; Spink, pp. 13–15. *franchises* confirmed by Adhémar Fabri in "De la féodalité à la communauté," pp. 132–133; Frédéric Gardy describes Geneva's political institutions in the fifteenth century in "Genève au xve siècle," pp. 140–143; Eugène Choisy discusses the Edicts of 1543 and Calvin's role in their preparation in "La Réforme calvinienne," pp. 240–243. Spink's account of this period differs in some respects. He agrees that the Conseil Général played a preponderant role in the fifteenth century but not a legislative role, since Geneva was then governed by customary law under the episcopate regime. He also notes that as early as 1460 the Conseil Général chose syndics from a list of candidates nominated by the Petit Conseil (Spink, p. 5).

6. Jean-Pierre Ferrier, "Le xviiie siècle: politique intérieure et extérieure," in *Histoire de Genève des origines à 1789*, pp. 402–412; Fazy, pp. 98–107; Spink, pp. 13–15. The text of Second Syndic Jean-Robert Chouet's speech has been reprinted with an

introduction by W.-A. Liebeskind in "Le discours du syndic Chouet sur la nature du gouvernement de l'Etat de Genève," in *Mélanges d'histoire et de littérature offerts à Monsieur Charles Gilliard* (Lausanne, Switzerland: F. Rouge, 1944), pp. 394–400. Liebeskind interprets Chouet's speech as a plea for representative democracy since Chouet insists that the Conseil Général, although sovereign in principle, had wisely delegated the exercise of sovereignty to the Petit and Grand Conseils. In a sequel to this article, "Un débat sur la démocratie genevoise: Chouet et Fatio au Conseil général (5 mai 1707)," in *Mélanges Georges Sauser-Hall* (Neuchâtel, Switzerland: Delachaux et Niestlé, 1952), pp. 99–107, Liebeskind compares the arguments of Chouet and Fatio and concludes that Chouet was arguing for indirect democracy and Fatio for direct democracy. Rousseau's hostility toward representation may well have originated in response to arguments like those set forth by Chouet.

7. According to Ferrier (p. 413), the Conseil Général voted 780 to 271 to dispense with the requirement for quinquennial meetings. Rousseau, however, argued in the *Lettres écrites de la montagne* that this singular vote had been achieved through illegal procedures and probably through terror and fraud as well (*O.C.* III, 856–857). Fazy agrees with Rousseau, whom he accepts as an authority on this matter as on many others in his interpretation of Genevan history (Fazy, pp. 110–112). Both Rousseau and Fazy consider it unthinkable that a free people could voluntarily surrender one of the cornerstones of its freedom. Spink also thinks this vote may have been fraudulent (Spink, p. 15). Textual confirmation for Rousseau's point of view is provided by Jean-Daniel Candaux in his notes to the *Lettres écrites de la montagne*, in *O.C.* III, 1701–1703.

8. Launay, *Rousseau écrivain politique*, 13–66. Launay strongly emphasizes the importance of life in the Saint-Gervais quarter in the formation of Rousseau's political thought. For a similar view, see Patrick F. O'Mara, "Jean-Jacques and Geneva: the Petty Bourgeois Milieu of Rousseau's Thought," *The Historian* (Feb. 1958), pp. 127–152.

9. Quoted in Ferrier, p. 420.

10. Ferrier, p. 420. Jean-Jacques Burlamaqui was an older contemporary of Rousseau, a professor of law at the University of Geneva and the semi-official theorist of the Genevan constitution during the eighteenth century. His *Principes du droit politique*—which, incidentally, was the subtitle of Rousseau's *Contrat social*—was published in 1751, i.e., at precisely the right time to have maximum impact on Rousseau, whose political thought was in ferment at that time. This circumstantial evidence for Burlamaqui's influence on Rousseau prompted a number of late nineteenth- and early twentieth-century scholars, among them Émile Faguet, Gustave Lanson, Charles Borgeaud, Georges Beaulavon, and Gaspard Vallette, to identify Burlamaqui as a principal source of Rousseau's political thought. This view was been challenged by more recent scholarship. Bernard Gagnebin admits that Rousseau may have borrowed a few phrases from Burlamaqui but argues that Rousseau borrowed few political concepts and that Burlamaqui had himself borrowed most of these from Pufendorf. On such fundamentals as their conceptions of the state of nature, the social contract, and sovereignty, the two Genevan political theorists were in marked disagreement. *Burlamaqui et le droit naturel* (Genève: Éditions de la Frégate, 1944), Chapter 5, "Jean-Jacques Burlamaqui et Jean-Jacques Rousseau," pp. 252–269. Derathé relies heavily on Gagnebin in his own analysis of Burlamaqui's influence on

Rousseau (*Rousseau et la science politique*, pp. 84–89). Among their other differences, Burlamaqui was an avowed supporter of representative government (see Ray Forrest Harvey, *Jean-Jacques Burlamaqui: a Liberal Tradition in American Constitutionalism* [Chapel Hill: University of North Carolina Press, 1937], p. 37).

Rousseau's only reference to Burlamaqui by name appears in the preface to the *Discours sur l'inégalité*, where he invoked the jurist's authority in support of the banal assertion that the idea of law is relative to the nature of man (*O.C.* III, 124). It is probable that Rousseau had Burlamaqui in mind on several occasions when he criticized the school of natural law, most notably when he attacked the notion of the divisibility of sovereignty in the *Contrat social* (*O.C.* III, 369). Burlamaqui strongly favored the distribution of the attributes of sovereignty among several different persons or corporate bodies to achieve a kind of balance of powers. As Derathé notes, Rousseau vehemently opposed this idea in the *Contrat social* by insisting on the indivisibility of sovereignty (*O.C.* III, 1455 and 1483).

11. Spink, pp. 17–18.

12. Ferrier, pp. 429–430.

13. François d'Ivernois, *An Historical and Political View of the Constitution and Revolutions of Geneva in the Eighteenth Century*, trans. from the French by John Farrell (Dublin: Wilson, 1784), pp. 75–76.

14. Ferrier, pp. 414–416. One of these supporters was Toussaint-Pierre Lenieps, who became a banker in Paris and was one of Rousseau's closest Genevan friends during his residence in France. *O.C.* III, 1441–1442.

15. Ferrier, pp. 429–440.

16. *Ibid.*, pp. 440–442.

17. Spink, pp. 26–29.

18. *O.C.* II, 1129. Cf. Launay's analysis of this poem in *Rousseau écrivain politique*, pp. 82–86.

19. Spink makes the same point in the course of emphasizing Rousseau's ignorance of the Genevan constitution prior to his return to Geneva in 1754. Rousseau's ignorance was widely shared by the bourgeoisie who participated in the political struggles of the 1730s. Even after 1754 Rousseau continued to share De Luc's false conception and idealization of the Genevan constitution and to reject the views of Micheli and his friend Lenieps, who almost alone among the bourgeoisie had penetrated to the realities of the constitution. Spink, pp. 30–39.

20. Among the items in his inheritance was a copy of the pamphlet that Micheli du Crest had written in 1728 criticizing the system of fortifications. Rousseau found much to praise in the work but had mixed feelings about Micheli himself, whom he described as "a man of great talent, learning, and enlightenment" but "too revolutionary" (*Confessions*, in *O.C.* I, 216–217). Ivernois rendered an equally mixed judgment on the legendary Pierre Fatio, whom he reproached for being too impetuous and having excessive confidence in the understanding and constancy of his contemporaries. "*Fatio* was too eager to reform the constitution of his country; his design proved abortive, because he strove to compleat the reform at once, and his fellow citizens lost not only their most illustrious defender, but, soon after, the most precious advantages he had obtained for them" (Ivernois, pp. 54–55).

21. *Confessions*, in *O.C.* I, 215. In a letter to Madame de Warens written in late July 1737, Rousseau spoke with obvious pride and perhaps some exaggeration of the

warm reception accorded him by La Closure, who had received him "le plus gracieusement et j'ose dire le plus familiérement du monde." *Correspondance complète de Jean-Jacques Rousseau,* edited by R. A. Leigh (Genève: 1965), I, 45.

22. *O.C.* I, 215–216.

23. *O.C.* I, 392; *The Confessions of Jean-Jacques Rousseau,* trans. by J. M. Cohen (1953; rpt. Baltimore: Penguin, 1971), p. 365.

24. *Confessions,* in *O.C.* I, 393–396. Brief biological sketches of each of the acquaintances mentioned are provided in *O.C.* I, 1456–1459. The information about the taxes is supplied in a note, *O.C.* I, 1456. For more detailed accounts of Rousseau's activities during this visit to Geneva, see Guéhenno, I, 306–313, and Gaspard Vallette, *Jean-Jacques Rousseau Genevois* (Paris: Plon-Nourrit; Genève: Jullien, 1911), pp. 85–96. As Vallette aptly remarks, by this visit Rousseau became doubly Genevan, once by birth and now by choice (Vallette, p. 96). His attachment to Geneva, or to the ideal he associated with Geneva, was in some ways correspondingly more intense than it would have been if he had never left his native city.

25. Rousseau's letter to Perdriau, 28 November 1754, in *Correspondance compléte,* III, 55–60.

26. *Correspondance complète,* III, 63.

27. *Ibid.,* pp. 136–137.

28. This is in part the explanation suggested by Guéhenno, I, 304.

29. Vallette, pp. 97, 241–242, and Masters, p. 230 of his translation of the second *Discours,* among others, stress the fact that Rousseau addressed the citizens as sovereign lords and the magistrates only as honored lords and thus emphasized the subordinate position of the magistrates. It is quite possible, however, that Rousseau meant no more by this distinction than many other writers on Geneva's constitutional history, including some patricians, who accepted the sovereignty of the Conseil Général in principle but knew that it was not sovereign in reality.

30. Rousseau's letter to Chouet, June 4, 1755, and Chouet's letter to Rousseau, June 18, 1755, are both included in the *Correspondance complète,* III, 132–134.

31. Rousseau's letter to Chouet, July 20, 1755, in *Correspondance complète,* III, 143.

32. *Confessions,* in *O.C.* I, 395.

33. E.g., Vallette, pp. 96–98, and Guéhenno, I, 316, 320.

34. *Confessions,* in *O.C.* I, 395.

35. See the views of Gagnebin and Raymond in their notes to the *Confessions,* in *O.C.* I, 1450; also Spink, pp. 42–43.

36. See his letters to Madame Dupin and Lenieps, both written in July 1754, in which he declared his eagerness to return to Paris. *Correspondance complète,* III, 13, 16.

37. Spink, p. 32, makes this point in reference to the 1740s, but his insight is equally applicable to the time when Rousseau wrote the *Dédicace* and probably even later. Cf. Jean Terrasse, *Jean-Jacques Rousseau et la quête de l'âge d'or* (Bruxelles: Palais des Académies, 1970), pp. 123–124.

38. *O.C.* III, 111–121; Masters trans., pp. 78–90.

39. *O.C.* III, 116–117; Masters trans., p. 85.

40. *O.C.* III, 117–118. Cf. Starobinski's note, *O.C.* III, 1291.

41. Characteristics 1–4, 6–7, 10, and 12 were unlikely to arouse controversy, and characteristic 13 was not controversial in principle, although many Genevans might

have found it difficult to respect individual magistrates. Characteristic 8 was probably untrue and recognized as such by most Genevans, although the treaty signed with the Kingdom of Sardinia in June 1754 may have led many to agree with Rousseau that Geneva was henceforth free from foreign entanglement. Whatever the appearances, the reality was that Geneva was heavily dependent on foreign powers. The constitution under which the city was governed in 1754 was the direct result of the intervention of France, Zurich, and Bern in 1737–1738, and the same three powers would be called on again in the 1760s to settle Geneva's domestic quarrels.

42. Mario Einaudi, one of the few commentators who stresses Rousseau's position on the legislative initiative in his discussion of the *Dédicace*, does not relate what Rousseau says about it to the Genevan political controversies of the eighteenth century. Einaudi argues that Rousseau, recognizing the revolutionary implications of the sweeping grant of legislative powers he had made to the people, wanted to reassure his readers that he understood the importance of carefully drafting and presenting new laws (Einaudi, pp. 160–162). In reality, it is unlikely that Rousseau intended anything more by this assertion than the moderate bourgeoisie and even some patricians did who made similar sweeping assertions; none of them, including Rousseau, intended that ordinary citizens should have sweeping legislative powers.

43. *O.C.* III, 112; Masters trans., p. 79.

44. *Contrat social* II, 2, in *O.C.* III, 369.

THREE. THE YEARS OF WITHDRAWAL

1. Sven Stelling-Michaud, "Écrits sur l'abbé de Saint-Pierre," *O.C.* III, cxx–cxxxi. Stelling-Michaud elaborates on Rousseau's debt to Saint-Pierre in "Ce que Jean-Jacques doit à l'abbé de Saint-Pierre," in *Études sur Contrat social de Jean-Jacques Rousseau*, pp. 34–45. For another comparison of the political ideas of Saint-Pierre and Rousseau, see Merle L. Perkins, *The Moral and Political Philosophy of the Abbé de Saint-Pierre* (Genève: Droz, 1959), Chapter 8, "The Political Theories of Saint-Pierre and Rousseau," pp. 97–133. Perkins emphasizes Rousseau's debt to the abbé, not only with regard to his theory of international relations but also with regard to his theory of democratic sovereignty.

2. Saint-Pierre's proposal for European confederation and Rousseau's critique of that proposal will be discussed in Chapter 6 in conjunction with Rousseau's suggestion, at the end of *Contrat social* III, 15, that confederation provides a solution to the problem of maintaining sovereignty vis-à-vis other states while relying on primary assemblies for legislation, which presupposes a small state. The dates of composition of Rousseau's extracts and critiques of Saint-Pierre's writings are uncertain. Vaughan contends that the *Extrait de la Paix Perpétuelle* and the *Extrait de la Polysynodie*, as well as Rousseau's *Jugements* on these two works, were completed in 1756 (Vaughan, I, 359 ff.), but Stelling-Michaud argues that Rousseau did not complete all four pieces until as late as 1758 or 1759 (*O.C.* III, cxxiv–cxxvi, cxxxii, cxlvi–cxlvii).

3. *Polysynodie*, in *O.C.* III, 617–634.

4. *Jugement sur la Polysynodie*, in *O.C.* III, 635–645. Rousseau's objections to Saint-Pierre's plans could well be made against his own argument in the *Contrat social*, Book II, Chapter 3, "Si la volonté générale peut errer," where he argues, very much as Saint-Pierre argued in *Polysynodie*, that the general will is what is left over after private interests have canceled each other (*O.C.* III, 371).

5. Hendel, I, 223–225.

6. *O.C.* III, 637–644.

7. Bernard Guyon, *O.C.* II, xx.

8. For a brief analysis of the political significance of *La Nouvelle Héloïse,* see Michel Launay, *"La Nouvelle Héloïse,* son contenu et son public," in *Jean-Jacques Rousseau et son temps: politique et littérature au XVIIIᵉ siècle,* by Michel Launay and others (Paris: A.-G. Nizet, 1969), pp. 179–184. *La Nouvelle Héloïse* also figures prominently in Judith Shklar's *Men and Citizens,* which includes a brief summary of the work in an appendix, pp. 232–234.

9. Letter XXIII of Part I, in *O.C.* II, 76–84.

10. *Confessions,* in *O.C.* I, 324.

11. *Ibid.,* p. 394. Cf. Guyon's note, *O.C.* II, 1387.

12. *Correspondance complète,* III, 249–250.

13. *O.C.* II, 79–81.

14. In *Contrat social* III, 4, Rousseau dismisses direct democracy as a utopian form of government (*O.C.* III, 404–406), but in Book IV, Chapter 1, he refers favorably to what appears to be a direct democracy like that of the Haut-Valais: "When we see among the happiest people in the world bands of peasants regulating the affairs of state under an oak tree, and always acting wisely, can we help feeling a certain contempt for the refinements of other nations, which employ so much skill and mystery to make themselves at once illustrious and wretched?" (*O.C.* III, 437; Cranston trans., p. 149).

15. The decline of the way of life of Swiss mountaineers like those of the Haut-Valais is the subject of Benjamin R. Barber's *The Death of Communal Liberty: A History of Freedom in a Swiss Mountain Canton* (Princeton, N.J.: Princeton University Press, 1974). Much of what Barber says about direct democracy in the communes of the Graubünden also applies to the Valaisans. As Barber notes in his introduction, Rousseau is "an invisible presence throughout our study" (p. 16).

16. Shklar treats Rousseau's account of life in the Haut-Valais as one of two alternative utopias, the other being the city-state republic exemplified by ancient Sparta or modern Geneva. While it is clear that Rousseau regarded the Haut-Valais as a utopia, i.e., as a political and social system beyond the reach of moderns, it is not at all clear that he considered the Spartan or Genevan ideal as similarly utopian, especially in Shklar's sense of the term, i.e., as a device for criticizing his contemporaries rather than a model for them to imitate and transform into reality. Prior to Geneva's condemnation of the *Contrat social* and *Émile,* Rousseau believed that Geneva fairly closely approximated the ideal political system he presented in the *Contrat social* and thought that other peoples could study it with profit. In contrast, he never believed that the primitive political and social system of the Haut-Valais could be widely imitated, and even recognized that it had already begun its inevitable decline.

17. Cf. Guyon, *O.C.* II, 1388–1390.

18. *O.C.* II, 231–306.

19. *O.C.* II, 657–663. Guyon finds it odd that Rousseau should have added this account of Geneva so late in the novel—it was written after his *Lettre à d'Alembert*—and odder still that Rousseau should have been "cold, dry, even severe" toward Geneva so soon after praising it to the skies in his defense of his native city against d'Alembert's article in the *Encyclopédie* (*O.C.* II, 1752–1753). It is true that Rousseau

was critical of his fellow countrymen in Claire's letter (insofar as her views can be taken as those of Rousseau), especially for their obsessive concern with making money, but he remained a fervent admirer of Geneva's political system and its government. To cite just one example of this praise, Claire found more talent in the government of the little republic of Geneva than in that of vast empires, meaning France (O.C. II, 658). It seems to me that Guyon somewhat exaggerates Rousseau's criticism of his fellow Genevans and thereby sees a more radical change from the *Lettre à d'Alembert* than is warranted.

20. For a more detailed analysis of these passages, see Launay, *Rousseau écrivain politique*, pp. 282–288.

21. *Lettre à d'Alembert*, edited by M. Fuchs (Lillie, France: Librairie Giard; Genève: Librairie Droz, 1948), pp. 80–87; *Politics and the Arts: Letter to M. d'Alembert on the Theatre*, trans. with notes and introduction by Allan Bloom (1960; rpt. Ithaca, N.Y.: Cornell University Press, 1968), pp. 60–64.

22. *Confessions*, in *O.C.* I, 153.

23. *Lettre à d'Alembert*, Fuchs edition, pp. 80–86.

24. François Jost, *Jean-Jacques Rousseau Suisse* (Fribourg, Switzerland: Éditions Universitaires, 1961), I, 77–78. Jost, whose central thesis is that Rousseau's political and social thought was distinctly Swiss as well as Genevan, stresses that both Neuchâtel and Geneva, although not at that time part of the Helvetic Confederation, were nevertheless perceived by contemporaries as Swiss.

25. *O.C.* I, 495.

26. Vallette, pp. 134–135, 440. Elsewhere, however, Vallette describes the *Lettres écrites de la montagne* as "peut-être l'oeuvre la plus genevoise de Jean-Jacques Rousseau" (p. 325). Hendel describes the *Lettre à d'Alembert* as "a complete portrayal of the constitution and life of the people of Geneva, an ampler version of what he had sketched in the *Dedication* to his *Discourse on Inequality*" (Hendel, II, 7).

27. Fuchs, introduction to the *Lettre à d'Alembert*, pp. vii–xvii.

28. Du Pan's argument is quoted in Launay, *Rousseau écrivain politique*, p. 333.

29. Fuchs, introduction to the *Lettre à d'Alembert*, pp. xl–xli. See also Herbert Lüthy, *From Calvin to Rousseau: Tradition and Modernity in Socio-Political Thought from the Reformation to the French Revolution*, trans. from the French by Salvator Attanasio (New York: Basic, 1970), pp. 216–217, 267–268.

30. Launay, *Rousseau écrivain politique*, pp. 333–334. The text of De Luc's "Remarques de J. F. de Luc sur l'article *Genève* dans *l'Encyclopédie*, qui traite de la Comédie et des Comédiens," can be found in Fuchs' edition of the *Lettre à d'Alembert*, pp. 191–194.

31. *Lettre à d'Alembert*, pp. 86–87, 152–155.

32. Rousseau does not specify the time when the *cercles* replaced the *sociétés*, saying only that they arose during a time of civil unrest, but there is little doubt that he had in mind the period of unrest from 1734 to 1738. Most historians date the origin of the *cercles* to 1734, which is consistent with Rousseau's account. Cf. Launay, *Rousseau écrivain politique*, p. 20.

33. *Lettre à d'Alembert*, p. 136; Bloom trans., p. 101.

34. *Ibid.*, p. 142; Bloom trans., p. 105.

35. *Ibid.*, p. 173; Bloom trans., p. 129.

36. *Ibid.*, pp. 178–179; Bloom trans., p. 133.

37. *Ibid.*, pp. 168–182; Bloom trans., pp. 125–136.

38. Launay, *Rousseau écrivain politique*, pp. 19–28, 328–352.

39. Spink, pp. 27–28.

FOUR. THE PRINCIPLES OF POLITICAL RIGHT

1 Vaughan, I, 20.

2. Hubert, *Rousseau et l'Encyclopédie*, pp. 65–66.

3. Derathé, *Rousseau et la science politique*, p. 58.

4. *O.C.* III, lxxxiii–lxxxiv.

5. Geneva Manuscript I, 4, which Derathé calls the most important chapter of the entire manuscript, corresponds to *Contrat social* II, 1, in which Rousseau inserted in the second paragraph his claim that "the sovereign, which is simply a collective being, cannot be represented by anyone but itself—power can be delegated, but the will cannot be." This statement does not appear in the manuscript. Cf. Geneva Manuscript I, 4, *O.C.* III, 295, and *Contrat social* II, 1, *O.C.* III, 368. For Derathé's evaluation of this chapter of the manuscript, see *O.C.* III, 1416.

6. Geneva Manuscript I, 4, *O.C.* III, 295–296; *Contrat social* II, 1, in *O.C.* III, 368–369.

7. Geneva Manuscript I, 6, in *O.C.* III, 307; this passage is repeated in the *Contrat social* II, 4, in *O.C.* III, 374.

8. *O.C.* III, 250–251.

9. Geneva Manuscript I, 7, in *O.C.* III, 310. As if to emphasize the contrast with *Économie politique*, this question is followed by a long paragraph extracted from the earlier work. Cf. *Économie politique*, in *O.C.* III, 248–249; Geneva Manuscript I, 7, in *O.C.* III, 310.

10. Geneva Manuscript II, 2, in *O.C.* III, 315.

11. Geneva Manuscript II, 3, in *O.C.* III, 322.

12. *Ibid.*

13. Geneva Manuscript III, 1, in *O.C.* III, 335; cf. *Contrat social* III, 1, in *O.C.* III, 395.

14. *Confessions*, in *O.C.* I, 516.

15. *Confessions*, in *O.C.* I, 554, 560. Cf. the note by Gagnebin and Raymond to the latter page, *O.C.* I, 1547–1548.

16. Peter D. Jimack discusses the composition of *Émile* in his "La genèse et la rédaction de l'Émile de J.-J. Rousseau," *Studies on Voltaire and the Eighteenth Century*, XIII (Genève: Institut et Musée Voltaire, 1960), pp. 33–43. He argues that Rousseau began the preliminary version of *Émile*, the Favre manuscript, at the end of 1758 or the beginning of 1759 and completed it in November or December 1759. The final version of *Émile* was begun at the end of 1759 and completed in September or October 1760. Book V of *Émile*, which contains the outline of the *Contrat social*, was probably begun in May 1759 and completed in August of the same year.

17. *Émile* V, in *O.C.* IV, 842–843. For the date of the footnote, see *O.C.* IV, 1691.

18. Hendel, II, 171.

19. Hendel contends that the outline of the *Contrat social* in *Émile* was a preliminary sketch of a work yet to be written rather than a summary or extract of a completed work, as Rousseau describes it. Hendel, II, 170–171.

20. *O.C.* IV, 843.

21. This is perhaps the prevalent view. Cf. Gierke, *The Development of Political*

Theory, p. 247; Bloom, "Jean-Jacques Rousseau," p. 543; Derathé, *Rousseau et la science politique,* pp. 267–268.

22. Guéhenno (II, 6–7) suggests that Rousseau began to think of Geneva as a "lost" city following the disappointing reception of his *Lettre à d'Alembert,* which Rousseau attributed to Voltaire's growing influence.

23. *Contrat social* I, 4, in *O.C.* III, 355–356; Cranston trans., pp. 54–55. For the use and misuse that Rousseau makes of the works of Grotius and Hobbes in this chapter, see Derathé's notes in *O.C.* III, 1437–1442.

24. *The Spirit of the Laws,* I, 236. Derathé, who compares the arguments of Montesquieu and Rousseau against voluntary servitude, observes that Rousseau's main purpose in this chapter is to refute the notion of a pact of submission in favor of the thesis that sovereignty belongs only to the people (*O.C.* III, 1439).

25. Rousseau's critique of the natural law theorists is discussed in greater detail in chapter 7.

26. *Contrat social* I, 6, in *O.C.* III, 340; Cranston trans., p. 60. Cf. *Contrat social* II, 4, where Rousseau reiterates this view in the course of summarizing the advantages of the social contract: "So long as the subjects submit to such covenants alone, they obey nobody but their own will." *O.C.* III, 375; Cranston trans., p. 77.

27. Charles Eisenmann makes this criticism of Rousseau in his "La cité de Jean-Jacques Rousseau," in *Études sur le Contrat social de Jean-Jacques Rousseau,* pp. 197–199.

28. *Contrat social* I, 5: "Indeed, if there were no earlier agreement, then how, unless the election were unanimous, could there be any obligation on the minority to accept the decision of the majority? . . . The law of majority voting itself rests on a covenant, and implies that there has been on at least one occasion unanimity." *O.C.* III, 359; Cranston trans., p. 59. Cf. *Contrat social* IV, 2, in *O.C.* III, 440.

29. In a celebrated passage of the *Contrat social,* Rousseau declares that "whoever refuses to obey the general will shall be constrained to do so by the whole body, which means nothing other than that he shall be forced to be free." *Contrat social* I, 7, in *O.C.* III, 364; Cranston trans., p. 64. As Plamenatz notes in a commentary on this passage, this may be a paradoxical or perverse way of making a point, but it is hardly evidence that Rousseau was a traitor to liberty. Plamenatz sees it rather as one of many indications that Rousseau was struggling toward a new concept of freedom, one that he was unable to express clearly but that conceived freedom as a form of self-discipline or obedience to a higher law. Plamenatz, "Ce qui ne signifie autre chose sinon qu'on le forcera d'être libre," in *Rousseau et la philosophie politique,* pp. 137–152.

30. *Contrat social* I, 8, in *O.C.* III, 365; Cranston trans., p. 65. Note, however, that Rousseau is here defining moral freedom, which he distinguishes from natural and civil freedom.

31. *O.C.* III, 440–441; Cranston trans., pp. 153–154.

32. *O.C.* III, 441; Cranston trans., p. 154.

33. *Contrat social* I, 6, in *O.C.* III, 361; Cranston trans., p. 61.

34. The formulation of the Geneva Manuscript was still more explicit on this point: "Each one of us puts into the community his will, his goods, his powers and his person under the direction of the general will, and as a body we incorporate every member as an inalienable part of the whole." Geneva Manuscript I, 3, in *O.C.* III, 290.

35. *Contrat social* II, 1, in *O.C.* III, 368; Cranston trans., p. 69.
36. *Contrat social* III, 15, in *O.C.* III, 429–430; Cranston trans., p. 141.
37. *O.C.* III, 1416 and 1453–1454.
38. Geneva Manuscript I, 4, in *O.C.* III, 294–295.
39. As Derathé notes, Rousseau's arguments against voluntary servitude in *Contrat social* I, 4, which he probably wrote at a relatively late date, amplify and clarify his discussion of sovereignty in *Contrat social* II, 1 (*O.C.* III, 1437).
40. Cf. *Contrat social* I, 7, in *O.C.* III, 363, and II, 1, in *O.C.* III, 368.
41. *Contrat social* II, 4, in *O.C.* III, 373.
42. *Contrat social* II, 2, in *O.C.* III, 369.
43. Cf. Rousseau's footnote to the preceding passage, *O.C.* III, 369.
44. *Contrat social* II, 4, in *O.C.* III, 373.
45. Cf. *Contrat social* II, 6: ". . . when the people as a whole makes rules for the people as a whole, it is dealing only with itself. . . . And *this* is the kind of act which I call a law." *O.C.* III, 379; Cranston trans., p. 81.
46. *Contrat social* II, 2, in *O.C.* III, 369; II, 6, in *O.C.* III, 379.
47. Plamenatz, *Man and Society*, I, 394.
48. Plamenatz concludes his analysis of Rousseau's contention that will cannot be represented as follows: "The dictum is empty or useless or false. Do what you like with it, you will get no pearls of political wisdom out of it. Rousseau, as we shall see, has some strong arguments against representative democracy, but they have nothing to do with anything about the will which makes it incapable of being represented." Plamenatz, *Man and Society*, I, 394.
49. *Contrat social* II, 3, in *O.C.* III, 371–372. Madison took a similar stand on the issue of factions in *Federalist* #10. Cf. Derathé's note (*O.C.* III, 1456–1457), and also Plamenatz's discussion of Rousseau's view of factions in *Man and Society*, I, 396–399.
50. *Contrat social* II, 9, in *O.C.* III, 386; Cranston trans., p. 90.
51. *Contrat social* II, 9, in *O.C.* III, 387; Cranston trans., p. 91. The question of the appropriate size of a state is discussed in greater detail in chapter 6 in connection with Rousseau's contention in *Contrat social* III, 15, that popular assemblies can function only in small states.
52. *Contrat social* II, 11, in *O.C.* III, 391–392; Cranston trans., p. 96.
53. See especially *Contrat social* II, 9, in *O.C.* III, 384–385, and II, 11, in *O.C.* III, 392.
54. In *Contrat social* II, 10, Rousseau describes the kind of people suited to receive the laws of a lawgiver. He there requires that each citizen know and be known by every other citizen, that the citizens be able to do without other people and other states, and that no one be too rich or too poor. *O.C.* III, 390–391.
55. *Contrat social* II, 3, in *O.C.* III, 371; Cranston trans., p. 72. Hamilton appears to take the same position in *Federalist* #71, and his comments there may help to clarify Rousseau's position: "It is a just observation, that the people commonly *intend* the PUBLIC GOOD. This often applies to their very errors. But their good sense would despise the adulator, who should pretend that they always *reason right* about the *means* of promoting it. They know from experience, that they sometimes err; and the wonder is, that they so seldom err as they do. . . . When occasions present themselves in which the interests of the people are at variance with their inclinations, it is the duty of the persons whom they have appointed to be the guardians of those interests, to withstand the temporary delusion, in order to give them time and

opportunity for more cool and sedate reflection. Instances might be cited, in which a conduct of this kind has saved the people from very fatal consequences of their own mistakes, and has procured lasting monuments of gratitude to the men, who had courage and magnanimity enough to serve them at the peril of their displeasure." *The Federalist*, edited by Jacob E. Cooke (Cleveland: Meridian, 1961), pp. 482–483. The similarities between Rousseau's concept of the general will and Hamilton's concept of the public good are stressed by Cecilia M. Kenyon in her "Alexander Hamilton: Rousseau of the Right," *Political Science Quarterly*, 73, no. 2 (June 1958), 161–178.

56. In keeping with this dictum, Rousseau permitted withdrawal from the contract under certain conditions. See *Contrat social* III, 18, in *O.C.* III, 436.

57. *Contrat social* II, 6, in *O.C.* III, 380; Cranston trans., p. 83. Rousseau's entire discussion of the lawgiver was clearly influenced by his reading of Machiavelli, whose *Discourses* he cites in a footnote to *Contrat social* II, 7 (*O.C.* III, 384).

58. As Rousseau says in *Contrat social* II, 7: "For a newly formed people to understand wise principles of politics and to follow the basic rules of statecraft, the effect would have to become the cause: the social spirit which must be the product of social institutions would have to preside over the setting up of those institutions: men would have to have already become before the advent of law that which they become as a result of law. And as the lawgiver can for these reasons employ neither force nor argument, he must have recourse to the authority of another order, one which can compel without violence and persuade without convincing." *O.C.* III, 383; Cranston trans., pp. 86–87. On the basis of this view, it might be said that while Rousseau distrusts the people as they are, he is highly optimistic about what they might become in a well-governed polity established by a wise lawgiver. If, however, the institutions of the *Contrat social* can be taken as the model for the best polity he believes possible, his expectations about what people might become even in the best of circumstances are not particularly optimistic.

FIVE. POLITICAL INSTITUTIONS: THE ROLE OF GOVERNMENT

1. *Contrat social* III, 1, in *O.C.* III, 395; Cranston trans., p. 101.
2. *Contrat social* III, 1, in *O.C.* III, 396–398. Rousseau was aware of the limitations of this type of argument and in the end claimed that he resorted to geometrical language only to make his point more forcefully and in the fewest possible words. For two analyses of Rousseau's geometrical analogy, see Bertrand de Jouvenel, "Théorie des formes de gouvernement chez Rousseau," and Masters, *The Political Philosophy of Rousseau*, pp. 340–348.
3. *Contrat social* III, 1, in *O.C.* III, 399; Cranston trans., 106.
4. *Ibid.*
5. *Contrat social* III, 2, in *O.C.* III, 400–401.
6. *Contrat social* III, 15, in *O.C.* III, 430; Cranston trans., p. 142.
7. See especially *Contrat social* II, 2, in *O.C.* III, 369–371.
8. As Paul Bastid remarks, government for Rousseau was a necessary evil. "Rousseau et la théorie des formes de gouvernement," p. 325.
9. *Contrat social* III, 17, in *O.C.* III, 434.
10. *Contrat social* IV, 1, in *O.C.* III, 437.
11. *Contrat social* III, 4, in *O.C.* III, 404.
12. Cf. *Contrat social* II, 4, in *O.C.* III, 374.

5. ROLE OF GOVERNMENT

13. *Contrat social* III, 4, in *O.C.* III, 404.

14. *Contrat social* III, 4, in *O.C.* III, 405; Cranston trans., p. 113.

15. *Contrat social* III, 5, in *O.C.* III, 406–407; Cranston trans., p. 115. In *Contrat social* IV, 3, Rousseau accepts the use of the lot to fill minor offices but insists on election to fill all important public offices (*O.C.* III, 442–443).

16. *Contrat social* III, 5, in *O.C.* III, 407; Cranston trans., p. 115.

17. *Contrat social* III, 5, in *O.C.* III, 407–408. Elective aristocracy presupposes (1) a medium-sized state, which in Rousseau's mind was probably quite small by modern standards; (2) an upright people, but one whose morals are not so pure that execution of the law follows automatically from the declaration of the law; (3) some inequality of wealth, since Rousseau assumes that magistrates will normally be chosen from the wealthy, who alone have sufficient leisure to devote themselves to public office.

18. Vaughan, I, 36.

19. Cf. Raymond Polin, *La politique de la solitude: essai sur la philosophie politique de Jean-Jacques Rousseau* (Paris: Éditions Sirey, 1971), p. 184, who argues that Rousseau, like Locke, Hobbes, and Montesquieu, sought to establish an equilibrium between legislative and executive power.

20. *O.C.* III, 1477–1479. Cf. *Contrat social* III, 5, in *O.C.* III, 407.

21. E.g., *Contrat social* III, 3, in which he says that "in general, democratic government suits small states, aristocratic government suits states of intermediate size, and monarchy suits large states." *O.C.* III, 403–404; Cranston trans., p. 111.

22. *Contrat social* III, 6, in *O.C.* III, 408–409. Rousseau cited Machiavelli as an authority on this point and praised the *Prince* as "a handbook for republicans" (*O.C.* III, 409) because it unmasked the real motives and techniques of rulers. Praise of Machiavelli was rare among the *philosophes*. Perhaps Rousseau felt a special affinity for Machiavelli because he shared Machiavelli's city-state republican background. For an assessment of Machiavelli's influence on Rousseau, see Yves Lévy, "Machiavel et Rousseau," *Le Contrat social,* VI, no. 3 (mai–juin 1962), 163–174.

23. Cf. *Contrat social* III, 6, in *O.C.* III, 410, and II, 6, in *O.C.* III, 380. In a footnote to the latter passage he explicitly states that a monarchy can also be a republic (*O.C.* III, 380). In *Contrat social* III, 8, monarchies are contrasted with free states (*O.C.* III, 415).

24. This is the conclusion Derathé comes to in his essay "Rousseau et le problème de la monarchie." See also Derathé's note to *Contrat social* III, 6, in *O.C.* III, 1479–1484; Vaughan, I, 34–36, 74–76; and Bastid, pp. 321–322.

25. Cf. *O.C.* III, 639–645, and *Contrat social* III, 7, in *O.C.* III, 413–414.

26. As Derathé notes, *Contrat social* III, 8, "That all forms of government do not suit all countries," is out of place in a work that supposedly deals with the "principes du droit politique." Derathé suggests that Rousseau included this chapter partly out of deference to Montesquieu, partly to pad the work a little, and partly to minimize the radicalism of the main thesis (*O.C.* III, 1484).

27. See Ronald Grimsley's introduction to his edition of *Du Contrat social,* p. 42.

28. Jouvenel uses this phrase to characterize the *Contrat social* as a whole, not just the chapters on the tendency of government to abuse its powers ("Rousseau the Pessimistic Evolutionist," p. 85). Shklar uses similar language in describing the chapters on government as "an account of how republics degenerate and die" (Shklar, p. 208).

29. *Contrat social* III, 11, in *O.C.* III, 424; Cranston trans., p. 134.

30. *Ibid.*

31. *Contrat social* III, 10, in *O.C.* III, 421. Cf. Chevallier, "Le mot et la notion de gouvernement chez Rousseau," especially pp. 308–309.

32. *Contrat social* III, 11, in *O.C.* III, 424; Cranston trans., p. 135.

33. *Contrat social* III, 12, in *O.C.* III, 425; Cranston trans., p. 136.

34. *Contrat social* III, 11, in *O.C.* III, 424–425.

35. Derathé points out that Rousseau adopted this argument from Hobbes' *Leviathan*, Chapter 26 (*O.C.* III, 1487).

36. Once again Rousseau's debt to Machiavelli, and to the classical republican tradition generally, is evident.

37. *Contrat social* III, 14, in *O.C.* III, 427–428; Cranston trans., p. 139. The last phrase of this quote, "où se trouve la Réprésenté, il n'y a plus de Réprésentant," appears at first glance to mean that when the people are *not* assembled they *are* represented. Derathé explains this oddity by interpreting *représenté* to mean the sovereign people and *représentant* to mean the government. He notes that in *Contrat social* III, 5, Rousseau specifically states that the people must be represented in the executive function (*O.C.* III, 1488). If the terminological ambiguity is thus easily clarified, however, the practical distinction between representation of the legislative and executive powers appears much less significant than Rousseau portrays it to be.

38. *Contrat social* III, 15, in *O.C.* III, 428–429. For Rousseau's view of the joyfulness of political participation, see Ronald Grimsley, "Rousseau and the Problem of Happiness," in *Hobbes and Rousseau*, pp. 442–443.

39. *Contrat social* III, 15, in *O.C.* III, 429; Cranston trans., p. 141.

40. *Ibid.*, p. 430.

41. *Ibid.*, p. 431; Cranston trans., pp. 142–143. Derathé, commenting on this "awkward passage" (*passage embarrassé*) of the *Contrat*, observes that Rousseau indirectly eulogizes the very slavery he previously condemned in Book I (*Rousseau et la science politique*, p. 276). Rousseau's suggestion that in certain situations freedom presupposes slavery may not be so farfetched as it appears. Just as Rousseau contended that Spartan liberty was based on slavery, Edmund S. Morgan has recently argued that republican liberty in colonial Virginia was based on slavery (*American Slavery, American Freedom: the Ordeal of Colonial Virginia* (New York: Norton, 1975), pp. 369–387).

42. *Contrat social* III, 15, in *O.C.* III, 431; Cranston trans., p. 143.

43. *Contrat social* I, 6, in *O.C.* III, 362.

44. Jouvenel, "Théorie des formes de gouvernement chez Rousseau," pp. 344–347. Jouvenel aptly summarizes what he sees as Rousseau's emphasis on the psychological value of participation: "The subject of the *Social Contract* is not the social contract, but social affection." Jouvenel, "Rousseau's Theory of the Forms of Government," in *Hobbes and Rousseau*, p. 487. (The English essay is in part a translation of the French essay, in part a revised version of the earlier essay.) Plamenatz provides a very useful analysis of Rousseau's view of participation in his *Man and Society*, I, 400–401, 411–418. Among those who argue for the intrinsic value of participation in Rousseau's political theory is Carole Pateman, *Participation and Democratic Theory*, pp. 22–27. Pateman describes Rousseau's ideal as a society in which "men are to be ruled by the logic of the operation of the political situation that they themselves created," i.e., no one will be able to achieve anything without cooperating with all the other members of society (p. 23).

45. *O.C.* III, 459.

46. *O.C.* III, 393–394.

47. John W. Chapman, *Rousseau—Totalitarian or Liberal?*, pp. 86–88.

48. Lester Crocker, *Rousseau's Social Contract*, p. 81. J. L. Talmon makes the same point in *The Origins of Totalitarian Democracy* (New York: Praeger, 1960), p. 47: "There is nothing Rousseau insists on more than the active and ceaseless participation of the people and of every citizen in the affairs of the State. . . . The Republic is in a continuous state of being born. In the pre-democratic age Rousseau could not realize that the originally deliberate creation of men could become transformed into a Leviathan, which might crush its own makers. He was unaware that total and highly emotional absorption in the collective political endeavour is calculated to kill all privacy, that the excitement of the assembled crowd may exercise a most tyrannical pressure, and that the extension of the scope of politics to all spheres of human interest and endeavour, without leaving any room for the process of casual and empirical activity, was the shortest way to totalitarianism." And because he could not anticipate all this, Talmon argues, Rousseau unwittingly provided the political theory that gave rise to totalitarian democracy.

49. *Rousseau's Social Contract*, p. 69. See also Crocker's "Rousseau et la voie du totalitarisme," in *Rousseau et la philosophie politique*, pp. 108–112.

50. Talmon, pp. 48–49.

51. R. A. Leigh, "Liberté et autorité dans le *Contrat social*," in *Jean-Jacques Rousseau et son oeuvre: problèmes et recherches* (Paris: Klincksieck, 1964), pp. 249–264. Leigh's essay, although brief, is an incisive critique of the totalitarian thesis in general and of Talmon's thesis in particular.

52. *O.C.* III, 375; Cranston trans., p. 77.

Six. Political Institutions: The People as Legislator

1. *Contrat social* III, 13, in *O.C.* III, 426; III, 18, in *O.C.* III, 435. The frequency of these assemblies should vary according to the strength of the government; i.e., the stronger the government, the more frequently the assemblies should meet.

2. *Contrat social* III, 15, in *O.C.* III, 430; Cranston trans., p. 141.

3. *Contrat social* IV, 1, in *O.C.* III, 438–439; Cranston trans., p. 151. Rousseau also seems to rule out debate by the people in *Contrat social* II, 3, in which he specifies as one of the conditions for realizing the general will that citizens not communicate among themselves during their deliberations (*O.C.* III, 371).

4. Ferrier, pp. 407–410.

5. *Édits de la République de Genève* (Genève: Chez Les Frères Detournes, 1735), pp. 78, 81, 85.

6. *Amtliche Sammlung der ältern Eidgenössischen Abschiede. Die Eidgenössischen Abschiede aus dem Zeitraume von 1712 bis 1743*, bearbeitet von Daniel Albert Fechter (Basel: Baur'schen, 1860), Bd. VII, Abteilung 1, p. 1399.

7. *Édit de pacification de 1782* (Genève: Pellet, 1782), pp. 5–6.

8. *The Political Writings of James Harrington: Representative Selections*, edited with an introduction by Charles Blitzer (Indianapolis: Bobbs-Merrill, 1955), p. 61.

9. *O.C.* III, 1492–1493. Derathé explains Rousseau's opposition to a popular legislative initiative as the result of his horror of innovation; Rousseau was more concerned with maintaining the laws established at the initiative of the lawgiver than in enacting new laws. One might add that Rousseau, as in many other instances in the *Contrat social*, was simply following in the footsteps of the Genevan bourgeoi-

sie, most of whom accepted the view of De Luc that the legislative initiative should be confined to the Petit Conseil.

Launay contests the view that Rousseau opposed a popular legislative initiative in *Contrat social* IV, 1. He argues that Rousseau had abandoned the opposition expressed in the *Dédicace* and now saw the right to vote as only *one* of the steps in the legislative process that belonged to the people. Launay derives this interpretation from an analysis of Rousseau's discussion of the Roman system of voting in Book IV. See Launay, *Rousseau écrivain politique*, pp. 445–447. While it is true that Rousseau does not explicitly reject a popular legislative initiative in *Contrat social* IV, 1—he says only that it is "a right which the government always takes great care to assign only to its own members"—it is nevertheless farfetched to discover in this passage a hidden meaning that Rousseau does specifically reject elsewhere.

10. *Contrat social* III, 13, in *O.C.* III, 426.

11. *O.C.* III, 432–433.

12. *Contrat social* III, 17, in *O.C.* III, 433; Cranston trans., p. 145.

13. *Ibid.*, pp. 433–434. As Derathé points out, following Dreyfus-Brisac, Rousseau here uses the same argument as Hobbes in *De Cive* VII, which shows how the body politic begins as a primitive democracy and transforms itself into aristocracy or monarchy (*O.C.* III, 1490). In *Contrat social* II, 4, however, Rousseau condemns the Athenians for confusing executive and legislative functions by appointing and dismissing magistrates instead of allotting these functions to the government (*O.C.* III, 374). Presumably, then, it is proper for a people to combine these functions only at the institution of a new government, not on a continuing basis.

14. *Contrat social* III, 17, in *O.C.* III, 434; Cranston trans., p. 146.

15. *O.C.* III, 442; Cranston trans., p. 155.

16. *Contrat social* IV, 3, in *O.C.* III, 442; Cranston trans., p. 155.

17. *Contrat social* IV, 3, in *O.C.* III, 442–443. Derathé notes that Rousseau expresses a very different opinion of the Genevan bourgeoisie in the *Lettres écrites de la montagne*, where he describes the bourgeoisie as an intermediate order between the rich and the poor (*O.C.* III, 1494).

18. Launay, e.g., argues that by elevating the Genevan bourgeoisie to the same status as the Venetian aristocracy Rousseau was in effect contesting the pretensions of the Petit Conseil to the monopolization of the government (*Rousseau écrivain politique*, p. 446).

19. Rousseau's expectation that the government in an elective aristocracy would normally be self-perpetuating may explain his paternalistic suggestion that a poor man should be elected to office once in a while just to show that merit is a more important consideration than wealth. Cf. *Contrat social* III, 4, in *O.C.* III, 408.

20. *Contrat social* III, 18, in *O.C.* III, 435–436; Cranston trans., p. 148.

21. *Ibid.*, p. 435; Cranston trans., p. 147.

22. Shklar contends that periodic assemblies are not only essentially preventive but that "Their positive function is symbolic and ritualistic. They actually *do* very little." Even the people's role in voting on the two propositions is essentially passive, and the assemblies in general serve primarily as "a device for keeping their country before their eyes, and their public selves intact." Shklar, *Men and Citizens*, p. 20 (cf. also pp. 180–184). Certainly the role of the people is more passive than Rousseau's basic political concepts would lead one to believe, but Shklar possibly underrates the importance Rousseau attaches to the two propositions put before each as-

sembly. On this occasion the people is active in the sense that it puts the two propositions to itself, so to speak; i.e., the propositions are presented in accordance with the constitution, not according to the discretion of the government. In Rousseau's view, this apparently provided ample opportunity for the people to take action whenever there is a need for action.

23. *Contrat social* III, 18, in *O.C.* III, 434; Cranston trans., p. 146.

24. *Ibid.*, pp. 434–435. In his discussion of elective aristocracy in *Contrat social* III, 5, Rousseau stresses the importance of determining the procedure for electing magistrates at the time a government is established in order to avoid a degeneration into hereditary aristocracy (*O.C.* III, 407).

25. *O.C.* III, 1490–1491.

26. *O.C.* III, 426; Cranston trans., p. 137.

27. *Contrat social* IV, 3, in *O.C.* III, 443.

28. *Contrat social* III, 12, in *O.C.* III, 425; Cranston trans., p. 136.

29. *Ibid.*, pp. 425–426. These population figures, while obviously not exact, are nevertheless sufficiently accurate for Rousseau's purposes. For more precise data on the citizen population, see Léon Homo, *Roman Political Institutions from City to State* (1929; rpt. New York: Barnes and Noble, 1962), pp. 74–79, 91–92.

30. *Contrat social* III, 15, in *O.C.* III, 430.

31. Vaughan, II, 109. See also Vaughan, I, 38.

32. Ernest Hunter Wright, *The Meaning of Rousseau* (London: Oxford University Press, 1929), p. 86.

33. *O.C.* III, 1495.

34. Masters, *The Political Philosophy of Rousseau*, pp. 305–306.

35. Cousin, "J.-J. Rousseau interprète des institutions romaines dans le *Contrat social*," in *Études sur le Contrat social de Jean-Jacques Rousseau*, pp. 13–14. Although Rousseau's account of Roman history is often inaccurate, it is usually sufficiently accurate for purposes of the point he makes; he does not concoct history out of whole cloth, even though he often bends it to suit his own needs. What is most striking about the Roman example he praises is not the historical inaccuracy of his account but the fact that in many crucial respects both Roman reality and his perception of that reality appear inconsistent with his basic political concepts.

36. *Rousseau écrivain politique*, pp. 443–444.

37. *Contrat social* IV, 4, in *O.C.* III, 444–446. Cousin points out that Rousseau, by celebrating the superiority of rural mores, adds to the distortions of the traditional sources that he uses some new distortions of his own (Cousin, pp. 17–18).

38. This system of voting is described in *O.C.* III, 447–451. The quotation is from *O.C.* III, 451.

39. *Contrat social* IV, 4, in *O.C.* III, 451–452; Cranston trans., pp. 166–167.

40. *Ibid.*, p. 449; Cranston trans., p. 163.

41. *Contrat social* IV, 5, in *O.C.* III, 453–454; also IV, 4, in *O.C.* III, 451. It is important to bear in mind that what Rousseau calls the tribunate in *Contrat social* IV, 5, is not identical with the tribunes of Rome.

42. Launay, *Rousseau écrivain politique*, pp. 448–451.

43. The dictatorship is discussed in *Contrat social* IV, 6 (*O.C.* III, 455–458), and the censorial tribunal in IV, 7 (*O.C.* III, 458–459).

44. *Contrat social* IV, 5, in *O.C.* III, 454; Cranston trans., p. 169. This at any rate is how Rousseau characterizes the tribunate. As Cousin points out, it would be mis-

leading to say that the Roman tribune's powers were purely negative (Cousin, pp. 25–26).

45. Kurt von Fritz, *The Theory of the Mixed Constitution in Antiquity: A Critical Analysis of Polybius' Political Ideas* (New York: Columbia University Press, 1954), p. 219.

46. Roman assemblies played the same kind of passive role in legislation that Rousseau envisioned for the ideal popular assemblies of the *Contrat*. In both cases the people's legislative function was limited to voting on proposals submitted by the government with no possibility of debate or amendment by the people. See Hans Julius Wolff, *Roman Law: An Historical Introduction* (Norman: University of Oklahoma Press, 1951), p. 38.

47. Wolff, pp. 26–27. In *Contrat social* IV, 2, Rousseau notes that the division of Rome into patricians and plebeians effectively meant that Rome was "two states in one," which he singles out as an inherent defect in the Roman system (*O.C.* III, 439).

48. *Contrat social* IV, 3, in *O.C.* III, 443; Cranston trans., p. 157.

49. *Contrat social* III, 15, in *O.C.* III, 431; Cranston trans., p. 143.

50. *Contrat social* II, 9, in *O.C.* III, 386; Cranston trans., p. 90.

51. *Laws* V, 737–738; *The Collected Dialogues of Plato, Including the Letters*, edited by Edith Hamilton and Huntington Cairns (Princeton, N.J.: Princeton University Press, 1963), p. 1323.

52. *Politics* VII, 4; *The Politics of Aristotle*, edited and trans. by Ernest Barker (New York: Oxford University Press, 1962), p. 292.

53. Dahl and Tufte, *Size and Democracy* (Stanford, Calif.: Stanford University Press, 1973), *passim*. I have relied heavily on this work in my discussion of the problem of size. The findings of this study are summarized on pp. 134–136 and in the Epilogue, pp. 137–142.

54. *Contrat social* III, 3, in *O.C.* III, 403–404.

55. Cf. Dahl and Tufte, p. 6.

56. *Contrat social* III, 8, in *O.C.* III, 418–419; Cranston trans., pp. 128–129.

57. *Contrat social* III, 13, in *O.C.* III, 426–427. He makes the same point even more forcefully in the Geneva Manuscript II, 3: "a fundamental rule for all well constituted and legitimately governed societies would be that one be able to easily assemble all the members every time it would be necessary. . . . It follows from this that the state must limit itself to a single city at the most; for if there are several, the capital will always be the *de facto* sovereign and the others will be subjects, a type of constitution in which tyranny and abuse are inevitable." *O.C.* III, 322.

58. *Contrat social* III, 13, in *O.C.* III, 427; Cranston trans., p. 138. The phrase "estates of the country" is curious since it would normally refer to a representative assembly. His use of the same phrase in *Économie politique* (*O.C.* III, 265) has already been mentioned. In his *Projet de constitution pour la Corse* he does not use this particular phrase, but he does appear to recommend a system of assembling the people at different times in different places (cf. *O.C.* III, 907) similar to that he recommends in *Contrat social* III, 13.

59. *Ibid.* Cf. Geneva Manuscript II, 3: "What enabled the small states of Greece to subsist was that they themselves were surrounded by other small states and amounted to a great power when they were united for the common interest." *O.C.* III, 325.

60. *Contrat social* III, 15, in *O.C.* III, 431; Cranston trans., p. 143.

6. PEOPLE AS LEGISLATOR

61. *Ibid.* Interestingly, Dahl and Tufte arrive at a similar conclusion two centuries later. After demonstrating that current democratic theory is inadequate because it fails to deal systematically with the problem of the relationship between size and democracy, they suggest the direction in which democratic theorists should look for solutions to this problem. Dahl and Tufte, p. 139.

62. Foreword to the *Contrat social,* in *O.C.* III, 349; conclusion, *Contrat social* IV, 9, in *O.C.* III, 470.

63. Vaughan, I, 95. D'Antraigues' account of this is included in Vaughan, II, 135–136. The fact that both French revolutionaries and counterrevolutionaries could legitimately cite Rousseau's authority is still another indication of the ambivalence that pervades his political thought. Joan McDonald argues that the counterrevolutionaries actually had the best of it, i.e., that they were able to invoke Rousseau's authority with less distortion of his writings than the revolutionaries were, although both sides naturally used Rousseau for their own purposes (*Rousseau and the French Revolution, 1762–1791* [London: Athlone Press, 1965], *passim*). She stresses the use that the counterrevolutionaries made of Rousseau's opposition to representative government, which the counterrevolutionaries cited to attack the legitimacy of the National Assembly. Iring Fetscher, who also emphasizes the conservative aspects of Rousseau's political thought, closely follows McDonald's thesis in a chapter added to the second edition of his *Rousseaus politische Philosophie* (Chapter 5, pp. 263–282). Neither McDonald nor Fetscher mentions any of the writings of Albert Soboul, who has demonstrated that Rousseau exerted a profound influence on the *sans-culottes* and other radical groups, who cited Rousseau's authority in support of their attempts at direct democracy in the Parisian sections. See Albert Soboul, "L'audience des Lumières sous la Révolution: Jean-Jacques Rousseau et les classes populaires," in *Utopie et institutions au XVIIIᵉ siècle,* pp. 289–303; "Jean-Jacques Rousseau et le jacobinisme," in *Études sur le Contrat social de Jean-Jacques Rousseau,* pp. 405–424. For an account of the political theory of the *sans-culottes,* see Soboul's *The Parisian Sans-Culottes and the French Revolution, 1793–4,* trans. by Gwynne Lewis (Oxford, England: Clarendon Press, 1964). The various interpretations of Rousseau's influence on the French Revolution are reviewed by Lionello Sozzi in "Interprétations de Rousseau pendant la Révolution," *Studies on Voltaire and the Eighteenth Century,* 64 (1968), 187–223.

64. *Émile* V, in *O.C.* IV, 848–849. By *droit public* Rousseau means that part of international law dealing with treaties, leagues, confederations, negotiations, and questions of a similar nature. By *droit politique,* which is of course the principal subject of the *Contrat social,* he means that body of law dealing with the origin of the state, the nature and limits of civil authority, the various forms of government, etc. Derathé, *Rousseau et la science politique,* pp. 393–396.

65. Rousseau makes this explicit in a footnote to this passage in which he says that the extract of the abbé's work provides the reason *for* such an association of states, his own critique the reasons *against* (*Émile* V, in *O.C.* IV, 848). The *Extrait du Projet de paix perpétuelle* was published in 1761, Rousseau's *Jugement sur le Projet de paix perpétuelle* in 1782 (*O.C.* IV, 1692).

66. *O.C.* III, 564–565. Stelling-Michaud notes that Rousseau contributes one example of the ancients, the Amphyctionic League, to those mentioned by Saint-Pierre and suggests that although Rousseau appears to agree with the abbé that the modern examples of confederation are superior to those of the ancients—one of the rare oc-

casions when Rousseau favors moderns over ancients—he still seeks out ancient examples to buttress his case. Stelling-Michaud also points out that Montesquieu presents a similar argument in *Esprit des lois* IX, 1, and mentions the same three modern examples of confederation cited by Saint-Pierre and Rousseau.

67. *Jugement sur le Projet de paix perpétuelle*, in *O.C.* III, 595–600.

68. Subtitled *Essai sur le système de politique étrangère de J.-J. Rousseau* (Paris: Alphonse Picard, 1900).

69. Windenberger, pp. 49–51.

70. *Ibid.*, Chapter VI, pp. 189–236.

71. Both Vaughan and Derathé agree that Windenberger's reconstruction of Rousseau's view of confederation is plausible, although Vaughan objects to specific features of Windenberger's argument and Windenberger's view of Rousseau as an individualist. Cf. Vaughan, I, 97–102; Derathé, *Rousseau et la science politique*, p. 277.

72. Windenberger, p. 223.

73. *Ibid.*, pp. 208–221.

SEVEN. THE SOURCES OF ROUSSEAU'S VIEW OF REPRESENTATION

1. *O.C.* III, 430.

2. Hanna F. Pitkin, *The Concept of Representation*, pp. 2–3. See also the "Appendix on Etymology," pp. 241–252, where she traces the various uses of the term.

3. Gustave Glotz, *The Greek City and Its Institutions* (1929; rpt. New York: Barnes and Noble, 1969), pp. 152–168, 208–219. Whereas direct democracy was the fundamental principle of Athenian democracy, elements of representative democracy were not wholly lacking. One recent study goes so far as to claim that the typical polis "contained so much representative machinery that little more than a shift in the emphasis on the various organs of government was needed to transform it into a representative government." J. A. O. Larsen, *Representative Government in Greek and Roman History* (Berkeley: University of California Press, 1966), p. 4. This "representative machinery" was embodied principally in the institution of the council, whose 500 members were chosen through a combination of election and lot, and who exercised extensive power, including an important role in legislation.

4. *Larsen*, p. 14. On this point Rousseau refused to follow in the footsteps of his acknowledged master, Plato, who distrusted common opinion.

5. *Dédicace*, in *O.C.* III, 114; Masters trans., p. 82.

6. *Contrat social* III, 12–15, in *O.C.* III, 425–431. Similar examples of praise for the Spartans' public-spiritedness can be found throughout his writings, among them *Considérations sur le gouvernement de Pologne* (*O.C.* III, 956–959); "Parallèle entre les deux républiques de Sparte et de Rome" (*O.C.* III, 538–539); and "Histoire de Lacédémone" (*O.C.* III, 544–548).

7. H. Michell, *Sparta* (Cambridge: Cambridge University Press, 1964), pp. 136–146.

8. "Parallèle entre les deux républiques de Sparte et de Rome," in *O.C.* III, 538–543; also *Contrat social* III, 11, in *O.C.* III, 424.

9. E.g., *Lettres écrites de la montagne*, in *O.C.* III, 809.

10. Cobban, *Rousseau and the Modern State*, pp. 43–44.

11. Gierke, *The Development of Political Theory*, p. 247.

12. Shklar, *Men and Citizens*, p. 94. Emphasis added.

7. SOURCES

13. *Contrat social* III, 15, in *O.C.* III, 430; Cranston trans., p. 141. Elsewhere in the *Contrat* he spoke of feudal government as "an irrational system if there ever was one, and contrary both to natural justice and to all sound polity." *Contrat social* I, 4, in *O.C.* III, 357; Cranston trans., p. 56.

14. Rousseau's *Histoire de Genève* includes this appraisal of feudalism: "The feudal system degraded human nature and there were no longer any men, properly speaking." *Oeuvres complètes,* edited by Michel Launay, III, 385–386.

15. *Contrat social* I, 6 (*O.C.* III, 360; Cranston trans., p. 60); I, 8 (*O.C.* III, 365; Cranston trans., p. 65); II, 12 (*O.C.* III, 394; Cranston trans., p. 99).

16. Derathé, *Rousseau et la science politique,* pp. 270–273.

17. Gay, *The Enlightenment,* I, 207–217; II, 482.

18. Derathé, *Rousseau et la science politique,* pp. 51–62, 252–269.

19. The index to Volume III of the Pléiade edition of the *Oeuvres complètes* indicates that, among the major political theorists, only Plato was mentioned by name more often than Grotius.

20. *O.C.* III, 118.

21. One of the few favorable references to Grotius appears in *Contrat social* III, 18, where Grotius's authority is cited in support of the proposition that under certain circumstances a citizen can rightfully withdraw from the body politic (*O.C.* III, 436).

22. *Émile* V, in *O.C.* IV, 863.

23. *Contrat social* II, 2, in *O.C.* III, 370. Rousseau included Grotius's translator Barbeyrac in this accusation, a charge that Derathé considers grossly unfair in view of Barbeyrac's Lockean liberalism (*O.C.* III, 1456).

24. *O.C.* III, 352–359. He neglected to mention that Grotius also stipulated the rights of the people when they shared sovereignty with their rulers. Derathé's notes to the early chapters of the *Contrat social* help greatly to clarify Rousseau's argument and explain his motives in singling out Grotius for special attention and also to distinguish Grotius's less extreme position from the one charged against him by Rousseau (*O.C.* III, 1435–1443). Cf. Derathé's *Rousseau et la science politique, pp.* 71–78.

25. *O.C.* III, 183.

26. *O.C.* III, 355. Cf. Starobinski's note to the relevant passage of the *Discours sur l'inégalité,* in *O.C.* III, 1355.

27. *Discours sur l'inégalité,* in *O.C.* III, 136; *Économie politique,* in *O.C.* III, 263; *Lettres écrites de la montagne,* in *O.C.* III, 844.

28. *Émile* I, in *O.C.* IV, 288.

29. Derathé, *Rousseau et la science politique,* pp. 102–104, 332–344. Derathé believes that Rousseau read both *De Cive* and *Leviathan.* Georges Davy points out several fundamental similarities between the political theories of Hobbes and Rousseau vis-à-vis the traditional school of natural law in "Le corps politique selon le *Contrat social* de J.-J. Rousseau et ses antécédents chez Hobbes," in *Études sur le Contrat social de Jean-Jacques Rousseau,* pp. 65–93.

30. *Émile* V, in *O.C.* IV, 836.

31. The passage from *L'État de guerre* appears in *O.C.* III, 611. Cf. Stelling-Michaud's notes to this passage, *O.C.* III, 1557, and Derathé's comments in his *Rousseau et la science politique,* pp. 105–106.

32. Derathé, *Rousseau et la science politique,* pp. 104–105. The relevant portions of the article are included in the selections from the *Encyclopédie* edited by Alain Pons (Paris: J'ai Lu, 1963), p. 363.

33. *De Cive* VII, 5, in *Man and Citizen,* edited with an introduction by Bernard Gert (Garden City, N.Y.: Doubleday, 1972), p. 195.

34. *De Cive* VII, 8, in *Man and Citizen,* p. 197.

35. *De Cive* VII, 11, in *Man and Citizen,* p. 198.

36. *Leviathan,* Part I, Chapter 16, edited with an introduction by Michael Oakeshott (Oxford, England: Blackwell, n.d.), p. 107. For an analysis of Hobbes's theory of representation, see Derathé, *Rousseau et la science politique,* pp. 400–402.

37. Hendel, II, 169.

38. Cobban suggests that this criticism of the traditional system of representation was implicit even in Locke and that Rousseau was only drawing the logical conclusions of Locke's own arguments (Cobban, *Rousseau and the Modern State,* p. 44).

39. Derathé, *Rousseau et la science politique,* pp. 270–277.

40. Jean Fabre points to the vigorous Genevan reaction to the *Contrat* as evidence that Rousseau's remarks struck home and were thus presumably based on an adequate knowledge of Genevan institutions and politics ("Réalité et utopie dans la pensée politique de Rousseau," *Annales de la Société Jean-Jacques Rousseau,* 35 (1959–1962, pp. 195–201). Other commentators assert the Genevan inspiration of the *Contrat* more emphatically. Gaspard Vallette's *Jean-Jacques Rousseau Genevois,* which Spink cites as a reliable guide (cf. Spink, *Jean-Jacques Rousseau et Genève,* p. vii), remains one of the essential works on the Genevan origins of Rousseau's political thought despite its age. Guglielmo Ferrero describes the *Contrat* as "une oeuvre genevoise, inspirée par les institutions de Genève, ses crises, les luttes qu'elles avaient engendrées" and stresses Rousseau's distinction between the sovereign and the prince, the people and the government, as the point of contact between Geneva and the *Contrat* ("Genève et le *Contrat social,*" p. 145). Marcel Raymond contends that Rousseau was familiar with Genevan institutions both in theory and practice and that he took these institutions as his model, not precisely as they were but as they easily could have been with only slight revision ("Rousseau et Genève," in *Jean-Jacques Rousseau* (Neuchâtel Switzerland: Éditions de la Baconnière, 1962), pp. 229–230). The differences between these interpretations are essentially differences of emphasis; all agree that Geneva was a major factor if not indeed the primary inspiration in the writing of the *Contrat social.*

41. *O.C.* III, 351; Cranston trans., p. 49. Derathé finds this homage to Geneva pale in comparison with the glowing tribute to Geneva in the *Dédicace* (*O.C.* III, 1433).

42. Vallette, p. 175; cf. also 209–210.

43. The "sovereign body" that Rousseau refers to in the introductory paragraph quoted above is clearly the Conseil Général. Cf. Derathé's note, *O.C.* III, 1432–1433.

44. All of these parallels are discussed by Vallette, pp. 185–199. Vallette sees the *Contrat* as a radical indictment of the ruling patriciate because he sees the demands of the bourgeois oppositionists as radical. For example, he considers the *droit de représentation* a form of legislative initiative even though the bourgeoisie itself subsequently recognized that the *droit de représentation* did not give them the right to initiate legislation but only the right to supervise, in some unspecified way, the execution of the laws. (The *droit de représentation* is examined in detail in the following chapter.) Vallette does not mention Rousseau's acceptance of the patriciate's monopolization of the nominating power.

45. Vallette, pp. 190–191.

46. *Lettres écrites de la montagne*, in *O.C.* III, 809.

47. *Ibid.*

48. *Ibid.*, p. 810. Candaux adds that not even the Spanish Inquisition expressly condemned the *Contrat social* (*O.C.* III, 1665).

49. Even Spink does not claim that Rousseau was wholly ignorant of Geneva and its history, only that he deceived himself on the political realities of his native city. See Spink's remarks in the discussion following the essay by Fabre, "Réalité et utopie dans la pensée politique de Rousseau," p. 219.

50. Spink, *Jean-Jacques Rousseau et Genève*, pp. 83–90.

51. *O.C.* III, clxxxiv–cxc. See also Candaux's note to the above-quoted passage from *Lettres écrites de la montagne*, in *O.C.* III, 1664–1665.

52. Launay, *Rousseau écrivain politique*, pp. 13–66.

53. Spink, pp. 53, 216–217, 223–226.

54. Guéhenno, II, 88–91.

55. *Correspondance complète*, XII, 98.

EIGHT. GENEVAN EXPATRIATE: LETTRES ÉCRITES DE LA MONTAGNE

1. At one point Vallette calls the *Lettres écrites de la montagne* "peut-être l'oeuvre la plus genevoise de Jean-Jacques Rousseau" (p. 325), but elsewhere, as previously noted, he identifies the *Lettre à d'Alembert* as "l'un des plus complètement genevois" of all Rousseau's writings (p. 134), and in his conclusion he says unequivocally that the *Lettre à d'Alembert* was "l'écrit le plus genevois de Rousseau" (p. 440).

2. Ferrier, pp. 446–447; Vallette, pp. 246–253.

3. Vallette thinks both charges justified (pp. 243–245), but Spink considers the charge of French influence at best superfluous and the charge of Voltaire's influence completely without foundation (pp. 215–217).

4. Spink argues in Part III, Chapter 2 of his work that most of the allegations of procedural irregularities in Rousseau's condemnation were unfounded, but he agrees with Pictet and Rousseau (who devotes *Lettre* V to a critique of what he saw as procedural irregularities in his condemnation) that the Petit Conseil violated Rousseau's procedural rights by not giving him an opportunity to defend himself prior to condemning his writings. Spink, pp. 229–238.

5. For the composition of the *Lettre à Christophe de Beaumont*, see Henri Gouhier's introduction to the work in *O.C.* IV, clxix–clxxvii.

6. *Confessions* XII, in *O.C.* I, 550.

7. *Ibid.*, pp. 609–610. Cf. Vallette's account, pp. 258–265.

8. *Confessions* XII, in *O.C.* I, 610; Cohen trans., p. 563.

9. Cf. Vallette, pp. 267–293; Candaux, in *O.C.* III, clxiii–clxiv.

10. Spink, p. 71. Spink sees the *Lettres écrites de la montagne* as the first of three works—the other two being Rousseau's proposals for Corsica and Poland—in which there are definite indications of an evolution in Rousseau's methodology. Instead of "setting aside all the facts," as Rousseau put it in the *Discours sur l'inégalité* (*O.C.* III, 132), he now argues on the basis of the facts.

11. Candaux, *O.C.* III, clxvii–clxxv. Rousseau conceived the outline of the first six letters as early as July 1762. In a letter of July 24, 1762, to his Genevan friend Mar-

cet de Mézières, he sketched six basic points that eventually became the basis for the first six letters of the *Lettres écrites de la montagne* (*Correspondance complète*, XII, 96–98; Candaux, *O.C.* III, clxvii). For a detailed account of the documentation Rousseau used in writing the *Lettres*, see Candaux, *O.C.* III, clxxxii–cxc.

12. Candaux, *O.C* III, clxxv; Vallette, p. 294.

13. Quoted in Vallette, pp. 286–287.

14. *Ibid.*, pp. 280–287.

15. *Lettres écrites de la montagne* IX, in *O.C.* III, 869–874.

16. *Lettre* VII, in *O.C.* III, 820–823; see also *Lettre* VIII, in *O.C.* III, 836–837.

17. Article I reads as follows: "Tous les differens Ordres qui composent le Gouvernement de GENEVE, Savoir les quatre Sindics, le Conseil des Vint Cinq, le Conseil des Soixante, le Conseil des Deux Cent, et le Conseil General, conserveront chacun leurs Droits et Attributions particulières provenant de la Loi fondamentale de l'Etat, et il ne sera fait à l'avenir aucun changement au présent Réglement, en sorte que l'un des susdit Ordres ne pourra donner atteinte, ni rien enfreindre au préjudice des Droits et Attributs de l'autre." *O.C.* III, 1678.

18. *Lettres écrites de la montagne* VII, in *O.C.* III, 823–824.

19. Article III begins "Les Droits et Attributions du Conseil General légitimement Assemblé demeureront invariablement fixés et limités aux Articles suivans," then proceeds to enumerate the six rights in question, namely, those concerning legislation, election, confederation, war and peace, new taxes, and fortification. *O.C.* III, 1680.

20. *Lettre* VII, in *O.C.* III, 825–826.

21. *Ibid.*, p. 826.

22. Article V: "Toutes les Matières qui seront portées au Conseil General, ne pourront y être proposées que par les Sindics, Petit et Grand Conseils." Article VI: "Il ne pourra rien être porté au Conseil des Deux Cent, qu'auparavant il n'ait été traité et aprouvé dans le Conseil des Vint Cinq; et il ne sera rien porté au Conseil General, qui n'ait été auparavant traité et aprouvé dans le Conseil des Deux Cent." *O.C.* III, 1683.

23. *Lettre* VII, in *O.C.* III, 827–829.

24. *Lettre* VIII, in *O.C.* III, 837.

25. Article XLIV: "Tous les Articles contenus au présent Réglement auront à l'avenir force de Loix, et ne pourront être susceptibles d'aucun changement, quel qu'il puisse être, que du consentement du Conseil General légitimement assemblé par le Petit et Grand Conseil." *O.C* III, 1691.

26. Spink, p. 75.

27. *O.C.* III, 1695–1696. "Les Citoyens et Bourgeois conformément à l'Edit du 26. May 1707. auront droit de faire telles Représentations qu'ils jugeront convenables au bien de l'Etat à Messieurs les Sindics ou Procureur General; sous l'expresse défense de commetre aucune sorte de violence, à peine de châtiment suivant l'exigence du cas."

28. *Lettre* VIII, in *O.C.* III, 841–844.

29. *O.C.* III, 1695.

30. *Lettre* VIII, in *O.C.* III, 844–847.

31. Even Launay, who argues that Rousseau favored a popular legislative initiative in the *Contrat social* despite his previous opposition in the *Dédicace*, admits that Rousseau accords the Petit Conseil the right to propose *new* laws. Launay nonethe-

less insists that Rousseau's criticism of Article III of the *Règlement implies* a right of popular legislative initiative. *Rousseau écrivain politique,* pp. 447–448.

32. Vaughan, II, 187–188.

33. Derathé, *Rousseau et la science politique,* p. 297; see also Derathé's note to *Contrat social* IV, 1, in *O.C.* III, 1492–1493.

34. Vallette singles out these two characteristics in the course of explaining the eagerness of the bourgeoisie to withdraw their *représentations of* 1763 at even the slightest hint of a concession by the patriciate (p. 280), but they apply equally to Rousseau.

35. *Lettres écrites de la montagne* VIII, in *O.C.* III, 847–848.

36. Cf. Candaux, *O.C.* III, 1697.

37. *Lettre* VIII, in *O.C.* III, 848–850.

38. Spink, pp. 73–74.

39. Article II reads in part: "Les Sindics ne pourront être pris que dans le Conseil des Vint Cinq; les Membres du Conseil des Vint Cinq ne pourront être choisis qu'entre les Citoyens du Conseil des Deux Cent . . ." (*O.C.* III, 1678).

40. *Lettre* VII, in *O.C.* III, 814–818, 824–825.

41. *Ibid.,* p. 825. Candaux confirms the accuracy of this part of Rousseau's account (*O.C.* III, 1678–1679). See also Frédéric Gardy, "Genève au XVᵉ siècle," in *Histoire de Genève des origines à 1789,* pp. 140–141.

42. *Histoire de Genève,* in *Oeuvres complètes* (ed. Launay), III, 390. For the composition and publication of the *Histoire de Genève,* see Launay's brief introduction on p. 381 and also Candaux, *O.C.* III, clxxiii.

43. For this last point, see *Histoire de Genève,* in *Oeuvres complètes* (ed. Launay), III, 389. Rousseau's comparison of the episopate and the republic is on pp. 394–397. The most thorough analysis of the *Histoire de Genève* is that by Jean Terrasse, *Jean-Jacques Rousseau et la quête de l'âge d'or,* pp. 147–155. Terrasse points out a number of errors in Rousseau's account that he thinks prove that Rousseau lacked a profound knowledge of Genevan history even at the time he wrote the *Histoire de Genève* and the *Lettres écrites de la montagne.* Terrasse contends that Rousseau rewrote history to support his preconceived notion that all governments tend to degenerate. It seems to me that Terrasse exaggerates the importance of Rousseau's distortions of history by imposing standards of scholarship that few if any historians followed at the time. The distortions in Rousseau's account were not simply the result of his personal whims or biases but reflected a view of Genevan history widely shared by the leadership of the bourgeoisie.

44. *Lettre* IX, in *O.C.* III, 870. Candaux confirms the accuracy of Rousseau's observation and also supplies the date of the abolition of the Edict of 1543 which had imposed the requirement in question (*O.C.* III, 1709).

45. *Lettre* VII, in *O.C.* III, 814. "Ce qui importeroit dans cette affaire seroit de pouvoir rejetter tous ceux entre lesquels on vous force de choisir."

46. *O.C.* III, 1669–1670.

47. *Lettre* I, in *O.C.* III, 687. Cf. Candaux's notes, *O.C.* III, 1578. In *Lettre* VIII Rousseau insists that he prefers permanent exile to disturbing the public tranquility of Geneva (*O.C.* III, 852).

48. *Dédicace,* in *O.C.* III, 112.

49. *Contrat social* I, 1, in *O.C.* III, 351.

50. *Lettre* VII, in *O.C.* III, 813–814.

51. *Ibid.*, pp. 814–815.

52. *Ibid.*, pp. 826–829.

53. *Lettre* VIII, in *O.C.* III, 854–858. Candaux points out that the real reason for the decline was the tendency toward oligarchy during the latter part of the sixteenth century. *O.C.* III, 1701.

54. Cf. Candaux, *O.C.* III, 1698–1699.

55. *Lettre* VIII, in *O.C.* III, 852–854. In 1766 the Genevan *cercles*, which by this time had largely replaced the assemblies of bourgeois companies, were permitted to elect twenty-four delegates to represent the bourgeoisie in negotiations with the foreign mediators who had intervened following the political impasse reached in January of that year as a result of the persistent refusal of the Conseil Général to elect the nominees of the Petit Conseil. Ferrier, p. 452.

56. *Lettre* IX, in *O.C.* III, 875–876.

57. *O.C.* III, 430.

58. *Confessions* XI, in *O.C.* I, 582; Cohen trans., p. 537.

59. *O.C.* III, 1000.

60. *Lettre* VII, in *O.C.* III, 824.

61. *Ibid.*, pp. 830–831. Candaux points out that Rousseau somewhat exaggerates the attendance at earlier meetings of the Conseil Général and understates the attendance at more recent meetings. *O.C.* III, 1685–1686.

62. *Lettre* VII, in *O.C.* III, 830–832.

63. *Lettre* IX, in *O.C.* III, 874–875.

64. Candaux quotes the pertinent passage from Lenieps' letter of October 18, 1763, in *O.C.* III, 1711.

65. *Lettre* IX, in *O.C.* III, 877–879.

66. *Ibid.*, pp. 878–879. For the point about the ineffectiveness of the Conseil Général's power of the purse, see *Lettre* VII, in *O.C.* III, 814.

67. *Histoire de Genève*, in *Oeuvres complètes* (ed. Launay), III, 389–397; *Lettre* VII, *passim.*

68. *Lettre* VII, in *O.C.* III, 835. Candaux suggests that Rousseau here outdoes even Micheli du Crest in his attack on the patriciate (*O.C.* III, 1668–1669, 1690). This may be true if one considers only the violence of the language Rousseau uses to characterize the patriciate, but unlike Micheli, Rousseau does not follow up this virulent criticism with the kind of radical demands that would threaten the patriciate's monopoly of political power.

69. *Lettre* IX, in *O.C.* III, 893–897.

NINE. ROUSSEAU AS LAWGIVER: CORSICA AND POLAND

1. *Contrat social* II, 10, in *O.C.* III, 391.

2. Sven Stelling-Michaud, "Introduction" to the *Projet de constitution pour la Corse,* in *O.C.* III, cxcix.

3. For a contemporary account of Paoli's constitution, see James Boswell's *An Account of Corsica: The Journal of a Tour to That Island,* 2nd ed. (London: Dilly, 1768), pp. 144–163. Boswell visited Rousseau just prior to his trip to Corsica. Matthieu Fontana's *La constitution de Généralat de Pascal Paoli en Corse (1755–1769)* (Paris: Bonvalot-Jouve, 1907) is a thorough study of the constitution but hardly less glowing in its praise of Paoli than Boswell's account. For briefer but more critical studies of Paoli's constitution, see Pierre Antonetti, *Histoire de la Corse* (Paris: Éditions Laffont, 1973),

pp. 349–364 and references; also Paul Arrighi, *La vie quotidienne en Corse au XVIIIe siècle* (Paris: Hachette, 1970), pp. 117–128.

The political theory of the Corsican revolution is examined by Fernand Ettori in "Du droit des peuples à disposer d'eux-mêmes: la révolte des Corses et la théorie de la souveraineté," in *Images du peuple au dix-huitième siècle* (Paris: Armand Colin, 1973), pp. 177–185. Ettori contends that as a result of the key role played by the Corsican clergy in formulating the theory used to justify the revolution, that theory owed more to traditional Christian teachings than to the contract and natural law theories that were prevalent in the eighteenth century.

4. Stelling-Michaud, *O.C.* III, cxcix–cci; Vaughan, II, 292–293. On the nature of Paoli's constitution, see Antonetti, p. 349, and Peter Adam Thrasher, *Pasquale Paoli: An Enlightened Hero, 1725–1807* (n.p.: Archon, 1970), p. 82.

5. Thadd E. Hall, *France and the Eighteenth-Century Corsican Question* (New York: New York University Press, 1971), pp. 162–186. Ernestine Dedeck-Héry stresses Buttafuoco's desire to reestablish the prerogatives of the Corsican nobility against the views of both Paoli and Rousseau in her *Jean-Jacques Rousseau et le Projet de constitution pour la Corse: histoire des pourparlers de J.-J. Rousseau avec ses correspondants corses et des répercussions de ces pourparlers dans le monde des lettres* (Philadelphia: University of Pennsylvania Press, 1932), pp. 52–53, 103–104. Stelling-Michaud supports this thesis in *O.C.* III, ccii–ccvii.

6. Stelling-Michaud, *O.C.* III, ccii–ccix; Vaughan, II, 293–295.

7. While this rule is hardly surprising in itself, Rousseau's application of it is rather surprising. Just as there is an incongruity between the radical principles of Books I and II of the *Contrat*, on the one hand, and his acceptance of Genevan institutions as the model for the institutions of Book III, so too his wholehearted acceptance of Corsican institutions tends to render the basic principles of the *Contrat* almost irrelevant to the whole project.

8. Rousseau apparently envisioned that the entire citizenry of Corsica would assemble on at least one occasion in a kind of literal enactment of the original social contract. "Toute la nation Corse se reunira par un serment solemnel en un seul corps politique dont tant les corses qui doivent la composer que les individus seront desormais les membres." *O.C.* III, 943.

9. Among the fragments found in Rousseau's miscellaneous papers relating to the *Projet* are two that may indicate his approval of the Consulte Générale: "Les Gardes des Loix pourront convoquer les états généraux toutes les fois qu'il leur plaira, et depuis le jour de la convocation jusqu'au lendemain de l'assemblée l'autorité du grand Podestat et du conseil d'état sera suspendue." "Les Etats une fois convoqués extraordinairement par le Senat ne pourront se dissoudre que le Senat ou le grand Podestat ne soient cassés." *O.C.* III, 944–945. Franz Neumann takes these fragments as evidence that Rousseau here accepted representative government. "Types of Natural Law," in *The Democratic and Authoritarian State: Essays in Political and Legal Theory*, edited with a preface by Herbert Marcuse (1957; rpt. New York: Free Press, 1964), p. 92, footnote #30. Neumann's interpretation may be correct, but it is also possible that these fragments were simply Rousseau's notes on the existing constitution of Corsica, which, apart from the terminology, they accurately reflect, rather than his own recommendations.

10. *O.C.* III, 907; trans. by Frederick Watkins, in *Rousseau: Political Writings* (London: Nelson, 1953), p. 286.

11. *O.C.* III, 907–914. That Switzerland rather than Geneva is proposed as the

model is an interesting departure from the *Contrat social*, where Swiss mountaineers are mentioned in passing as "the happiest people in the world" (*O.C.* III, 437) but otherwise receive scant attention. Rousseau attributed this change of models to Corsica's size, but it may also reflect his recent disenchantment with Geneva.

12. Stelling-Michaud gives the following definition of a *piève:* "La piève était la circonscription administrative que formait le groupement de plusieurs communes; elle correspondait à peu près au canton actuel." *O.C.* III, 1728. Arrighi places the number of *pièves* at this time between 55 and 61 (p. 117).

13. Arrighi, pp. 117–120; Antonetti, pp. 349–352.

14. Jean Fabre, "Introduction" to the *Considérations sur le gouvernement de Pologne,* in *O.C.* III, ccxxi–ccxxiii, ccxxxiii.

15. *Ibid.,* pp. ccxxiv–ccxxviii. Fabre elaborates on the contrasting views of Voltaire and Grimm, on the one hand, and Rousseau, on the other, in his *Stanislaus-Auguste Poniatowski et l'Europe des Lumières* (Strasbourg, France: Université de Strasbourg, 1952), pp. 21–52, and in his "Jean-Jacques Rousseau et le destin polonais," *Europe* (nov.-déc. 1961), 206–227. For a broader analysis of French opinion of Poland at this time, see Ryszard W. Woloszynski, "La Pologne vue par l'Europe au XVIIIe siècle," *Acta Poloniae Historica,* X (1965), 22–42. The fundamental realism of Rousseau's political proposals is convincingly argued by Fabre in his "Réalité et utopie dans la pensée politique de Rousseau," especially pp. 205–216.

16. These are the dates of composition given by Fabre, *O.C.* III, ccxvii, who relies mainly on evidence presented by Otto Forst-Battaglia in "Un peu de lumière sur les *Considérations*," *Annales de la Société Jean-Jacques Rousseau,* XVII (1926), 97–119. Prior to Forst-Battaglia's article, and even in many works published since then, the dates of composition given by Vaughan (II, 390–395), October 1771 to April 1772, were generally accepted. Fabre acknowledges that Rousseau must have made some changes in the manuscript after June 1771, but he contends that Rousseau cannot have written the *Considérations* as late as Vaughan suggests, for by that time the Confederates had been defeated in battle beyond all hope of recovering, and Rousseau would have had no reason to identify himself with their cause.

17. Fabre, *O.C.* III, ccxxv–ccxxxvi; see also Fabre's note, *O.C.* III, 1735.

18. Fabre, "Jean-Jacques Rousseau et le destin polonais," pp. 207–208; also *O.C.* III, ccxli.

19. *O.C.* III, 953–954, 961, 970–971, 1037, 1041.

20. *Ibid.,* pp. 970–971, 978, 1010. Rousseau used the term *Gouvernements fédératifs* in this context, but he did not always distinguish clearly between federation and confederation, and in this instance he may have wished to avoid confusion with the Confederation of Bar. In any event, there is little doubt that the system he outlined in the *Considérations* was a federation rather than a confederation in terms of the distinctions made by Windenberger since Rousseau vested final legislative authority in the national diet rather than in the dietines.

21. *Contrat social* III, 15, in *O.C.* III, 430; Cranston trans., p. 141.

22. *O.C.* III, 973; Watkins trans., p. 185. Emphasis added.

23. *O.C.* III, 980–981.

24. Rousseau made this proposal in *O.C.* III, 1024–1029. It will be recalled that he had previously explicitly opposed the extension of the franchise to the *natifs* and *habitants* of Geneva even though these two groups were surely better prepared for citizenship according to his criteria than were the Polish serfs.

25. *Rousseau et la science politique,* pp. 279–280.

26. *O.C.* III, 978–980. Quotation on p. 980; Watkins trans., p. 194.

27. *Ibid.*, p. 1000.

28. Rousseau may have perceived Poland's political institutions, including the imperative mandate, as prefeudal rather than feudal in origin. This at least was the view of Rulhière in his *Histoire de l'anarchie de Pologne*. Cf. Fabre's comments on this, *O.C.* III, 1741.

29. P. Skwarczynski, "The Constitution of Poland Before the Partitions," in *The Cambridge History of Poland* (Cambridge, England: Cambridge University Press, 1951), II, 56.

30. *O.C.* III, 994–998.

31. *Ibid.*, p. 979; Watkins trans., p. 193.

32. Skwarczynski identifies six types of dietine: (1) prediet dietines summoned by the king to elect deputies to the diet and prepare their instructions; (2) election dietines summoned by sheriffs to elect local officials; (3) dietines composed of deputies of the nobility whose function was to elect judges; (4) dietines of report—what Rousseau called *dietines de relations*—to review the work of deputies to the diet; (5) hooded dietines, which formed into confederations during an interregnum and temporarily exercised considerable powers; (6) economic dietines, which assessed taxes imposed by the diet and also imposed additional taxes on their own authority, maintained the local militia, and generally contributed to the radical decentralization of the state's administration. Skwarczynski, pp. 57–58.

33. The average membership of the thirty-degree dietines was approximately 25,000 to 30,000, depending on which estimate of the population of the Polish nobility one accepts. L. R. Lewitter, "Poland Under the Saxon Kings," *The New Cambridge Modern History* (Cambridge, England: Cambridge University Press, 1957), VII, 366, gives figures of two or three dozen magnates and 1 million lesser noblemen. Franklin L. Ford, *Europe: 1780–1830* (New York: Holt, Rinehart and Winston, 1970), p. 41, estimates a maximum of 750,000 noblemen in mid-eighteenth-century Poland.

34. *O.C.* III, 979–980.

35. *Ibid.*, p. 972; Watkins trans., p. 183.

36. *Ibid.*, pp. 974, 1012–1020; Watkins trans., pp. 186–187. Rousseau did not use the term *guerilla warfare*, but from his description of what he called "la petite guerre," he clearly intended what would now be called guerilla warfare.

37. *Ibid.*, pp. 1024–1029; Watkins trans., p. 253. Rousseau seems to have contemplated separate representation for free peasants in the dietines and for the burghers in the diet, at least as temporary expedients pending the elevation of all persons to the equal status of citizen. *O.C.* III, 1027.

38. Lewitter, pp. 365–366.

39. *O.C.* III, 964–965.

40. *Ibid.*, pp. 1001–1002. It was in keeping with the uncharacteristically radical reforms advocated by Rousseau in those sections of the *Considérations* dealing with the franchise and the merit system that he should here call into question one of the most basic tenets of even liberal eighteenth-century thought, namely, that the right to vote presupposed economic independence.

41. *Ibid.*, pp. 966–970. He apparently did not intend to include the children of burghers and peasants in this system of public education, at least not in the beginning. Their public education would take place rather in public games, festivals, and ceremonies designed to instill in them love of their country and its law. All ranks of

society would participate together in these public events. Rousseau believed that this would simultaneously strengthen the feelings of a common bond and reinforce the people's respect for their leaders. *O.C.* III, 962–964. All of these devices are highly reminiscent of his proposals in the *Lettre à d'Alembert*.

42. *Ibid.,* pp. 1019–1029.

43. *Ibid.,* pp. 975–978.

44. Skwarczynski, p. 55; Fabre, *O.C.* III, 1768.

45. *O.C.* III, 985–994. The senate would thus be composed of 89 senator-deputies, i.e., senators elected for two-year terms by the diet and eligible to participate in legislation as well as administration, and 89 senators-for-life, who would have purely administrative duties. Of these 89 senators-for-life, 72 would be elected by the dietines, 16 bishops would be appointed by the king, and the archbishop of Gniezno, the ranking religious leader, would be elected by the diet. These figures are derived from Rousseau's account plus the information on the actual number of senators of various categories supplied by Fabre, *O.C.* III, 1768.

Rousseau listed the following powers as appropriate to the king: "To preside over the diet, the senate and all corporate groups, to examine strictly the conduct of all office-holders, to take great pains to maintain justice and the integrity of all the law courts, to preserve order and tranquility in the state, to maintain its position abroad, to command its armies in time of war, to inaugurate useful works in time of peace, these are the duties which particularly pertain to his royal office." *O.C.* III, 993; Watkins trans., p. 211.

46. *Ibid.,* pp. 1029–1036.

BIBLIOGRAPHY

I. Works by Rousseau

Wherever possible, I have cited the Pléiade edition of Rousseau's works, *Oeuvres complètes*, édition publiée sous la direction de Bernard Gagnebin et Marcel Raymond (Paris: Éditions Gallimard, 1959 to date), which includes extremely useful introductions and notes. Four volumes have been published to date, including most of Rousseau's political writings. Citations to this edition are indicated by *O.C.* followed by the volume number.

For works not yet published in the Pléiade edition, I have used the *Oeuvres complètes*, edited by Michel Launay (Paris: Éditions du Seuil, 1971), 3 v.

For Rousseau's *Lettre à d'Alembert sur les spectacles*, which does not appear in either the Pléiade or Launay editions, I have used the edition by M. Fuchs (Lille, France: Librairie Giard; Genève: Librairie Droz, 1948).

A new edition of Rousseau's correspondence is now in the process of publication, and I have used this wherever possible: *Correspondance complète de Jean-Jacques Rousseau*, edited by R. A. Leigh (Genève: 1965 to date).

All translations from Rousseau's works are my own unless indicated otherwise, but I have borrowed freely from the following existing translations:

The Confessions. Translated with an introduction by J. M. Cohen. Baltimore: Penguin, 1954.

The First and Second Discourses. Edited, with introduction and notes by Roger D. Masters; translated by Roger D. and Judith R. Masters. New York: St. Martin's, 1964.

The Social Contract and Discourses. Translated with an introduction by G. D. H. Cole. New York: Dutton, 1950.

Politics and the Arts: Letter to M. d'Alembert on the Theatre. Translated with notes and introduction by Allan Bloom. Ithaca, N.Y.: Cornell University Press, 1960.

The Social Contract. Translated and introduced by Maurice Cranston. Baltimore: Penguin, 1968.

Rousseau: Political Writings. Translated and edited by Frederick Watkins. New York: Nelson, 1953.

II. Works by Other Authors

Acomb, Frances. *Anglophobia in France, 1763–1789: An Essay in the History of Constitutionalism and Nationalism.* Durham, N.C.: Duke University Press, 1950.

Amtliche Sammlung der ältern Eidgenössischen Abschiede. Die Eidgenössichen Abschiede aus dem Zeitraume von 1712 bis 1743, bearbeitet von Daniel Albert Fechter. Basel: Baur'schen, 1860.

Antonetti, Pierre. *Histoire de la Corse.* Paris: Éditions Robert Laffont, 1973.

Aristotle. *The Politics of Aristotle.* Trans. with an introduction, notes, and appendixes by Ernest Barker. New York: Oxford University Press, 1962.

Arrighi, Paul. *La vie quotidienne en Corse au XVIIIe siècle.* Paris: Hachette, 1970.

Barber, Benjamin R. *The Death of Communal Liberty: A History of Freedom in a Swiss Mountain Canton.* Princeton, N.J.: Princeton University Press, 1974.

Barker, Ernest. "Introduction" to *Social Contract: Essays by Locke, Hume, and Rousseau.* 1947; rpt. New York: Oxford University Press, 1962.

Bastid, Paul. "Rousseau et la théorie des formes de gouvernement," in *Études sur le Contrat social de Jean-Jacques Rousseau,* pp. 315–327.

Besterman, Theodore. *Voltaire.* New York: Harcourt, Brace and World, 1969.

Birch, A. H. *Representation.* New York: Praeger, 1971.

Bloom, Allan. "Jean-Jacques Rousseau," in *History of Political Theory.* 2nd ed. Edited by Leo Strauss and Joseph Cropsey. Chicago: Rand McNally, 1972.

Bonno, Gabriel. *La constitution britannique devant l'opinion française de Montesquieu à Bonaparte.* Paris: Honoré Champion, 1931.

Boswell, James. *An Account of Corsica: The Journal of a Tour to That Island.* 2nd ed. London: Dilly, 1768.

Broome, J. H. *Rousseau: A Study of His Thought.* London: Arnold, 1963.

Chapman, John W. *Rousseau—Totalitarian or Liberal?* New York: Columbia University Press, 1956.

Chevallier, Jean-Jacques. "Le mot et la notion de *gouvernement* chez Rousseau," in *Études sur le Contrat social de Jean-Jacques Rousseau,* pp. 291–313.

Choisy, Eugène. "La réforme calvinienne," in *Histoire de Genève des origines à 1789,* pp. 231–255.

Citizen of Geneva: Selections from the Letters of Jean-Jacques Rousseau. Edited by Charles William Hendel. New York: Oxford University Press, 1937.

Cobban, Alfred. *Rousseau and the Modern State.* 2nd ed. London: George Allen and Unwin, 1964.

Cousin, Jean. "J.-J. Rousseau interprète des institutions romaines dans le *Contrat social,*" in *Études sur le Contrat social de Jean-Jacques Rousseau,* pp. 13–34.

Crocker, Lester G. *Jean-Jacques Rousseau: A New Interpretative Analysis of His Life and Works.* New York: Macmillan, 1968–1973. 2 v.

——. "Rousseau et la voie du totalitarisme," in *Rousseau et la philosophie politique,* pp. 99–136.

——. *Rousseau's Social Contract: An Interpretive Essay.* Cleveland: Case Western Reserve University Press, 1968.

Dahl, Robert, and Edward R. Tufte. *Size and Democracy.* Stanford, Calif.: Stanford University Press, 1973.

Davy, Georges. "Le corps politique selon le *Contrat social* de J.-J. Rousseau et ses antécédents chez Hobbes," in *Études sur le Contrat social de Jean-Jacques Rousseau,* pp. 65–93.

Dedeck-Héry, Ernestine. *Jean-Jacques Rousseau et le Projet de constitution pour la Corse: histoire des pourparlers de J.-J. Rousseau avec ses correspondants corses et des répercussions de ces pourparlers dans le monde des lettres.* Philadelphia: University of Pennsylvania Press, 1932.

Dedieu, Joseph. *Montesquieu et la tradition politique anglaise en France*. Paris: Victor Lecoffre, 1909.

Derathé, Robert. *Jean-Jacques Rousseau et la science politique de son temps*. 2nd ed. Paris: J. Vrin, 1970.

——. "Les philosophes et le despotisme," pp. 57–75 in *Utopie et institutions au XVIIIe siècle: le pragmatisme des Lumières*. Textes recueillis par Pierre Francastel. Paris: Mouton, 1963.

——. "Les rapports de l'exécutif et du législatif chez J.-J. Rousseau," in *Rousseau et la philosophie politique*, pp. 153–169.

——. "Montesquieu et Jean-Jacques Rousseau." *Revue internationale de philosophie*, 9 (1955), 366–386.

——. "Rousseau et le problème de la monarchie." *Le Contrat social*, 6, no. 3 (mai–juin 1962), 165–168.

Diderot, Denis. *Oeuvres politiques*. Edited by Paul Vernière. Paris: Garnier, 1963.

Édit de pacification de 1782. Genève: Pellet, 1782.

Édits de la République de Genève. Genève: Les Frères Detournes, 1735.

The Eighteenth-Century Constitution, 1688–1815: Documents and Commentary. Edited by E. Neville Williams. Cambridge, England: Cambridge University Press, 1960.

Einaudi, Mario. *The Early Rousseau*. Ithaca, N.Y.: Cornell University Press, 1967.

Eisenmann, Charles. "La cité de Jean-Jacques Rousseau," in *Etudes sur le Contrat social de Jean-Jacques Rousseau*, pp. 191–201.

The Encyclopédie of Diderot and d'Alembert: Selected Articles. Edited by John Lough. Cambridge, England: Cambridge University Press, 1954.

Encyclopédie ou Dictionnaire raisonné des sciences, des arts, et des métiers, 1751–1772. Edited by Alain Pons. Paris: J'ai Lu, 1963.

Ettori, Fernand. "Du droit des peuples à disposer d'eux-mêmes: la révolte des Corses et la théorie de la souveraineté," pp. 177–185 in *Images du peuple au dix-huitième siècle*. Paris: Armand Colin, 1973.

Études sur le Contrat social de Jean-Jacques Rousseau. Actes des journées d'étude tenues à Dijon les 3, 4, 5, et 6 mai 1962. Paris: Société Les Belles Lettres, 1964.

Fabre, Jean. "Jean-Jacques Rousseau et le destin polonais." *Europe* (nov.–déc. 1961), 206–227.

——. "Réalité et utopie dans la pensée politique de Rousseau." *Annales de la Société Jean-Jacques Rousseau*, 35 (1959–1962), 179–221.

——. *Stanislaus-Auguste Poniatowski et l'Europe des Lumières.* Strasbourg, France: Université de Strasbourg, 1952.

Favre, Edouard, and Paul-F. Geisendorf. "Les Combourgeoisies avec Fribourg et Berne," in *Histoire de Genève des origines à 1789,* pp. 171–186.

Fazy, Henri. *Les constitutions de la République de Genève: étude historique.* Paris: Librairie Fischbacher, 1890.

The Federalist. Edited with an introduction and notes by Jacob E. Cooke. Cleveland: Meridian Books, 1961.

Ferrero, Guglielmo. "Genève et le *Contrat social.*" *Annales de la Société Jean-Jacques Rousseau,* 23 (1934), 137–152.

Ferrier, Jean-Pierre. "Le xviiie siècle: politique intérieure et extérieure," in *Histoire de Genève des origines à 1789,* pp. 401–482.

Fetscher, Iring. "Rousseau, auteur d'intention conservatrice et d'action révolutionnaire," in *Rousseau et la philosophie politique,* pp. 51–75.

——. *Rousseaus politische Philosophie: zur Geschichte des demokratischen Freiheitsbegriffs.* 2nd ed. Neuwied am Rhein: Luchterhand, 1968.

Fink, Zera S. *The Classical Republicans: An Essay in the Recovery of a Pattern of Thought in Seventeenth Century England.* Evanston, Ill.: Northwestern University Press, 1945.

Fontana, Matthieu. *La constitution du Généralat de Pascal Paoli en Corse (1755–1769).* Paris: Bonvalot-Jouve, 1907.

Ford, Franklin L. *Europe: 1780–1830.* New York: Holt, Rinehart and Winston, 1970.

——. *Robe and Sword: The Regrouping of the French Aristocracy after Louis XIV.* 1953; rpt. New York: Harper and Row, 1965.

Forst-Battaglia, Otto. "Un peu de lumière sur les *Considérations.*" *Annales de la Société Jean-Jacques Rousseau,* 17 (1926), 97–119.

Fritz, Kurt von. *The Theory of the Mixed Constitution in Antiquity: A Critical Analysis of Polybius' Political Ideas.* New York: Columbia University Press, 1954.

Gagnebin, Bernard. *Burlamaqui et le droit naturel.* Genève: Éditions de la Frégate, 1944.

Gardy, Frédéric. "Genève au xve siècle," in *Histoire de Genève des origines à 1789,* pp. 139–169.

Gay, Peter. *The Enlightenment: An Interpretation.* 2 v. New York: Random House, 1966–1969.

——. *The Party of Humanity: Essays in the French Enlightenment.* New York: Norton, 1971.

——. *Voltaire's Politics: The Poet as Realist.* New York: Vintage, 1965.

Gierke, Otto von. *The Development of Political Theory.* Translated by Bernard Freyd. New York: Norton, 1939.

Glotz, Gustave. *The Greek City and Its Institutions.* 1929; rpt. New York: Barnes and Noble, 1969.

Grandjean, Henri. "De la féodalité à la Communauté," in *Histoire de Genève des origines à 1789*, pp. 91–137.

Grimsley, Ronald. "Introduction" to *Du Contrat social.* Oxford, England: Clarendon Press, 1972.

——. "Rousseau and the Problem of Happiness," in *Hobbes and Rousseau*, pp. 437–461.

Groethuysen, Bernard. *Jean-Jacques Rousseau.* Paris: Gallimard, 1949.

Guéhenno, Jean. *Jean-Jacques Rousseau.* 2 v. Trans. by John and Doreen Weightman. New York: Columbia University Press, 1967.

Hall, Thadd E. *France and the Eighteenth-Century Corsican Question.* New York: New York University Press, 1971.

Harrington, James. *The Political Writings of James Harrington: Representative Selections.* Edited by Charles Blitzer. Indianapolis: Bobbs-Merrill, 1955.

Harvey, Ray Forrest. *Jean Jacques Burlamaqui: A Liberal Tradition in American Constitutionalism.* Chapel Hill: University of North Carolina Press, 1937.

Havens, George R. "Introduction" to *Discours sur les sciences et les arts.* New York: Modern Language Association of America, 1946.

Haymann, Franz. "La loi naturelle dans la philosophie politique de J.-J. Rousseau." *Annales de la Société Jean-Jacques Rousseau*, 30 (1943–1945), 65–110.

Hendel, Charles W. *Jean-Jacques Rousseau: Moralist.* 2 v. London: Oxford University Press, 1934.

Hill, Christopher. *Reformation to Industrial Revolution.* Baltimore: Penguin, 1969.

Histoire de Genève des origines à 1789. Publiée par la Société d'Histoire et d'Archéologie de Genève. Genève: Jullien, 1951.

Hobbes, Thomas. *Leviathan.* Edited with an introduction by Michael Oakeshott. Oxford, England: Blackwell, n.d.

——. *Man and Citizen.* Edited with an introduction by Bernard Gert. Garden City, N.Y.: Doubleday, 1972.

Hobbes and Rousseau: A Collection of Critical Essays. Edited by Maurice Cranston and Richard S. Peters. Garden City, N.Y.: Doubleday, 1972.

Holbach, Paul Henri Thiry, Baron d'. *La politique naturelle, ou Discours sur les vrais principes du gouvernement.* Londres: 1773.
——. *Système sociale, ou Principes naturels de la morale et de la politique.* Londres: 1773.
Homo, Léon. *Roman Political Institutions from City to State.* 1929; rpt. New York: Barnes and Noble, 1962.
Hubert, René. *Rousseau et l'Encyclopédie: essai sur la formation des idées politiques de Rousseau (1742–1756).* Paris: Gamber, 1928.
Ivernois, François d'. *An Historical and Political View of the Constitution and Revolutions of Geneva in the Eighteenth Century.* Trans. from the French by John Farrell. Dublin: Wilson, 1784.
Jean-Jacques Rousseau. Neuchâtel, Switzerland: Éditions de la Baconnière, 1962.
Jimack, Peter D. "La genèse et la rédaction de l'*Émile* de J.-J. Rousseau." *Studies on Voltaire and the Eighteenth Century,* 13 (1960), 33–43.
Jost, François. *Jean-Jacques Rousseau Suisse.* Fribourg, Switzerland: Éditions Universitaires, 1961.
Jouvenel, Bertrand de. "Essai sur la politique de Rousseau," pp. 1–160 in *Du Contrat social.* Genève: Éditions du Cheval Ailé, 1947.
——. "Rousseau's Theory of the Forms of Government," in *Hobbes and Rousseau,* pp. 484–497.
——. "Rousseau the Pessimistic Evolutionist." *Yale French Studies,* 28 (Fall–Winter 1961–1962), 83–96.
——. "Théorie des formes de gouvernement chez Rousseau." *Le Contrat social,* 6, no. 6 (nov–dec. 1962), 343–351.
Kenyon, Cecilia M. "Alexander Hamilton: Rousseau of the Right." *Political Science Quarterly,* 73, no. 2 (June 1958), 161–178.
Krafft, Olivier. *La politique de Jean-Jacques Rousseau: aspects méconnus.* Paris: Pichon et Durand-Auzias, 1958.
Larsen, J. A. O. *Representative Government in Greek and Roman History.* Berkeley: University of California Press, 1966.
Laski, Harold J. *Political Thought in England: Locke to Bentham.* London: Oxford University Press, 1919.
Launay, Michel. *Jean-Jacques Rousseau écrivain politique (1712–1762).* Cannes: C. E. L.; Grenoble: A.C.E.R., 1971.
——. "*La Nouvelle Héloïse,* son contenu et son public," pp. 179–184 in *Jean-Jacques Rousseau et son temps: politique et littérature au XVIIIᵉ siècle.* Paris: Nizet, 1969.
Leigh, R. A. "Liberté et autorité dans le *Contrat social,*" pp. 249–264

in *Jean-Jacques Rousseau et son oeuvre: problèmes et recherches*. Paris: Klincksieck, 1964.

Lévy, Yves. "Machiavel et Rousseau." *Le Contrat social*, 6, no. 3 (mai–juin 1962), 169–174.

Lewitter, L. R. "Poland Under the Saxon Kings," in *The New Cambridge Modern History*. Cambridge, England: Cambridge University Press, 1957.

Liebeskind, W.-A. "Le discours du syndic Chouet sur la nature du gouvernement de l'Etat de Genève," pp. 394–400 in *Mélanges d'histoire et de littérature offerte à Monsieur Charles Gilliard*. Lausanne, Switzerland: F. Rouge, 1944.

——. "Un débat sur la démocratie genevoise: Chouet et Fatio au Conseil général (5 mai 1707)," pp. 99–107 in *Mélanges Georges Sauser-Hall*. Neuchâtel, Switzerland: Delachaux et Niestlé, 1952.

Locke, John. *Two Treatise of Government*. Edited by Peter Laslett. Rev. ed. New York: Cambridge University Press, 1963.

Lough, John. *The Encyclopédie*. London: Longman, 1971.

Lüthy, Herbert. *From Calvin to Rousseau: Tradition and Modernity in Socio-Political Thought from the Reformation to the French Revolution*. Translated by Salvator Attanasio. New York: Basic, 1970.

McDonald, Joan. *Rousseau and the French Revolution, 1762–1791*. London: Athlone Press, 1965.

Masters, Roger D. *The Political Philosophy of Rousseau*. Princeton, N.J.: Princeton University Press, 1968.

——. "The Structure of Rousseau's Political Thought," in *Hobbes and Rousseau*, pp. 401–436.

Michell, H. *Sparta*. Cambridge, England: Cambridge University Press, 1964.

Monter, E. William. *Calvin's Geneva*. New York: Wiley, 1967.

Montesquieu, Charles Secondat, Baron de. *The Spirit of the Laws*. Trans. by Thomas Nugent, with an introduction by Franz Neumann. 2 v. New York: Hafner, 1949.

Morgan, Edmund S. *American Slavery, American Freedom: The Ordeal of Colonial Virginia*. New York: Norton, 1975.

Mornet, Daniel. *Les origines intellectuelles de la révolution française, 1715–1787*. 6th ed. Paris: Armand Colin, 1967.

Naef, Henri. "L'émancipation politique et la Réforme," in *Histoire de Genève des origines à 1789*, pp. 187–217.

Neumann, Franz. *The Democratic and Authoritarian State: Essays in Political and Legal Theory*. Edited with a preface by Herbert Marcuse. New York: Free Press, 1957.

O'Mara, Patrick F. "Jean-Jacques and Geneva: The Petty Bourgeois Milieu of Rousseau's Thought." *The Historian* (Feb. 1958), 127–152.

Palmer, Robert R. *The Age of the Democratic Revolution: A Political History of Europe and America, 1760–1800.* 2 v. Princeton, N.J.: Princeton University Press, 1959.

Pateman, Carole. *Participation and Democratic Theory.* Cambridge, England: Cambridge University Press, 1970.

Perkins, Merle L. *Jean-Jacques Rousseau on the Individual and Society.* Lexington: University Press of Kentucky, 1974.

———. *The Moral and Political Philosophy of the Abbé de Saint-Pierre.* Genève: Droz, 1959.

Pitkin, Hanna Fenichel. *The Concept of Representation.* Berkeley: University of California Press, 1967.

Plamenatz, John. "Ce qui ne signifie autre chose sinon qu'on le forcera d'être libre," in *Rousseau et la philosophie politique,* pp. 137–152.

———. *Man and Society.* 2 v. New York: McGraw-Hill, 1963.

Plato. *The Collected Dialogues of Plato, Including the Letters.* Edited by Edith Hamilton and Huntington Cairns. Princeton, N.J.: Princeton University Press, 1963.

Plumb, J. H. *England in the Eighteenth Century (1714–1815).* Baltimore: Penguin, 1969.

Pole, J. R. *Political Representation in England and the Origins of the American Republic.* New York: St. Martin's, 1966.

Polin, Raymond. *La politique de la solitude: essai sur la philosophie politique de Jean-Jacques Rousseau.* Paris: Éditions Sirey, 1971.

Raymond, Marcel. "Rousseau et Genève," in *Jean-Jacques Rousseau,* pp. 225–237.

Robbins, Caroline. *The Eighteenth-Century Commonwealthman: Studies in the Transmission, Development and Circumstance of English Liberal Thought from the Restoration of Charles II Until the War with the Thirteen Colonies.* Cambridge, Mass.: Harvard University Press, 1959.

Rousseau et la philosophie politique. Annales de philosophie politique, special publication no. 5. Paris: Presses Universitaires de France, 1965.

Sabine, George H. *A History of Political Theory.* 3rd ed. New York: Holt, Rinehart and Winston, 1961.

Schmitt, Eberhard. *Repräsentation und Revolution: eine Untersuchung zur Genesis der kontinentalen Theorie und Praxis parlamentarischer*

Repräsentation aus der Herrschaftspraxis des Ancien régime in Frankreich (1760–1789). München: Verlag C. H. Beck, 1969.

Sée, Henri. *L'évolution de la pensée politique en France au XVIIIe siècle*. Paris: Giard, 1925.

Shklar, Judith. *Men and Citizens: A Study of Rousseau's Social Theory*. Cambridge, England: Cambridge University Press, 1969.

Skwarczynski, P. "The Constitution of Poland Before the Partitions," in *The Cambridge History of Poland*. Cambridge, England: Cambridge University Press, 1951.

Soboul, Albert. "L'audience des Lumières sous la Révolution: Jean-Jacques Rousseau et les classes populaires," pp. 289–303 in *Utopie et institutions au XVIIIe siècle: le pragmatisme des Lumières*. Paris: Mouton, 1963.

——. "Jean-Jacques Rousseau et le jacobinisme," in *Études sur le Contrat social de Jean-Jacques Rousseau*, pp. 405–424.

——. *The Parisian Sans-Culottes and the French Revolution, 1793–1794*. Translated by Gwynne Lewis. Oxford, England: Clarendon Press, 1964.

Sozzi, Lionello. "Interprétations de Rousseau pendant la Révolution." *Studies on Voltaire and the Eighteenth Century*, 64 (1968), 187–223.

Spink, John Stephenson. *Jean-Jacques Rousseau et Genève: essai sur les idées politiques et religieuses de Rousseau dans leur relation avec la pensée genevoise au XVIIIe siècle*. Paris: Boivin, 1934.

Starobinski, Jean. *Jean-Jacques Rousseau: la transparence et l'obstacle*. 2nd ed. Paris: Gallimard, 1971.

——. "Rousseau & Modern Tyranny." *The New York Review of Books*, Nov. 29, 1973, pp. 20–25.

Stelling-Michaud, Sven. "Ce que Jean-Jacques doit à l'abbé de Saint-Pierre," in *Études sur le Contrat social de Jean-Jacques Rousseau*, pp. 35–45.

Talmon, J. L. *The Origins of Totalitarian Democracy*. New York: Norton, 1960.

Terrasse, Jean. *Jean-Jacques Rousseau et la quête de l'âge d'or*. Bruxelles: Palais des Académies, 1970.

Thrasher, Peter Adam. *Pasquale Paoli: An Enlightened Hero, 1725–1807*. n.p.: Archon Books, 1970.

Vallette, Gaspard. *Jean-Jacques Rousseau Genevois*. Paris: Plon-Nourrit; Genève: Jullien, 1911.

Vaughan, C. E. *The Political Writings of Jean-Jacques Rousseau.* 2 v. 1915; rpt. New York: Wiley, 1962.

Weil, Eric. "J.-J. Rousseau et sa politique." *Critique,* 8, no. 56 (Jan. 1952), 3–28.

Weinstein, Fred, and Gerald M. Platt. *The Wish to Be Free: Society, Psyche, and Value Change.* Berkeley: University of California Press, 1969.

Weis, Eberhard. *Geschichtsschreibung und Staatsauffassung in der französischen Enzyklopädie.* Wiesbaden: Franz Steiner Verlag, 1956.

Weulersee, Georges. *La physiocratie à la fin du règne de Louis XV (1770–1774).* Paris: Presses Universitaires de France, 1959.

Wilson, Arthur M. *Diderot.* New York: Oxford University Press, 1972.

——. "The Development and Scope of Diderot's Political Thought." *Studies on Voltaire and the Eighteenth Century,* 27 (1963), 1871–1900.

Windenberger, J.-L. *La république confédérative des petits états: essai sur le système de politique étrangère de J.-J. Rousseau.* Paris: Picard, 1900.

Wolff, Hans J. *Roman Law.* Norman: University of Oklahoma Press, 1951.

Woloszynski, Ryszard W. "La Pologne vue par l'Europe au XVIIIe siècle." *Acta Poloniae Historica,* 10 (1965), 22–42.

Wright, Ernest Hunter. *The Meaning of Rousseau.* London: Oxford University Press, 1929.

Index